Theoretical Foundations of Health Education and Health Promotion

Theoretical Foundations of Health Education and Health Promotion

Second Edition

Manoj Sharma, MBBS, CHES, PhD
Professor, Health Promotion & Education
Professor, Public Health
University of Cincinnati

John A. Romas, MPH, PhD, LPC
Professor Emeritus, Department of Health Science
Minnesota State University

JONES & BARTLETT
LEARNING

World Headquarters

Jones & Bartlett Learning
40 Tall Pine Drive
Sudbury, MA 01776
978-443-5000
info@jblearning.com
www.jblearning.com

Jones & Bartlett Learning
Canada
6339 Ormindale Way
Mississauga, Ontario L5V 1J2
Canada

Jones & Bartlett Learning
International
Barb House, Barb Mews
London W6 7PA
United Kingdom

Jones & Bartlett Learning books and products are available through most bookstores and online booksellers. To contact Jones & Bartlett Learning directly, call 800-832-0034, fax 978-443-8000, or visit our website, www.jblearning.com.

Substantial discounts on bulk quantities of Jones & Bartlett Learning publications are available to corporations, professional associations, and other qualified organizations. For details and specific discount information, contact the special sales department at Jones & Bartlett Learning via the above contact information or send an email to specialsales@jblearning.com.

Production Credits

Publisher, Higher Education: Cathleen Sether
Senior Acquisitions Editor: Shoshanna Goldberg
Senior Associate Editor: Amy L. Bloom
Editorial Assistant: Prima Bartlett
Production Manager: Julie Champagne Bolduc
Production Assistant: Sean Coombs
Associate Marketing Manager: Jody Sullivan
V.P., Manufacturing and Inventory Control: Therese Connell
Composition: Glyph International

Cover Design: Scott Moden
Assistant Photo Researcher: Rebecca Ritter
Cover Images: (background) © Vladitto/ ShutterStock, Inc.; (top) © StockLite/ ShutterStock, Inc.; (left) © Yuri Arcurs/ ShutterStock, Inc.; (right) © Lisa F. Young/ShutterStock, Inc.
Printing and Binding: Malloy, Inc.
Cover Printing: Malloy, Inc.

Photo credits: 1, © Monkey Business Images/ShutterStock, Inc.; 39, © Mauro Bighin/ShutterStock, Inc.; 73, © GWImages/ShutterStock, Inc.; 95, © Richard Langs/ShutterStock, Inc.; 121, © Dmitriy Shironosov/ ShutterStock, Inc.; 145, © shippee/ShutterStock, Inc.; 173, © Scott O. Smith/ShutterStock, Inc.; 201, © John Wade/Alamy; 227, © kwest/ShutterStock, Inc.; 251, © Dmitriy Shironosov/ShutterStock, Inc.

Library of Congress Cataloging-in-Publication Data
Sharma, Manoj.
  Theoretical foundations of health education and health promotion / Manoj Sharma,
John A. Romas.—2nd ed.
    p. ; cm.
  Includes bibliographical references and index.
  ISBN 978-0-7637-9611-2 (pbk. : alk. paper)
  1. Health promotion. 2. Health education. I. Romas, John Albert. II. Title.
  [DNLM: 1. Health Education—methods. 2. Health Promotion—methods. 3.
Models, Theoretical. WA 18]
  RA427.8.S495 2011
  613—dc22
                              2010029707

6048

Printed in the United States of America
14 13 12 11 10   10 9 8 7 6 5 4 3 2 1

CONTENTS

PREFACE

We have been extremely pleased with the response that the *First Edition* of *Theoretical Foundations of Health Education and Health Promotion* received from its readership. This book has been used in both undergraduate courses and introductory graduate-level courses. We hope we will receive the same love, support, and admiration with the launch of this *Second Edition*.

The field of health education and health promotion has evolved from the early days of focusing on information dissemination to knowledge-based programs to present-day theory-based behavior change interventions. This introductory text for undergraduate students, entry-level graduate students, and practitioners working in the field summarizes common theories from the behavioral and social sciences that are being used in health education and health promotion. Hence this book is required reading for all students in public health and health education.

Theoretical Foundations of Health Education and Health Promotion provides an accessible, uniform approach to understanding the theories commonly used in health education and health promotion. Each theory is described in a consistent and uniform manner and discussed in simple language with an emphasis on practical applications. The book is neither overwhelming nor too short, and is compatible for teaching in a quarter or a semester-long course. The information presented here is in consonance with the core competencies for entry-level practitioners described by the National Commission for Health Education Credentialing (NCHEC) and provides a useful review for those preparing to take the certification examination. The book is also useful for those preparing for the Certified in Public Health (CPH) exam administered by the National Board of Public Health Examiners (NBPHE). Each chapter offers several learning tools to aid readers in understanding and learning to apply theory-based behavior change interventions:

- Key concepts and chapter objectives begin each chapter and help readers focus their attention and retain important information.
- Chapter summaries conclude each chapter and provide an opportunity for readers to prepare for exams and master key concepts effectively by reinforcing important topics and key terms. Key terms and their definitions are also provided in the glossary at the end of the book.

- Boxed quotations highlight the theorists or important aspects of the theory and provide a direct flavor of the actual theory.
- Each chapter begins with a discussion of the historical genesis and constitutive constructs of the theory. This foundation is followed by a clear delineation of the constructs of the theory, which helps readers understand the process by which the theory is reified and used in health education and health promotion. This process of simplification of constructs helps the health education and health promotion student to apply these constructs in designing programs.
- New to the *Second Edition*, Application Exercises in each chapter present a case study that urges readers to apply concepts discussed in the chapter and to retrieve additional applications from the literature.
- Each discussion of theory is accompanied by a practical Skill-Building Activity in the context of planning and evaluation along with a set of application questions. This activity will assist readers in mastering the application of the theory to community, school, worksite, or patient care settings.
- Up-to-date examples of applications from current literature are included throughout the text and serve as ideas for designing interventions and resources for initiating literature review.
- Each chapter includes a Websites to Explore section that encourages readers to participate in a specific interactive activity to enhance their learning on the topic.

INSTRUCTOR AIDS

We have prepared a set of PowerPoint slides for each chapter that instructors can use for classroom lectures. Instructors also have access to a series of online TestBank questions for each chapter. Instructor resources and additional resources for students may be accessed at http://health.jbpub.com/foundations/2e.

ACKNOWLEDGMENTS

We want to thank all of the reviewers who read through this text and provided invaluable advice: Carl Fertman, PhD, CHES, University of Pittsburgh; Deborah A. Fortune, North Central Carolina University; Wendelyn Inman, PhD, Tennessee State University; Dr. Jacqueline E. Sharpe, Old Dominion University; and Joshua H. West, PhD, MPH, Brigham Young University. A special appreciation is extended to graduate students at the University of Cincinnati who have used this book in the course HPE 781: Social and Behavioral Change in Public Health and provided excellent suggestions.

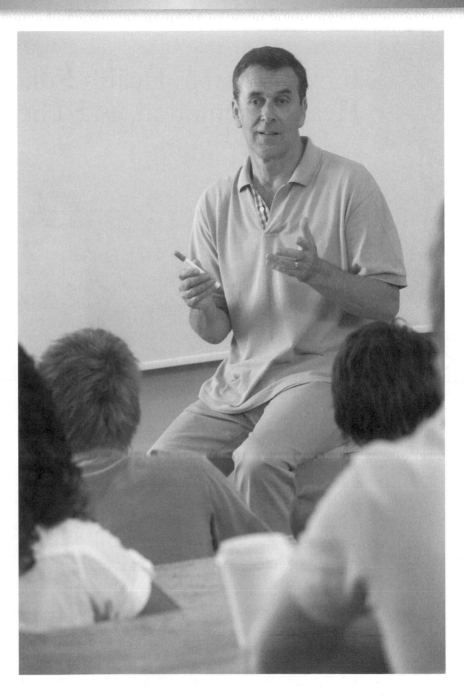

CHAPTER 1

Introduction to Health Education, Health Promotion, and Theory

AFTER READING THIS CHAPTER YOU SHOULD BE ABLE TO

- Define health, health behavior, health education, and health promotion
- Identify the limitations of the traditional definition of health
- Differentiate between health education and health promotion
- Define terms related to antecedents of behavior
- Delineate community-related terms
- List the responsibilities of certified health education specialists
- Explain the role of theory in health education and health promotion
- Name different types of theories and provide examples
- Identify 10 national health education organizations

HEALTH, BEHAVIOR, AND HEALTH BEHAVIOR

Health is an age-old concept. In Old English the idea appeared as *haelen* ("to heal"), and in Middle English as *helthe*, meaning to be sound in body, mind, and spirit. The classic Greek definition of medicine was to "prolong life and prevent disease," or in other words to keep people healthy (Cook, 2004). Similarly, medicine in ancient India was called *Ayurveda*, or the science of life or health. By the 17th century, most medical textbooks commonly used the word *restoration*. By the end of the 19th century, the word *health* was considered colloquial and was replaced with the word *hygiene*, which was considered more scientific (Cook, 2004).

After the Second World War, the word *health* resurfaced with the formation of the World Health Organization (WHO), a global entity. Around the same time, the Hygienic Laboratory in the United States was renamed the National Institutes of Health. In 1948, WHO defined health in its constitution as "a state of complete physical, mental, and social well-being and not merely the absence of disease or infirmity" (WHO, 1974, p. 29). This definition of health has received a lot of criticism over the years for a number of reasons.

First, the use of the word *state* is misleading. Health is dynamic and changes from time to time. For example, a person may be healthy in the morning and then develop a headache in the afternoon and thus not be in the "state" of health. Second, the dimensions mentioned in the definition are inadequate to capture the variations in health. One such dimension is the spiritual dimension (Perrin & McDermott, 1997). Bensley (1991) has identified six perspectives related to the spiritual dimension of health: (1) sense of fulfillment, (2) values and beliefs of community and self, (3) wholeness in life, (4) well-being, (5) God or a controlling power, and (6) human–spiritual interaction. None of these concepts are included in WHO's definition. Another dimension that is not mentioned is the political dimension. Do the rich get sick more often, or do the poor? Who controls greater resources to health? Do the rich or the poor have a greater burden of mortality? All these and many other questions pertaining to the politics of health must be explicitly mentioned in the definition for it to be meaningfully complete.

Third, the word *well-being* is very subjective. A definition must be more objective, and subjectivity should be minimized. Fourth, the way in which health is defined makes it very difficult to measure. McDowell and Newell (1987) pointed out that "just as language molds the way we think[,] our health measurements influence (and are influenced by) the way we define and think about health" (p. 14); in other words, health and measurement are inextricably linked. Fifth, WHO's definition of health presents an idealistic or utopian view. It would be impossible to find anyone who embodies all the attributes presented in the definition. Thus the definition of health lacks practical applications.

Sixth, in the WHO definition health is presented as an end product, whereas most people perceive health as a means of achieving something that they value more highly. For example, people want to be healthy so that

> *Health is a state of complete physical, mental, and social well-being and not merely the absence of disease or infirmity.*
>
> —World Health Organization (1974, p. 29)

they can raise their families. Finally, the WHO definition of health is written from an individualistic perspective in which health is defined for one person. It lacks a community orientation, which is much needed for something as complex as health. These limitations of the WHO definition are summarized in **Table 1.1**.

The original WHO definition has been modified in subsequent discussions at the world level. In November 1986, the first International Conference on Health Promotion was held in Ottawa, Canada (WHO, 1986). At that conference the Ottawa Charter for Health Promotion was drafted. In the charter, health was defined more broadly:

> [H]ealth has been considered less as an abstract state and more as a means to an end which can be expressed in functional terms as a resource which permits people to lead an individually, socially, and economically productive life. Health is a resource for everyday life, not the object of living. It is a positive concept emphasizing social and personal resources as well as physical capabilities. (WHO, 1986, p. 1)

Another important basic concept is **behavior**. *Merriam-Webster's Dictionary* defines behavior as "anything that an organism does involving action and response to stimulation." The key word is "action." A behavior is any overt action, conscious or unconscious, with a measurable frequency, intensity, and duration. "Frequency" refers to how many times the behavior occurs in a given time period. For example, we may classify someone as being active who participates in some sort of physical activity 5 days a week. "Intensity" refers to how intensely or how hard the behavior is performed. For example, we may say that a behavior is mildly intense, moderately intense, or vigorous depending on the effect it has on the heart rate or the number of calories burned.

TABLE 1.1   Limitations of the World Health Organization's Definition of Health

Health is dynamic, not a state.

The dimensions are inadequate.

The definition is subjective.

Measurement is difficult.

The definition is idealistic rather than realistic.

Health is not an end but a means.

The definition lacks a community orientation.

"Duration" refers to the amount of time spent on each session. For example, physical activity may last for 20 minutes on any given day.

Any behavior is influenced by factors at five levels. The first level pertains to individual factors. For example, a person's attitude helps determine his or her behavior. A person who is partaking in physical activity may believe that physical activity is refreshing. The second level pertains to interpersonal factors. For example, the person may be exercising because his or her spouse requested it. The third level pertains to institutional or organizational factors. For example, there may be a policy at the workplace that requires every person to work out for an hour, and that may be the reason the person is performing the physical activity. The fourth level pertains to community factors. For example, if the only available parking is 10 minutes away from where the person lives or works, this may be the main reason the person is physically active. The final level in determining behavior is the role of public policy factors. For example, laws and policies requiring the use of seat belts while driving may make a person perform that particular behavior.

> *A* behavior is any overt action, conscious or unconscious, with a measurable frequency, intensity, and duration.

Now let us focus our attention on defining health behavior. The World Health Organization (1998, p. 8) defines health behavior as "any activity undertaken by an individual regardless of actual or perceived health status, for the purpose of promoting, protecting or maintaining health, whether or not such behavior is objectively effective toward that end." David Gochman (1982, p. 167, 1997, p. 3) defines health behavior as "those personal attributes such as beliefs, expectations, motives, values, perceptions, and other cognitive elements; personality characteristics, including affective and emotional states and traits; and behavioral patterns, actions, and habits that relate to health maintenance, to health restoration, and to health improvement." Three key foci of health behavior are clear in these definitions: maintenance of health, restoration of health, and improvement of health.

These foci correspond to the three levels of prevention: namely, primary prevention, secondary prevention, and tertiary prevention (Modeste & Tamayose, 2004; Pickett & Hanlon, 1998). **Primary prevention** refers to preventive actions taken prior to the onset of a disease or injury with the intention of removing the possibility of their ever occurring. **Secondary prevention** refers to actions that block the progression of an injury or disease at its incipient stage. **Tertiary prevention** refers to actions taken after the onset of disease or an injury with the intention of assisting the individual with the disease or disability. The actions for primary, secondary, and tertiary level care are taken at individual, interpersonal, organizational, community, and public policy levels. Hence health behavior can be defined as all actions with a potentially measurable frequency, intensity, and duration performed at the individual, interpersonal, organizational, community, or public policy level for primary, secondary, or tertiary prevention.

Some health behaviors have positive attributes, such as promoting physical activity or eating five or more servings of fruits and vegetables. Other health behaviors focus on extinguishing negative attributes, such as smoking or binge drinking. These behaviors can be categorized as risk behaviors and protective behaviors. The World Health Organization (1998, p. 18) defines risk behaviors as "specific forms of behavior which are proven to be associated with increased susceptibility to a specific disease or ill-health." For example, indiscriminate sexual behavior is a risk behavior for sexually transmitted diseases, including HIV/AIDS. Protective behaviors aim to protect a person from developing ill-health or a specific disease. For example, a person may be immunized against tetanus and thus prevent the disease. Green and Kreuter (2005) divided protective behaviors into two categories: health-directed and health-related behaviors. Health-directed behaviors are actions a person consciously pursues for health improvement or health protection, such as seeking an immunization, getting a physical examination, eating a low-fat food, or using a condom. Health-related behaviors are actions performed for reasons other than health but that have health effects. An example is an individual who is trying to lose weight in order to improve his or her appearance.

HEALTH EDUCATION AND HEALTH PROMOTION

Health education professionals facilitate modification of health behaviors. Health education has been defined in several ways. Downie, Fyfe, and Tannahill (1990) defined it as "[c]ommunication activity aimed at enhancing positive health and preventing or diminishing ill-health in individuals and groups through influencing the beliefs, attitudes and behavior of those with power and of the community at large" (p. 28). The 2000 Joint Committee on Health Education and Promotion Terminology (Gold & Miner, 2002, p. 3) defined health education as "any combination of planned learning experiences based on sound theories that provide individuals, groups, and communities the opportunity to acquire information and the skills needed to make quality health decisions." The World Health Organization (1998, p. 4) defined health education as "compris[ing] consciously constructed opportunities for learning involving some form of communication designed to improve health literacy, including improving knowledge, and developing life skills which are conducive to individual and community health." Green and Kreuter (2005, p. G-4) defined health education as "any planned combination of learning experiences designed to predispose, enable, and reinforce voluntary behavior conducive to health in individuals, groups or communities."

From these definitions some things are clear. First, health education is a systematic, planned application, which qualifies it as a science. Second, the delivery of health education involves a set of techniques rather than just one, such as preparing health education informational brochures, pamphlets, and videos; delivering lectures; facilitating role plays or simulations; analyzing case studies; participating and reflecting in group discussions; reading; and interacting in computer-assisted training. In the past, health education encompassed a wider range of functions, including community mobilization, networking, and advocacy, which are now embodied in the term **health promotion**. Third, the primary purpose of health education is to influence antecedents of behavior so that healthy behaviors develop in a voluntary fashion (without any coercion). The common antecedents of behavior are awareness, information, knowledge, skills, beliefs, attitudes, and values. Finally, health education is performed at several levels. It can be done one-on-one, such as in a counseling session; it can be done with a group of people, such as through a group discussion; it can be done at an organizational level, such as through an employee wellness fair; or it can be done at the community level, such as through a multiple-channel, multiple-approach campaign.

Since the publication of *Healthy People: The Surgeon General's Report on Health Promotion and Disease Prevention* (U.S. Department of Health and Human Services [USD-HHS], 1979), the term *health promotion* has gained popularity and continues to gain strength. This term has been used in the *Objectives for the Nation* (USDHHS, 1980), *Healthy People 2000* (USDHHS, 1990), *Healthy People 2010* (USDHHS, 2000) and *Healthy People 2020* (USDHHS, 2009) reports. **Table 1.2** summarizes the 38 focus areas in *Healthy People 2020*, which underscore the importance of health promotion.

> Healthy People 2020 *reflects assessments of major risks to health and wellness, changing public health priorities, and emerging issues related to our nation's health preparedness and prevention.*
>
> —U.S. Department of Health and Human Services (2009)

Green and Kreuter (2005, p. G-4) defined health promotion as "any planned combination of educational, political, regulatory and organizational supports for actions and conditions of living conducive to the health of individuals, groups or communities." The 2000 Joint Committee on Health Education and Promotion Terminology (Gold & Miner, 2002, p. 4) defined health promotion as "any planned combination of educational, political, environmental, regulatory, or organizational mechanisms that support actions and conditions of living conducive to the health of individuals, groups, and communities." The *Ottawa Charter for Health Promotion* (WHO, 1986, p. 1) defined health promotion as "the process of enabling people to

TABLE 1.2 **Focus Areas in *Healthy People 2020***	
Access to health services	HIV
Adolescent health	Immunization and infectious diseases
Arthritis, osteoporosis, and chronic back conditions	Injury and violence prevention
Blood disorders and blood safety	Maternal, infant, and child health
Cancer	Medical product safety
Chronic kidney diseases	Mental health and mental disorders
Diabetes	Nutrition and weight status
Disability and secondary conditions	Occupational safety and health
Early and middle childhood	Older adults
Educational and community-based programs	Oral health
Environmental health	Physical activity and fitness
Family planning	Public health infrastructure
Food safety	Quality of life and well being
Genomics	Respiratory diseases
Global health	Sexually transmitted diseases
Health communication and health IT	Social determinants of health
Healthcare associated infections	Substance abuse
Hearing and other sensory or communication disorders	Tobacco use
Heart disease and stroke	Vision

increase control over, and to improve their health." The Ottawa Charter identified five key action strategies for health promotion:

- Build healthy public policy.
- Create physical and social environments supportive of individual change.
- Strengthen community action.

- Develop personal skills such as increased self-efficacy and feelings of empowerment.
- Reorient health services to the population and partnership with patients.

These action areas were confirmed in the *Jakarta Declaration on Leading Health Promotion into the 21st Century* in 1997 (WHO, 1997). In addition, the Jakarta Declaration identified five priorities for health promotion:

- Promote social responsibility for health.
- Increase investments for health development.
- Expand partnerships for health promotion.
- Increase community capacity and empower the individual.
- Secure an infrastructure for health promotion.

Once again, all these depictions of health promotion have some things in common. First, just like health education, health promotion is a systematic, planned application that qualifies as a science. Second, it entails methods beyond mere education such as community mobilization, community organization, community participation, community development, community empowerment, networking, coalition building, advocacy, lobbying, policy development, formulating legislation, and developing social norms. Third, unlike health education, health promotion does not endorse voluntary change in behavior but utilizes measures that compel an individual's behavior change. These measures are uniform and mandatory. Often the behavior change in health promotion comes from measures that an individual may not like, for example, an increase in insurance premium for a smoker. Finally, health promotion is done at the group or community level.

> *Health for all: The attainment by all people of the world of a level of health that will permit them to lead a socially and economically productive life.*
>
> —World Health Organization (1986, p. 4)

RESPONSIBILITIES AND COMPETENCIES FOR HEALTH EDUCATORS

The history of health education dates to the late 19th century, when the first academic programs emerged for training school health educators (Allegrante et al., 2004). The 2003 "Directory of Institutions Offering Undergraduate and Graduate Degree Programs in Health Education" listed 258 institutions offering baccalaureate, master's, and doctoral degrees in health education (American Association for Health Education, 2003).

As the profession of health education has grown, greater interest has arisen in establishing standards and holding professionals accountable to those standards.

In February 1978, a conference for health educators was convened in Bethesda, Maryland, to analyze the similarities and differences in preparing health educators from different practice settings and to discuss the possibility of developing uniform guidelines (National Commission for Health Education Credentialing [NCHEC], Society for Public Health Education [SOPHE], & American Association for Health Education [AAHE], 2006; U.S. Department of Health, Education and Welfare, 1978). Soon after, the Role Delineation Project was implemented, which looked at the role of the entry-level health education specialist and identified the desirable responsibilities, functions, skills, and knowledge for that level. These were verified by a survey of practicing health educators. The process led to the publication of *A Framework for the Development of Competency-Based Curricula for Entry-Level Health Educators* (NCHEC, 1985).

In 1986, the second Bethesda Conference provided consensus for the certification process, and in 1988, the National Commission for Health Education Credentialing was established. In 1989, a charter certification phase was introduced, during which time health educators could become certified by submitting letters of support and academic records. From 1990 to the present, the NCHEC has conducted competency-based national certification examinations. An individual who meets the required health education training qualifications, successfully passes the certification exam, and meets continuing education requirements is known as a **certified health education specialist (CHES)**. In 2006, there were 12,000 certified individuals (NCHEC, SOPHE, & AAHE, 2006). **Table 1.3** summarizes the responsibilities for entry-level health educators (NCHEC, 1985).

In 1992, the AAHE and SOPHE began to determine graduate-level competencies, and a Joint Committee for the Development of Graduate-Level Preparation Standards was formed. *A Competency-Based Framework for Graduate Level Health Educators* was

TABLE 1.3   Areas of Responsibilities for Entry-Level Health Educators
I.   Assess individual and community needs for health education
II.   Plan effective health education programs
III.   Implement health education programs
IV.   Evaluate the effectiveness of health education programs
V.   Coordinate the provision of health education services
VI.   Act as a resource person in health education
VII.   Communicate health and health education needs, concerns, and resources

published in 1999 (AAHE, NCHEC, & SOPHE, 1999). **Table 1.4** summarizes the responsibilities for graduate-level health educators. Beginning in October 2011, the NCHEC will hold exams for the advanced-level credential, Master Certified Health Education Specialist (MCHES) (Rehrig, 2010).

In 1998 the profession launched the National Health Educator Competencies Update Project (CUP), a six-year project to reverify the entry-level health education responsibilities, competencies, and subcompetencies and to verify the advanced-level competencies and subcompetencies (Airhihenbuwa et al., 2005; Gilmore, Olsen, Taub, & Connell, 2005). The CUP model identifies three levels of practice: (1) entry (competencies and subcompetencies performed by health educators with a baccalaureate or master's degree and less than 5 years of experience), (2) advanced 1 (competencies and subcompetencies performed by health educators with a baccalaureate or master's degree and more than 5 years of experience), and (3) advanced 2 (competencies and subcompetencies performed by health educators with a doctoral degree and 5 years or more of experience). The CUP model contains seven areas of responsibility, 35 competencies, and 163 subcompetencies, many of which are similar to previous models. **Table 1.5** summarizes the responsibilities. Research and advocacy have been combined to form Area IV, and communication and advocacy have been combined in Area VII. The CUP model also identifies six settings for health education (**Table 1.6**).

TABLE 1.4   Areas of Responsibilities for Graduate-Level Health Educators
I.   Assess individual and community needs for health education
II.   Plan effective health education programs
III. Implement health education programs
IV.   Evaluate the effectiveness of health education programs
V.   Coordinate the provision of health education services
VI.   Act as a resource person in health education
VII. Communicate health and health education needs, concerns, and resources
VIII. Apply appropriate research principles and techniques in health education
IX.   Administer health education programs
X.   Advance the profession of health education

TABLE 1.5   Areas of Responsibilities for Health Educators in the CUP Model

I.   Assess individual and community needs for health education

II.   Plan health education strategies, interventions, and programs

III. Implement health education strategies, interventions, and programs

IV.   Conduct evaluation and research related to health education

V.   Administer health education strategies, interventions, and programs

VI.   Serve as a health education resource person

VII. Communicate and advocate for health and health education

TABLE 1.6   Settings for Health Education Identified in the CUP Model

Community

School (K–12)

Health care

Business/industry

College/university

University health services

Health education is an important and integral function of public health. The Institute of Medicine (1988) defined three core functions of public health in its *Future of Public Health* report:

1. *Assessment*: Every public health agency should regularly and systematically collect, assemble, analyze, and make available information on the health of the community.
2. *Policy development*: Every public health agency should assist in the development of comprehensive public health policies.
3. *Assurance*: Every public health agency should ensure that services necessary to achieve agreed-upon goals in communities are provided either directly or by regulations or by other agencies.

Building on these identified functions, the Public Health Functions Steering Committee (1994) identified six public health goals and 10 essential public health services.

The six goals are to (1) prevent epidemics and the spread of disease, (2) protect against environmental hazards, (3) prevent injuries, (4) promote and encourage healthy behaviors, (5) respond to disasters and assist communities in recovery, and (6) assure the quality and accessibility of health services. The 10 essential public health services are to (1) monitor health status to identify community health problems; (2) diagnose and investigate health problems and health hazards in the community; (3) inform, educate, and empower people about health issues; (4) mobilize community partnerships to identify and solve health problems; (5) develop policies and plans that support individual and community health efforts; (6) enforce laws and regulations that protect health and ensure safety; (7) link people to needed personal health services and ensure the provision of health care when it is otherwise unavailable; (8) ensure the availability of a competent public health and personal health care workforce; (9) evaluate the effectiveness, accessibility, and quality of personal and population-based health services; and (10) research new insights and innovative solutions to health problems. It can be seen from both these lists that health education is a core and integral function of public health and that health educators are key public health functionaries.

The Institute of Medicine published *The Future of the Public's Health in the 21st Century* in 2002, which echoed the vision articulated in *Healthy People 2010* (USDHHS, 2000): healthy people in healthy communities. It emphasized the following key areas of action:

- Adopt a focus on population health that includes multiple determinants of health
- Strengthen the public health infrastructure
- Build partnerships
- Develop systems of accountability
- Emphasize evidence
- Improve communication

Once again, all of these functions underscore the inextricable linkage between public health and health education. Health education is an important subset of public health. Just as there is a NCHEC, since 2005 the National Board of Public Health Examiners (NBPHE, n.d.) has ensured that graduates from schools and programs of public health accredited by the Council on Education for Public Health (CEPH) have gained the required knowledge and skills related to public health. NBPHE is responsible for developing, preparing, administering, and evaluating a voluntary certification exam. People who pass this exam are called **Certified in Public Health (CPH).** The first exam was conducted in 2008 and certified about 500 individuals. The exam consists of questions from five core areas: biostatistics, epidemiology, environmental health sciences, health policy and management, and social and behavioral sciences along with seven cross-cutting areas: communication and informatics, diversity and culture, leadership, public health biology, professionalism, programs planning, and systems thinking.

CODE OF ETHICS FOR THE HEALTH EDUCATION PROFESSION

Ethics is a major area of philosophy that deals with the study of morality, and in recent years, interest in ethics has increased in all walks of life. Practicing ethical behavior provides a standard for performance in any profession. In the profession of health education, the earliest effort to develop a code of ethics was the 1976 code of ethics developed by the Society for Public Health Education (Taub, Kreuter, Parcel, & Vitello, 1987). A coalition of national health education organizations, composed of the American Academy of Health Behavior (AAHB), the American Association for Health Education (AAHE), the American College Health Association (ACHA), the American Public Health Association's (APHA) Public Health Education and Health Promotion (PHEHP) Section, APHA's School Health Education and Services (SHES) Section, the American School Health Association (ASHA), the Directors of Health Promotion and Education (DHPE), Eta Sigma Gamma, the Society for Public Health Education (SOPHE), and the Society of State Directors of Health, Physical Education and Recreation (SSDHPER) has developed a unified code of ethics for health educators (Coalition of National Health Education Organizations, 2004). The code of ethics has six areas, which are summarized in **Table 1.7**.

TABLE 1.7   Articles in the Code of Ethics for the Health Education Profession
Responsibility to the public: Supports principles of self-determination and freedom of choice for the individual
Responsibility to the profession: Exhibits professional behavior
Responsibility to employers: Accountable for professional activities and actions
Responsibility in the delivery of health education: Respects the rights, dignity, confidentiality, and worth of people
Responsibility in research and evaluation: Conducts oneself in accordance with federal and state laws, organizational and institutional policies, and professional standards
Responsibility in professional preparation: Provides quality education that benefits the profession and the public

HEALTH EDUCATION ORGANIZATIONS

Ten health education organizations exist at the national level. The following subsections provide a brief description of each of these organizations.

American Academy of Health Behavior (AAHB)

The American Academy of Health Behavior was established in 1998. The mission of this organization is to advance the practice of health education and health promotion through health behavior research. Its specific objectives are to:

- Foster and disseminate findings of health behavior, health education, and health promotion research through sponsorship of scientific meetings, symposia, and publications
- Recognize outstanding achievements in the areas of health behavior, health education, and health promotion research
- Facilitate collaborative research efforts by bringing its members in contact with each other through a membership directory, professional meetings, professional publications, and electronic media
- Advance health education and health promotion by influencing health policy and allocation of resources (government agencies, private foundations, universities, etc.) by developing and disseminating a cohesive body of knowledge in the area of health behavior research

Its website is www.aahb.org.

American Association for Health Education (AAHE)

The American Association for Health Education was established in 1937, but its parent organization, the Association of the American Alliance for Health, Physical Education, Recreation, and Dance (AAHPERD), was established in 1885. The AAHE is a membership organization representing 7500 health educators and health promotion specialists and is the oldest and largest health education association. It advances the profession by serving health educators and other professionals who strive to promote the health of all people. Its specific objectives are to:

- Develop and promulgate standards, resources, and services regarding health education to professionals and nonprofessionals
- Foster the development of national research priorities in health education and promotion
- Provide mechanisms for the translation of theory and research into practice and the translation of practice into theory and research

- Facilitate communication among members of the profession, the lay public, and other national and international organizations with respect to the philosophic basis and current application of health education principles and practices
- Provide technical assistance to legislative and professional bodies engaged in drafting pertinent legislation and related guidelines
- Provide leadership in promoting policies and evaluative procedures that will result in effective health education programs
- Assist in the development and mobilization of resources for effective health education and promotion

Its website is www.aahperd.org/aahe.

American College Health Association (ACHA)

The American College Health Association was established in 1920. The mission of the organization is to be the principal advocate and leadership organization for college and university health. The association provides advocacy, education, communications, products, and services, as well as promoting research and culturally competent practices to enhance its members' ability to advance the health of all students and the campus community. Its main objectives are:

- To support and promote systems and programs that produce optimum health outcomes for college students and campus communities
- To be the primary source of information, education, and consultation on health and health promotion issues affecting college and university students within the campus community
- To be the leading source of evidence-based knowledge about the field of college health
- To be the principal advocate for national public policy affecting the health of all college students and campus communities
- To develop and maximize the use of human, financial, and technological resources to ensure and sustain growth

Its website is www.acha.org.

American Public Health Association's (APHA) Public Health Education and Health Promotion (PHEHP) Section

The Public Health Education and Health Promotion Section was established in 1920. The parent organization, the American Public Health Association, was formed in 1872. The section has more than 3000 members. Its specific objectives are:

- To be a strong advocate for health education, disease prevention, and health promotion directed to individuals, groups, and communities in all activities of the association
- To encourage the inclusion of health education, disease prevention, and health promotion activities in all of the nation's health programs
- To stimulate thought, discussion, research, and programmatic applications aimed at improving the public's health
- To improve the quality of research and practice in all public health programs of health education, disease prevention, and health promotion
- To provide networking opportunities for persons whose professional interests and training include, but are not limited to, the disciplines of health education, health communication, health promotion, social marketing, behavioral and social sciences, and public relations
- To provide section members with opportunities to become informed and engaged in all of the activities and matters of concern to the association
- To facilitate collaboration with all of the association's boards, committees, special primary interest groups, caucuses, sections, and affiliates
- To provide section members with such benefits as the annual meeting program, continuing education opportunities, newsletters, and a structure for exercising association leadership
- To identify and recognize individuals who make outstanding and substantial contributions to health education, disease prevention, and health promotion

Its website is www.jhsph.edu/hao/phehp/.

American Public Health Association's School Health Education and Services (SHES) Section

The School Health Education and Services Section was established in 1942 and has more than 300 members. Its specific objectives are:

- To provide a section within the association that works independently, with other association substructures, and with external organizations toward the improvement of early childhood, school, and college health programs
- To interpret the functions and responsibilities of health agencies to day care, preschool, school, and college personnel
- To interpret early childhood, school, and college health education and service objectives to other public health personnel and assist them in integrating the objectives in their community

- To provide a forum for discussion of practices and research in early childhood, school, and college health
- To encourage the provision of health promotion programs within the school and college settings that address the needs of children and school personnel
- To encourage among interested association members the study and discussion of procedures and problems in early childhood, school, and college health services, health education, and environmental health programs

Its website is www.hsc.usf.edu/CFH/cnheo/apha-shes.htm.

American School Health Association (ASHA)

The American School Health Association was established in 1927 and has a membership of more than 3000. The mission of ASHA is to protect and promote the health of children and youth by supporting coordinated school health programs as a foundation for school success. Its specific objectives are:

- To promote interdisciplinary collaboration among all who work to protect and improve the health, safety, well-being, and school success of children, youth, families, and communities
- To provide professional development opportunities for all those associated with school health programs
- To provide advocacy for building and strengthening effective school health programs
- To advance a research agenda that promotes quality school health programs
- To fulfill these initiatives by acquiring human, fiscal, and material resources

Its website is www.ashaweb.org.

Directors of Health Promotion and Education (DHPE)

The Directors of Health Promotion and Education was established in 1946 and has more than 200 members. Its specific objectives are:

- To serve as a channel through which directors of public health education programs of states and territories of the United States may exchange and share methods, techniques, and information for the enrichment and improvement of public health education programs
- To establish position statements and make recommendations on legislation and public policy related to and having implications for public health education

- To participate with the Association of State and Territorial Health Officials (ASTHO) in promoting health and preventing disease
- To identify methods of improving the quality and practice of education, public health education, and health promotion
- To elicit cooperation and coordination with national, public, private, and voluntary agencies related to public health programs
- To provide a forum for continuing education opportunities in public health education and health promotion

Its website is www.dhpe.org/.

Eta Sigma Gamma (ESG)

Eta Sigma Gamma was established in 1967. It is the national professional health education honorary society. The specific objectives of this organization are:

- To support the planning, implementation, and evaluation of health education programs and resources
- To stimulate and disseminate scientific research
- To motivate and provide health education services
- To recognize academic achievement
- To support health education advocacy initiatives
- To promote professional standards and ethics
- To promote networking activities among health educators and related professionals

Its website is www.etasigmagamma.org.

Society for Public Health Education (SOPHE)

The Society for Public Health Education was established in 1950, and has more than 4000 members. The primary mission of SOPHE is to provide leadership to the profession of health education and to contribute to the health of all people through advances in health education theory and research and excellence in health education practice, and to promote public policies conducive to health. The specific objectives of this organization are:

- To expand the reach and effectiveness of advocacy efforts beyond SOPHE membership
- To promote the use of health education to eliminate health disparities

- To review, expand, and promote a dynamic research agenda for health education and behavioral sciences
- To support and enhance the professional preparation and training of health educators and public health professionals
- To proactively market health education
- To continually elevate SOPHE's performance in operations, governance, and resource development to achieve the strategic plan

Its website is www.sophe.org.

Society of State Directors of Health, Physical Education and Recreation (SSDHPER)

The Society of State Directors of Health, Physical Education and Recreation was established in 1926. The mission of SSDHPER is to provide leadership in facilitating and promoting initiatives to achieve national health and education goals and objectives. Its members supervise and coordinate programs in health, physical education, and related fields within state departments of education. Associate membership is available to individuals interested in the goals and programs of the society, but who do not work within a state education agency. Its specific objectives are:

- To help shape national and state policy defining and supporting comprehensive school health and physical education programs
- To link state health, physical education, and recreation leaders with their counterparts in other states
- To forge school–family–community linkages in support of school health, physical education, and recreation programs
- To foster professional growth and the development of leadership and advocacy skills
- To help resolve complex issues in education and health reform
- To provide leadership in the effort to link postsecondary institutions to school districts for improvement in curriculum, instruction, and assessment
- To provide a supportive network of professional and social relationships among members
- To provide training and workshops for members to help them increase capacity to improve comprehensive school health education and programs within their states

Its website is www.thesociety.org.

BASIC VOCABULARY IN HEALTH EDUCATION AND HEALTH PROMOTION

Health education and health promotion have their roots in several disciplines: biological science, behavioral science, economics, political science, and other social sciences. As in any other field, certain terms and jargon are common to health promotion and health education professionals. Some of these terms are presented in this section. These terms are used when we talk of the antecedents of health behavior change.

Awareness

A concept commonly used by health educators is developing awareness of health topics. To undergo any behavior change, the person first needs to become aware of what he or she is going to change. The *American Heritage Dictionary* defines being aware as "being mindful or heedful." The word *aware* implies knowledge gained through one's own perceptions or other means of information. **Awareness** refers to becoming conscious about an action, idea, object, person, or situation. An example of building awareness is a health educator screening a film about avian flu (bird flu) in a community in which there have been no cases of avian flu and no one knows about this disease. When people are already aware of an issue—for example, that smoking is harmful to health—there is no need to build awareness regarding that issue.

Information

After becoming aware of the need to make a behavior change, the person starts to gather facts about the change. The collection of facts related to an action, idea, object, person, or situation is called **information**. Health educators provide information on various health topics through pamphlets, brochures, flyers, compact discs, videos, and so forth.

Knowledge

After gathering information for making a behavior change, the person needs to learn facts and gain insights related to the action, idea, object, person, or situation. These facts and insights are called **knowledge**. Knowledge is part of the cognitive domain, and Bloom (1956) identified six categories of cognitive learning. The first level is knowledge, which entails recalling data or information—for example, reciting the symptoms of a disease or knowing safety procedures. The second level is comprehension, or understanding the meaning, translation, interpolation, and interpretation of instructions and problems. An example is the ability to state a problem in one's own words. The third level is application, which entails using a concept in a new situation. It also means applying what was learned in the classroom setting to novel situations in the workplace. The fourth level is analysis, in which the person is able to separate concepts into component parts so that their organizational structure may be understood. For example, a health educator collects information about a community and then prioritizes the needs to decide what program to offer in the community. The fifth level is synthesis, in which the parts are put together to form a whole, with emphasis on creating a new meaning or structure. The sixth and final level is evaluation, where one makes judgments about the value of ideas or materials. Knowledge can be tested using true/false or multiple-choice questions.

> *Science is organized knowledge.*
>
> —Herbert Spencer

Skills

Performing any action requires a set of psychomotor skills. Performance entails physical movement, coordination, and use of the motor skill. Development of these skills requires practice and is measured in terms of speed, precision, distance, procedures, or techniques in execution (Simpson, 1972). Seven categories, ranging from the simplest to the most complex skill, have been identified:

1. *Perception.* The ability to use sensory cues to guide motor activity.
2. *Set.* The readiness to act. It includes mind-set, which predetermines a person's response to different situations.
3. *Guided response.* Early stages in learning a complex skill, which include imitation and trial and error.
4. *Mechanism.* Learned responses have become habitual and the movements can be performed with some confidence and proficiency.
5. *Complex overt response.* Performance without hesitation; automatic performance.
6. *Adaptation.* Skills are well developed, and the individual can modify movement patterns to fit special requirements.
7. *Origination.* The person creates new movement patterns to fit a particular situation or specific problem.

Psychomotor skills are required in almost all health education programs. These are tested by demonstration and redemonstration. For example, in a cardiopulmonary resuscitation program, the instructor first shows the correct technique and then checks to see whether the participants have learned the technique correctly.

Health Literacy

The 2000 Joint Committee on Health Education and Promotion Terminology (Gold & Miner, 2002, p. 5) defined **health literacy** as "the capacity of an individual to obtain, interpret, and understand basic health information and services and the competence to use such information and services in ways that are health enhancing." Zarcadoolas, Pleasant, and Greer (2003) have suggested a four-part model to understand health literacy.

1. *Fundamental literacy/numeracy:* Competence in understanding and using printed language, spoken language, numerals, and basic mathematical symbols or terms. This domain is involved in a wide range of cognitive, behavioral, and social skills and abilities.
2. *Literacy pertaining to science and technology:* Understanding the basic scientific and technological concepts, technical complexity, the phenomenon of scientific un-certainty, and the phenomenon of rapid change.
3. *Community/civic literacy:* Understanding about sources of information, agendas, and methods of interpreting those agendas. It enables people to engage in dia-logue and decision making. It includes media interpretation skills and under-standing civic and legislative functions.
4. *Cultural literacy:* Understanding collective beliefs, customs, worldviews, and so-cial identity relationships to interpret and produce health information.

Beliefs

Beliefs are convictions that a phenomenon is true or real (Rokeach, 1970). In other words, beliefs are statements of perceived fact or impressions about the world. These are neither correct nor incorrect. For example, a student may enter a classroom and say that the classroom is big. She may be used to smaller classrooms, and thus from her perspective the current classroom seems big. Another student may enter the same classroom and say that it is small. He may be used to bigger classrooms and, thus, from his perspective the classroom is small.

Attitudes

Attitudes are relatively constant feelings, predispositions, or sets of beliefs directed toward an idea, object, person, or situation (Mucchielli, 1970). Put another way, atti-tudes are beliefs with an evaluative component. Attitudes have an affective component and demonstrate what one likes and what one does not like. For example, the student who found the room too small might qualify that belief by saying that it is "an ugly, small room." Since an evaluation has been made that the student dislikes the room, it becomes an attitude. Likewise, another student might find the same room to be a cozy, small room and thus demonstrate an attitude of liking the room.

Attitudes are usually measured by self-reporting scales, such as Likert scales. Likert scales list several sentences about an object and then ask respondents whether they strongly agree, agree, disagree, or strongly disagree with each statement. The scores are then summed to measure the respondent's attitude toward that object.

Values

A collection of beliefs and attitudes comprises a value system. Values are enduring beliefs or systems of beliefs regarding whether a specific mode of conduct or end state of behavior is personally or socially preferable (Rokeach, 1970). Let us take the example of the student who likes cozy, small classrooms. He also likes the students and the instructor in the classroom and likes the textbook that has been assigned by his instructor. He likes to read and to complete his assignments on time. Such a student can be said to have a value system that values education.

Community Mobilization

A community is a collection of people identified by a set of shared values. Working with communities is fundamental to the practice of health education. The first step in working with a community is community mobilization, which involves persuading community members to attend or participate in any activity planned by the health educator. The purpose of community mobilization is to enhance awareness on a given issue at the community level. Activities such as organizing a talk in the community, arranging a health fair, and bringing together key leaders of the community for a panel discussion are all methods used in community mobilization.

Community Organization

The second step for action at a community level is community organization. The term *community organization* was coined by American social workers in the late 1800s to describe their efforts with immigrants and indigent people (Minkler & Wallerstein, 1997). In community organization, community members identify needs, set objectives, prioritize issues, develop plans, and implement projects for community improvement in health and related matters. Green and Kreuter (2005, p. G-2) define community organization as "the set of procedures and processes by which a population and its institutions mobilize and coordinate resources to solve a mutual problem or to pursue mutual goals." Activities such as group discussions and committee meetings are common at this stage.

Community Participation

When community members actively participate in planning or implementing projects, it is called **community participation**. Community participation can take place regarding health-related matters or other civic matters. Community members must be in leadership roles for true community participation. Arnstein (1971) has identified eight different types of participation in a ladder of participation. At the bottom of the ladder there is no participation—only manipulation. Token participation entails the levels of information, consultation, and placation. Development of partnerships, delegation of power, and citizen control are levels of participation that are desirable.

Community Development

At the stage of **community development** local initiative and leadership in a community has been organized and stimulated so that changes in health or other matters are occurring. The key word in the concept of community development is *change* at the community level. Change can be measured by assessing changes in services or the provision of new services or by replacing existing policies or by incorporating new policies.

Community Empowerment

The concept of **community empowerment** is closely related to the Ottawa Charter definition of community action for health. The World Health Organization (1998, p. 6) defines it as "a process through which people gain greater control over decisions and actions affecting their health." In essence, empowerment is a process whereby individuals gain mastery over their lives in the context of changing their social and political environments. Empowerment can be a social, cultural, psychological, or political process. Individual empowerment is different from community empowerment. Individual empowerment is mainly about an individual gaining control over his or her personal life. Community empowerment entails individuals collectively gaining greater influence and control over the determinants of health and the quality of life in their community.

Networking

An important function of health promotion is to establish a network. Creating interdependent relationships with individuals, groups, and organizations to accomplish mutually set objectives in health or other matters is called **networking**.

Coalition Building

No single organization can effectively achieve changes in the health status of a community; collaboration between agencies, groups, and organizations is needed. A grouping of separate organizations in a community united to pursue a common goal related to health or other matters affecting a large number of people is called a **coalition**. It takes time and concerted effort to develop such coalitions; this art is called *coalition building*, and it is a vital function for achieving health promotion goals.

Advocacy

Advocacy is active support of an idea or cause that entails especially the act of pleading or arguing for something. Green and Kreuter (2005, p. G-1) define advocacy as "working for political, regulatory, or organizational change on behalf of a particular interest group or population." Advocacy in health is about creating a shift in public opinion and mobilizing the essential resources to support any issue or policy that affects the health of a community or a constituency. It is a vital function for achieving health promotion goals.

Lobbying

Lobbying is working with and influencing policy makers to develop an issue or a policy affecting the health of a community. It is an important activity in health promotion. Oftentimes health lobbyists have to compete with more powerful and resource-rich lobbyists from business or industry.

Policy Development

Policies are made by institutions or governments (local, state, or federal). Health promotion professionals work with institutional heads or other lawmakers to develop health policies. The process of developing a policy with ramifications for the health of communities is called **policy development**.

Legislation

Legislation are the laws passed by elected officials at the local, state, or federal level. Legislation has ramifications for the health of a large number of people. Health promotion professionals work at every step of the way to influence laws that foster healthy behaviors and help in extinguishing negative and unhealthy behaviors.

Development of Social Norms

Creating social acceptance for a practice, behavior, condition, policy, law, or environment that may affect the health in a community is called **development of social norms**. Health promotion professionals develop social norms so that healthy behaviors become acceptable and normative.

ROLE OF THEORY IN HEALTH EDUCATION AND HEALTH PROMOTION

Health education and health promotion have multiple influences from several disciplines. But the primary influence on health education is derived from the behavioral sciences, and health promotion is deeply embedded in the social sciences. It is from these behavioral and social sciences that the practice of health education and health promotion borrows the strategic planning of its methods.

The core concepts in behavioral and social sciences are organized in the form of theories. Theories are developed a result of research. Kerlinger and Lee (2000, p. 8) have defined theory as "a set of interrelated, concepts, definitions, and predispositions that present a systematic view of events or situations by specifying relations among variables in order to explain and predict the events or situations." In health education and health promotion, we are primarily interested in predicting or explaining changes in behaviors or environments. A theoretical foundation is becoming almost mandatory for practitioners of health education and health promotion. These days, even for entry-level health educators, competency in developing a logical scope and sequence plan for health education is a requirement (NCHEC, SOPHE, & AAHE, 2006). Graduate-level health educators must base their practice on accepted theory. Theories help us articulate assumptions and hypotheses regarding the strategies and targets of interventions (National Cancer Institute, 2005).

Polit and Hungler (1999) have classified theories into three types. Macro theories, or grand theories, purport to explain and describe large segments of the environment or human experience. Talcott Parsons's (1951) theory on social functioning is an example of a macro theory. Middle-range theories describe or explain phenomena such as specific behaviors. Albert Bandura's (1986, 2004) social cognitive theory is an example of a midrange theory. Finally, descriptive theories describe or explain a single discrete phenomenon, such as Hans Selye's (1974) explanation of general adaptation syndrome.

Glanz, Rimer, and Lewis (2002) have classified theories as explanatory theories, or theories of the problem, and change theories, or theories of action. Explanatory theories help describe and identify why a problem exists and search for modifiable constructs. Change theories guide the development of interventions and form the basis of evaluation.

Theories start from discussing concepts or ideas that are abstract entities. These are not measurable or observable. The concepts are adopted into theories and become known as constructs. For example, in social cognitive theory (Bandura, 1986, 2004), "self-efficacy" is a construct. When specific properties are assigned to the construct, it becomes an indicator. For example, a questionnaire examining self-efficacy may contain 10 items, which constitute what the construct means. A variable or quantitative score can be derived from each indicator, and this will vary from one individual to other. For example, in the 10-item questionnaire each item may be ranked from 1 to 5 and the summation may yield a score between 10 and 50. The constructs of a theory are constantly refined by empirical testing. A theory must be able to demonstrate predictive power. Behavioral theories must be able to make significant changes on affect (feelings or conation), thought (cognition), and action (volition). Ideally a theory provides practical guidance on what, why, and how. An ideal theory must be testable and must be generalizable. The constructs of the theory must be able to explain phenomena, which for health education and health promotion are behaviors or environmental conditions. **Figure 1.1** shows a generic depiction of a behavioral theory.

Theories derived from behavioral or social science help the practice of health education and health promotion in several ways. First, it helps in developing program objectives that are measurable. For example, if the health education program uses social cognitive theory (Bandura, 1986, 2004) to change physical activity behavior in elementary school students, then the objectives can be based on the following three constructs derived from the theory: (1) At the end of the program 80% of the participants are able to demonstrate positive change in their physical activity expectations score from before to after the intervention, (2) at the end of the program 80% of the participants are able to demonstrate positive change in their physical activity self-efficacy score from before to after the intervention, and (3) at the end of the program 80% of the participants are able to

There is nothing so practical as a good theory.

—Kurt Lewin

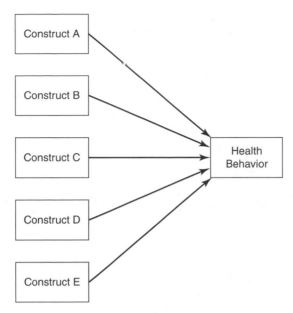

FIGURE 1.1   Generic depiction of a behavioral theory.

demonstrate positive change in their physical activity self-control score from before to after the intervention.

Second, the theory helps in identifying the method to use in health education or health promotion. For example, to change self-efficacy, the behavior must be taught in small steps, so demonstration could be used as a method. Third, the theory helps in deciding the timing of the intervention. For example, interventions that prevent use of tobacco should be implemented at the middle school level because that is when the behavior is beginning. Fourth, the theory helps in choosing the right mix of strategies and methods. In the earlier example, we were able to choose three constructs of the social cognitive theory because the theory suggests that those three constructs are important for early-stage adolescents.

Fifth, theory aids communication between professionals. The constructs of each theory remain the same in different applications, so readers can understand what was done across the studies. Sixth, the use of theory helps in replication of the program because the same constructs can be used from one intervention to the other. Finally, behavioral and social science theories help in designing programs that are more effective (have greater impact) and more efficient (take less time). These benefits are summarized in **Table 1.8**.

TABLE 1.8   Benefits of Theory in Health Education and Health Promotion
Helps in discerning measurable program outcomes
Specifies methods for behavior change
Identifies the timing for interventions
Helps in choosing the right mix of strategies
Enhances communication between professionals
Improves replication
Improves program efficiency and effectiveness

APPLICATION EXERCISE

Go to your library webpage and see if you have access to MEDLINE, CINAHL, and ERIC databases. If you have access, then conduct this exercise using those three databases. If not, go to the following website which has public domain Medline (PubMed): http://www.ncbi.nlm.nih.gov/sites/entrez.

Choose a health behavior that interests you, such as a physical activity behavior or a behavior of eating fruits and vegetables. Then choose a target population such as schoolchildren or worksite. Add the key words "theory," and "intervention" to your key words for a "behavior" and a "target population" and conduct a search for a theory-based health education or health promotion intervention. Choose one article from your library or Internet search and summarize it in 500 words.

SKILL-BUILDING ACTIVITY

Think of either a positive behavior or a negative behavior amenable to modification by health education. Choose a target population for whom this behavior would be most relevant. Now, using the SMART way of writing objectives shown in **Table 1.9**,

TABLE 1.9   The SMART Way to Write Objectives
S = Specific (what exactly is being changed and in whom)
M = Measurable (percentage of participants who will change)
A = Action verb (list, describe, identify, explain)
R = Realistic (must be achievable)
T = Time frame (end of the session, end of one year)

write at least three program objectives that would help bring about positive change in this behavior in your target population.

SUMMARY

Health is a means to achieve desirable goals in life while maintaining a multidimensional (physical, mental, social, political, economic, and spiritual) equilibrium that is operationalized for individuals as well as for communities. Health behaviors are actions with potentially measurable frequency, intensity, and duration performed at the individual, interpersonal, organizational, community, or public policy level for primary, secondary, or tertiary prevention. Health education is the systematic application of a set of techniques to voluntarily and positively influence health through changing the antecedents of behavior (awareness, information, knowledge, skills, beliefs, attitudes, and values) in individuals, groups, or communities. Health promotion is the process of empowering people to improve their health by providing educational, political, legislative, organizational, social, and community supports.

Health education and health promotion professionals assess individual and community needs; plan health education strategies, interventions, and programs; implement health education strategies, interventions, and programs; conduct evaluation and research related to health education; administer health education strategies, interventions, and programs; serve as health education resources; and communicate and advocate for health and health education. All these functions can be aided by the use of theories from the behavioral and social sciences. Theories help to discern measurable program outcomes, specify methods for behavior change, identify the timing for interventions, choose the right mix of strategies, enhance communication between professionals, improve replication, and improve program efficiency and effectiveness.

IMPORTANT TERMS

advocacy

attitudes

awareness

behavior

beliefs

certified health education specialist (CHES)

certified in public health (CPH)

coalition

code of ethics for health educators

community

community development

community empowerment

community mobilization

community organization

community participation

development of social norms

health

health behavior

health education

health literacy

health promotion

information   primary prevention
knowledge   secondary prevention
legislation   skills
lobbying   tertiary prevention
networking   values
policy development

REVIEW QUESTIONS

1. How has the World Health Organization defined health? Discuss the limitations of this definition of health.
2. Differentiate between health education and health promotion.
3. Differentiate among primary, secondary, and tertiary prevention.
4. What are the areas of responsibilities for entry-level health educators?
5. What are the differences in responsibilities for entry-level health educators and graduate-level health educators?
6. Identify at least five settings for health education.
7. Discuss at least five areas in the code of ethics for the health education profession.
8. Discuss the objectives of any one national-level health education organization.
9. Differentiate between attitudes and beliefs.
10. Differentiate between community mobilization and community empowerment.
11. Define theory. What are the benefits of using theory in health education and health promotion?

WEBSITES TO EXPLORE

American Alliance for Health, Physical Education, Recreation, and Dance (AAHPERD)

http://www.aahperd.org/

AAHPERD is an alliance of five national associations: American Association for Physical Activity and Recreation (AAPAR), American Association for Health Education (AAHE), National Association for Girls and Women in Sport (NAGWS), National Association for Sport and Physical Education (NASPE), and National Dance Association (NDA). The American Association for Health Education (AAHE) serves health educators and other professionals who promote the health of all people. AAHE encourages, supports, and assists health professionals concerned with health promotion through education and other systematic strategies. The website has information on interest areas, programs and events, professional development, issues and action, and publications. *Explore this website and locate internship and leadership opportunities.*

American Public Health Association (APHA)

http://www.apha.org/

The American Public Health Association (APHA) is the oldest and largest organization of public health professionals in the world, representing more than 50,000 members from more than 50 public health occupations including health education. APHA is an association of individuals and organizations that works to improve the public's health and to achieve equity in health status for all. APHA promotes the scientific and professional foundation of public health practice and policy, advocates the conditions for a healthy global society, emphasizes prevention, and enhances the ability of members to promote and protect environmental and community health. *Visit this website and read about the latest public health news.*

Eta Sigma Gamma (ESG)

http://www.etasigmagamma.org/

Eta Sigma Gamma was founded on the campus of Ball State University in Muncie, Indiana, on August 14, 1967. It is the national health education honorary society. The principal purpose of Eta Sigma Gamma is to elevate the standards, ideals, competence, and ethics of professionally trained men and women in and for the health science discipline. *Visit this website and find out more about the national officers of this organization. Does your university have a chapter? Find information on starting a chapter at your college or explore the criteria for joining an existing chapter.*

National Board of Public Health Examiners (NBPHE)

http:// http://www.nbphe.org/

The mission of NBPHE is to test the knowledge and skills of students and graduates from schools and programs of public health accredited by the Council on Education for Public Health (CEPH). *Explore this website and find the date of the next exam. Evaluate what you need to do to become eligible for this exam.*

National Commission for Health Education Credentialing (NCHEC)

http://www.nchec.org/

The mission of NCHEC is to improve the practice of health education and to serve the public and profession of health education by certifying health education specialists, promoting professional development, and strengthening professional preparation and practice. This organization credentials health educators in the United States. Requirements for the Certified Health Education Specialist (CHES) examination, dates for examinations, requirements for continuing education, and a forum for job seekers and employers are presented on the website. *Explore this website and find the date of the next exam. Evaluate what you need to do to become eligible for this exam.*

Society for Public Health Education (SOPHE)

http://www.sophe.org/

SOPHE was founded in 1950 and is an independent, international professional association made up of a diverse membership of health education professionals and students. Its mission is to provide leadership to the profession of health education and health promotion to contribute to the health of all people through advances in health education theory and research, excellence in health education practice, and the promotion of public policies conducive to health. The website presents news and announcements, benefits of joining, opportunities for continuing education, and advocacy. *Explore this website and find the date of the next SOPHE midyear or annual meeting. Visit the resources and links and learn about other health education organizations.*

World Health Organization (WHO)

http://www.who.int/en/

The website has information about the formation and organization of WHO, health information about all countries, alphabetical information about common health topics, a list of WHO publications, and a database of all WHO publications and WHO sites. *Read the constitution of the World Health Organization. Reflect on the successes and failures of this organization since its inception in 1948.*

REFERENCES AND FURTHER READING

Airhihenbuwa, C. O., Cottrell, R. R., Adeyanju, M., Auld, M. E., Lysoby, L., & Smith, B. J. (2005). The National Health Educator Competencies Update Project: Celebrating a milestone and recommending next steps to the profession. *American Journal of Health Education, 36,* 361–370.

Allegrante, J. P., Airhihenbuwa, C. O., Auld, M. E., Birch, D. A., Roe, K. M., & Smith, B. J. (2004). Toward a unified system of accreditation for professional preparation in health education: Final report of the National Task Force on Accreditation in Health Education. *Health Education and Behavior, 31,* 668–683.

American Association for Health Education. (2003). Directory of institutions offering undergraduate and graduate degree programs in health education. 2003 edition. *American Journal of Health Education, 34*(4), 219–235.

American Association for Health Education, National Commission for Health Education Credentialing, & Society for Public Health Education. (1999). *A competency-based framework for graduate-level health educators.* Allentown, PA: National Commission for Health Education Credentialing.

Arnstein, S. R. (1971). Eight rungs on the ladder of citizen participation. In E. S. Cahn & B. A. Passett (Eds.), *Citizen participation: Effecting community change* (p. 70). New York: Praeger.

Bandura, A. (1986). *Social foundations of thought and action.* Englewood Cliffs, NJ: Prentice-Hall.

Bandura, A. (2004). Health promotion by social cognitive means. *Health Education and Behavior, 31,* 143–164.

Bensley, R. J. (1991). Defining spiritual health: A review of the literature. *Journal of Health Education, 22*(5), 287–290.

Bloom, B. S. (1956). *Taxonomy of educational objectives. Handbook I: The cognitive domain.* New York: David McKay.

Coalition of National Health Education Organizations. (2004). *Code of ethics.* Retrieved from http://www.hsc.usf.edu/CFH/cnheo/ethics.htm

Cook, H. (2004). Historical keywords. Health. *Lancet, 364,* 1481.

Downie, R., Fyfe, C., & Tannahill, A. (1990). *Health promotion: Models and values.* Oxford, UK: Oxford University Press.

Gilmore, G. D., Olsen, L. K., Taub, A., & Connell, D. (2005). Overview of the National Health Educator Competencies Update Project, 1998–2004. *Health Education and Behavior, 32,* 725–737.

Glanz, K., Rimer, B. K., & Lewis, F. M. (2002). *Health behavior and health education. Theory, research, and practice* (3rd ed.). San Francisco: Jossey-Bass.

Gochman, D. S. (1982). Labels, systems, and motives: Some perspectives on future research. *Health Education Quarterly, 9,* 167–174.

Gochman, D. S. (1997). Health behavior research: Definitions and diversity. In D. S. Gochman (Ed.), *Handbook of health behavior research: Vol. 1. Personal and social determinants.* New York: Plenum Press.

Gold, R. S., & Miner, K. R., for the 2000 Joint Committee on Health Education and Promotion Terminology. (2002). Report of the 2000 Joint Committee on Health Education and Promotion Terminology. *Journal of School Health, 72,* 3–7.

Green, L. W., & Kreuter, M. W. (2005). *Health program planning: An educational and ecological approach* (4th ed.). Boston: McGraw-Hill.

Institute of Medicine. (1988). *Future of public health.* Washington, DC: National Academy Press.

Institute of Medicine. (2002). *The future of the public's health in the 21st century.* Washington, DC: National Academy Press.

Kerlinger, F. N., & Lee, H. B. (2000). *Foundations of behavioral research* (4th ed.). Fort Worth, TX: Harcourt College.

McDowell, I., & Newell, C. (1987). The theoretical and technical foundations of health measurement. In I. McDowell & C. Newell (Eds.), *Measuring health: A guide to rating scales and questionnaires* (pp. 10–42). New York: Oxford University Press.

Minkler, M., & Wallerstein, N. (1997). Improving health through community organization and community building. A health education perspective. In M. Minkler (Ed.), *Community organizing and community building for health*. New Brunswick, NJ: Rutgers University Press.

Modeste, N. M., & Tamayose, T. (Eds.). (2004). *Dictionary of public health promotion and education. Terms and concepts* (2nd ed.). San Francisco: Jossey-Bass.

Mucchielli, R. (1970). *Introduction to structural psychology*. New York: Funk and Wagnalls.

National Board of Public Health Examiners. (n.d.). *National Board of Public Health Examiners*. Retrieved from http://www.nbphe.org/about.cfm

National Cancer Institute. (2005). *Theory at a glance: A guide for health promotion practice* (2nd ed.). Washington, DC: U.S. Department of Health and Human Services. Retrieved May 20, 2006, from http://www.nci.nih.gov/theory/pdf

National Commission for Health Education Credentialing. (1985). *A framework for the development of competency based curricula for entry-level health educators*. New York: Author.

National Commission for Health Education Credentialing, Society for Public Health Education, & American Association for Health Education. (2006). *Competency-based framework for health educators—2006*. Whitehall, PA: Author.

Parsons, T. (1951). *The social system*. New York: Free Press.

Perrin, K. M., & McDermott, R. J. (1997). The spiritual dimension of health: A review. *American Journal of Health Studies, 13*(2), 90–99.

Pickett, G., & Hanlon, J. J. (1998). *Public health: Administration and practice* (10th ed.). St. Louis, MO: Mosby.

Polit, D. F., & Hungler, B. P. (1999). *Nursing research: Principles and methods* (6th ed.). Philadelphia: Lippincott.

Public Health Functions Steering Committee. (1994). *Public health in America*. Retrieved from http://www.health.gov/phfunctions/public.htm

Rehrig, M. (2010, Winter). The long awaited advanced credential, MCHES, Don't miss out. *The CHES Bulletin, 21*(1), 1.

Rokeach, M. (1970). *Beliefs, attitudes and values*. San Francisco: Jossey-Bass.

Selye, H. (1974). *The stress of life*. New York: McGraw-Hill.

Simpson, E. J. (1972). *The classification of educational objectives in the psychomotor domain*. Washington, DC: Gryphon House.

Taub, A., Kreuter, M., Parcel, G., & Vitello, E. (1987). Report from the AAHE/SOPHE Joint Committee on Ethics. *Health Education Quarterly, 14*(1), 79–90.

U.S. Department of Health, Education and Welfare. (1978). *Preparation and practice of community, patient, and school health educators: Proceedings of the workshop on commonalities and differences*. Washington, DC: Division of Allied Health Professions.

U.S. Department of Health and Human Services. (1979). *Healthy People: The surgeon general's report on health promotion and disease prevention*. Washington, DC: Author.

U.S. Department of Health and Human Services. (1980). *Promoting health—preventing disease. Objectives for the nation*. Washington, DC: Author.

U.S. Department of Health and Human Services. (1990). *Healthy People 2000. National health promotion and disease prevention objectives*. Washington, DC: Author.

U.S. Department of Health and Human Services. (2000). *Healthy People 2010* (Vols. 1–2). Washington, DC: Author.

U.S. Department of Health and Human Services. (2009). *Healthy People 2020: The road ahead*. Retrieved from http://www.healthypeople.gov/HP2020/default.asp

World Health Organization. (1974). Constitution of the World Health Organization. *Chronicle of the World Health Organization, 1*, 29–43.

World Health Organization. (1986). *Ottawa charter for health promotion, 1986*. Geneva, Switzerland: Author.

World Health Organization. (1997). *The Jakarta Declaration on leading health promotion into the 21st century*. Geneva, Switzerland: Author.

World Health Organization. (1998). *Health promotion glossary*. Retrieved from http://www.who.int/hpr/NPH/docs/hp_glossary_en.pdf

Zarcadoolas, C., Pleasant A., & Greer, D. S. (2003). Elaborating a definition of health literacy: A commentary. *Journal of Health Communication, 8*, 119–120.

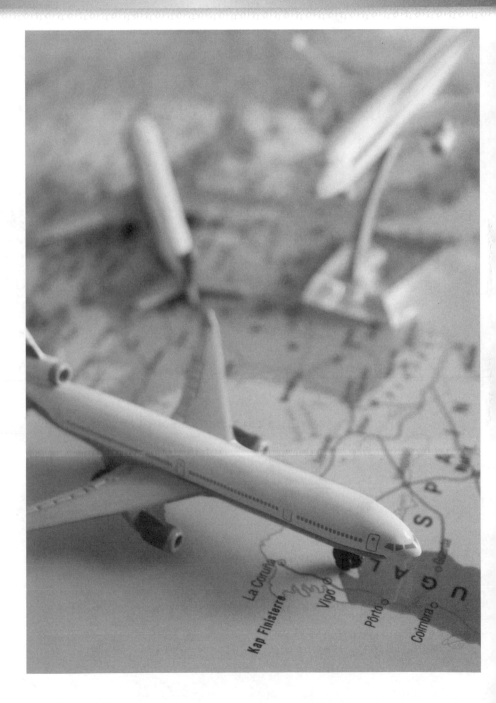

CHAPTER 2

Planning Models in Health Education and Health Promotion

AFTER READING THIS CHAPTER YOU SHOULD BE ABLE TO

- Differentiate between a theory and a model
- Apply the PRECEDE-PROCEED model of planning in health education and health promotion
- Identify the main components of the planned approach to community health (PATCH) model
- Describe the multilevel approach to community health (MATCH) model
- Narrate the steps and processes in the intervention mapping model
- Explain the assessment protocol for excellence in public health (APEXPH) model
- Explicate the comprehensive health education model (CHEM)
- Describe the model for health education planning (MHEP)
- Elaborate on the model for health education planning and resource development (MHEPRD)
- Explain the PEN-3 model
- Summarize the CDCynergy model

DIFFERENCES BETWEEN A MODEL AND A THEORY _____

A theory helps health education and health promotion programs identify program objectives, specify methods for facilitating behavior change, provide guidance about the timing of the methods, and select the methods of intervention. These are all very specific functions in the broad area of planning. Chapter 1 explained why planning skills are one of the seven essential responsibilities of health educators. In addition to setting objectives and selecting methods, planning functions may include assessing needs, prioritizing needs, allocating resources, matching human resources to tasks, and so on. To achieve these goals, health promotion and health education planning relies on various models.

A **model** can be characterized as a theory in its early stages. Models are eclectic, creative, simplified, miniaturized applications of concepts for addressing problems. Model makers present their ideas but may not yet have the empirical evidence through testing and experimentation that are required of a theory. Sometimes a model is thoroughly tested, yet the word "model" sticks as part of its name. Unlike theories, models do not provide guidance for micro-level management. An example of a model is the PRECEDE-PROCEED model (Green & Kreuter, 2005), which is used in planning health promotion and health education programs. This model provides guidance for planning at the macro level: what behaviors to target, what resources to tap, how to mobilize the community etc. A theory such as social cognitive theory provides guidance at the micro level; it tells which attitudes to change for making the behavior change, what activities to do with the target audience, what educational methods to employ, etc. **Table 2.1** summarizes the differences between a model and a theory.

TABLE 2.1 Comparison between a Model and a Theory	
Theory	**Model**
Explains or predicts phenomena	Simplified, miniaturized application of concepts for addressing problems
Micro-level guidance	Macro-level guidance
Empirically tested	Not enough empirical evidence
Based in previous literature	Creative
Usually parsimonious	Usually tries to cover a lot
Does not contain any model	May embody one or more theories
Example: Social cognitive theory	Example: PRECEDE-PROCEED model

> *Planning is bringing the future into the present so that you can so something about it now.*
>
> —Alan Lakein

The essential competencies identified by the Competencies Update Project (CUP) for health educators who are planning health education strategies, interventions, and programs are summarized in **Table 2.2**. To fulfill these competencies at the macro level, planning models are needed; to accomplish these functions at the micro level, theories are needed.

This chapter focuses on models that are used in planning health promotion and health education programs at the macro level. Later chapters emphasize micro-level planning using behavioral and social science theories. We begin with an overview of the various planning models and the process of planning. The models discussed in this chapter are the PRECEDE-PROCEED model (Green & Kreuter, 2005); planned approach to community health (PATCH) model (U.S. Department of Health and Human Services [USDHHS], 2005); multilevel approach to community health (MATCH) model (Simons-Morton, Greene, & Gottlieb, 1995); intervention mapping model (Bartholomew, Parcel, Kok, & Gottlieb, 2006); assessment protocol for excellence in public health (APEXPH) model (National Association of County and City Health Officials, 1991); comprehensive health education model (CHEM) (Sullivan, 1973); model for health education planning (MHEP) (Ross & Mico, 1980); model for health education planning and resource development (MHEPRD) (Bates & Winder, 1984); PEN-3 model (Airhihenbuwa, 1993); and the CDCynergy model (Centers for

TABLE 2.2   Competencies Identified by the Competencies Update Project for Health Educators Who Are Planning Health Education Strategies, Interventions, and Programs
A. Involve people and organizations in program planning
B. Incorporate data analysis and principles of community organization
C. Formulate appropriate and measurable program objectives
D. Develop a logical scope and sequence plan for health education practice
E. Design strategies, interventions, and programs consistent with specified objectives
F. Select appropriate strategies to meet objectives
G. Assess factors that affect implementation

Disease Control and Prevention [CDC], 2004). Linnan and colleagues (2005) surveyed instructors at 253 accredited graduate and undergraduate health education programs to gather information about planning and the professional preparation of health educators. Among survey respondents, 88% used the PRECEDE-PROCEED model in their teaching, and 62% used the planned approach to community health (PATCH) model. The following discussion presents the models in the order of their popularity as identified by these survey respondents.

PRECEDE-PROCEED MODEL

One of the most popular models in health education is the **PRECEDE-PROCEED model**, and approximately 1000 applications of this model have been published in the health field in the early 2000s (Green & Kreuter, 2005). The acronym PRECEDE stands for predisposing, reinforcing, and enabling constructs in educational/environmental diagnosis and evaluation. The acronym PROCEED stands for policy, regulatory, and organizational constructs in educational and environmental development.

The model originated in the 1970s from applications in hypertension trials (Green, Levine, & Deeds, 1975; Green, Levine, Wolle, & Deeds, 1979), cost-benefit evaluations of health education programs (Green, 1974), family planning studies (Green, 1970), and immunization campaigns (Rosenstock, Derryberry, & Carriger, 1959). The model was initially called PRECEDE (predisposing, reinforcing, and enabling constructs in educational diagnosis and evaluation) and remained popular under that name throughout the 1980s (Green, Kreuter, Deeds, & Partridge, 1980). In the 1980s the movement for health promotion grew very strong; in response, the model evolved and a number of health promotion functions were added. As a result, it came to be known as PRECEDE-PROCEED. In the 1990s the role of socioenvironmental approaches was strengthened even further, and the model emphasized the ecological approach. The latest edition of this model was published in 2005 (Green & Kreuter, 2005). For a detailed discussion of this model, see *Health Program Planning: An Educational and Ecological Approach* (Green & Kreuter, 2005). **Figure 2.1** depicts the model.

The eight phases of the PRECEDE-PROCEED model provide guidance in planning any health program. The first phase is *social assessment*. An assessment of community perceptions provides a starting point for identifying quality of life concerns, and methods such as asset mapping, social reconnaissance, nominal group process, the Delphi method, focus groups, central location intercept interviews, and surveys may be employed. Asset mapping is an assessment of the strengths, capacities, and skills of individuals and the existing resources in a community. In social reconnaissance,

FIGURE 2.1   Generic representation of the PRECEDE-PROCEED model for health, program planning, and evaluation that shows the main lines of causation from program inputs and determinants of health to outcomes by the direction of the arrows.

Note: From Green, L. W. & Kreuter, M. W. (2005). *Health program planning: An educational and ecological approach* (4th ed., p. 10). Boston: McGraw-Hill. Reproduced with permission from The McGraw-Hill Companies, Inc.

a point of entry into the community is chosen and local players are identified; this is followed by preparation of research and briefing materials and identification of leaders and representatives. This is followed in turn by field interviews and then analysis, reporting, and follow-up. In the nominal group process, community participants are recruited and are asked to reflect on a single question. The responses are collected and then ranked in importance by the participants to establish a priority list. In the Delphi method, a panel of experts is recruited and sent a questionnaire. Subsequent mailings of the questionnaire aim at deriving consensus, and the choices are narrowed at each iteration. Focus group discussions are small group discussions on a given topic moderated by a facilitator. Central location intercept interviews are conducted at shopping malls, churches, and other places where target population members can be found. These interviews typically include structured, close-ended questions. Surveys also consist of asking questions of the target population and can be done by mail, e-mail, online, or other means.

The second phase is *epidemiological assessment,* and it includes identifying the specific health problems that are contributing to or interacting with the quality of life concerns identified in the social assessment. This phase also identifies the causative factors in the three categories of genetics, behavior, and environment. Epidemiology assessment consists of two parts—descriptive and analytical—and attempts to gather information on both these aspects. In **descriptive epidemiology**, facts regarding the time, place, and population attributes of the health problem are collected through mortality (death), morbidity (illness), and disability rates. **Analytical epidemiology** examines the determinants of health. In this model analytical work translates into identifying behaviors and environments. Behaviors are of three types: proximal, or direct, actions affecting health; actions influencing the health of others; and distal actions affecting the organizational or policy environment. To diagnose behaviors that need to be targeted, the behavioral factors are rated in terms of importance and changeability. Behavioral objectives are developed for those behaviors that are judged to be more changeable and more important. To diagnose environments, environmental factors are rated in terms of importance and changeability. Environmental objectives also are determined by focusing on the more changeable and more important ones listed.

The third phase is *educational and ecological assessment*. In this phase, factors are classified into the hallmark categories of this model as predisposing, enabling, or reinforcing factors. **Predisposing factors** are antecedents to behavioral change that provide motivation for the behavior (for example, knowledge, beliefs, attitudes, values, perceptions). **Enabling factors** are antecedents to behavioral or environmental change that allow a motivation or environmental policy to be realized (for example, availability of resources, accessibility, laws, legislations, skills). **Reinforcing factors** follow a behavior and provide continuing reward for sustaining the behavior (for example, family, peers, teachers, employers, health providers, community leaders, or decision makers). In this phase the factors are identified and sorted, priorities are determined, and once again priorities within categories are identified using the criteria of changeability and importance.

The fourth phase is *administrative and policy assessment and intervention alignment.* In this phase the program components are aligned with priorities, resources needed to run the program are identified, barriers that may influence the program are addressed, and policies needed to run the program are developed. In aligning priority determinants with program components, ecological levels are first matched with program components, followed by mapping specific interventions, and finally pooling previous interventions to patch any gaps. This phase assesses aspects such as time, personnel, and budget.

The fifth phase is *implementation*. In this phase several factors may hinder or augment the impact of the program. These factors pertain to the program (such as resources and goals), the implementing organization (such as employee attributes, organizational goals, and organizational climate), the political milieu, and the environment (such as timing and other organizations).

The sixth phase is *process evaluation*. In this phase, the first evaluation is whether the intervention has been implemented in the manner in which it was planned. For example, if 10 activities were planned, have all of them been implemented, and to what extent have they been implemented? Second, the reception of the program at the site where it has been implemented is evaluated. Third, the attitudes of the recipients of the program are considered. How satisfied have they been with the program? What did they like and what did they dislike about the program? Fourth, the response of the person implementing the program is determined. What difficulties did he or she face while implementing the program? What things were easy to do? Finally, the competencies of the personnel involved are assessed. For example, if health education work was done, was it done by a certified health education specialist or someone else?

The seventh phase is *impact evaluation*. Impact evaluation assesses the immediate effect of the program on its target behaviors or environments and their predisposing, enabling, and reinforcing antecedents. For example, a program designed to combat obesity in a community would measure physical activity and consumption of fruits and vegetables.

The final phase is *outcome evaluation*. In this phase, changes in health status (such as mortality, morbidity, and disability indicators) and quality of life concerns (such as perceived quality of life and unemployment) are measured.

The PRECEDE-PROCEED model has been used in a variety of applications in health promotion and health education programming, including coalition building (Fisher et al., 1996), enhancing community participation (Lengerich et al., 2007; Watson, Horowitz, Garcia, & Canto, 2001), planning multiple-channel interventions (Hall & Best, 1997), developing health instruments (Chang, Brown, Nitzke, & Baumann, 2004), conducting needs assessments (Brouse, Basch, Wolf, & Shmukler, 2004; Hu, Wallace, Jones, & Liu, 2009; Li, Cao, Lin, Li, Wang, & He, 2009), implementing health risk appraisals at worksites (Bailey, Rukholm, Vanderlee, & Hyland, 1994), planning disease prevention programs at worksites (Wilkens, 2003), planning employee assistance programs at worksites (Dille, 1999), planning health programs in school settings (MacDonald & Green, 2001), weight management programs (Cole &

Horacek, 2009, 2010), training health care staff (Larson, Cohn, Meyer, & Boden-Albala, 2009; Macrina, Macrina, Horvath, Gallaspy, & Fine, 1996), improving self-care (Chiang, Huang, Yeh, & Lu, 2004), and ensuring compliance behaviors (Kang, Han, Kim, & Kim, 2006). **Table 2.3** summarizes these applications.

The developers of this model, Larry Green and Marshall Kreuter, teamed up with Robert Gold to develop a computerized software program designed to help health educators in academia who teach community health courses and assist practitioners in the field to plan and implement community health programs. The software is called EMPOWER (enabling methods of planning and organizing within everyone's reach) (Gold, Green, & Kreuter, 1998). The program provides a specific example in the area of breast cancer prevention and control and walks the user through the various steps of the PRECEDE-PROCEED model.

The PRECEDE-PROCEED model is by far the most popular and most researched model in the field of health promotion and health education. It has been in existence for four decades, and professional health educators are familiar with this model. It is very comprehensive and covers all areas of planning. The initiation of the

TABLE 2.3   Applications of the PRECEDE-PROCEED Model
Coalition building
Enhancing community participation
Planning multiple-channel interventions
Developing health instruments
Conducting needs assessments
Implementing health risk appraisals at worksites
Planning disease prevention programs at worksites
Planning employee assistance programs (EAPs) at worksites
Planning health programs in school settings
Weight management programs
Training health care staff
Improving self-care
Ensuring compliance behaviors

> *The hallmarks of the PRECEDE-PROCEED model are: (1) flexibility and scalability, (2) evidence-based process and evaluability, (3) its commitment to the principle of participation, and (4) its provision of a process for appropriate adaptation of evidence-based "best practices."*
>
> —Green and Kreuter
> (2005, p. 18)

model utilizes community inputs and participation, which is a big plus. The phased evaluation is also a strong feature of the model.

However, the model does have a few limitations. First, it is too comprehensive to be fully implemented in many situations. Health promotion and education funding may be allocated for work in a specific area, with no provision for social assessment or epidemiological assessment. In such cases, the model is implemented in a piecemeal fashion. Second, health promotion and education programs are often implemented on a limited basis. These programs may not account for changes in health outcomes, making evaluation impossible. Third, the model is a mixture of several theories, and it is not possible to discern which component of the model is working and to what extent. Finally, comparative studies with other models have not been done. Therefore, the relative utility of this model cannot be ascertained.

PLANNED APPROACH TO COMMUNITY HEALTH MODEL

The **planned approach to community health (PATCH) model** was developed in the mid-1980s by the Centers for Disease Control and Prevention in partnership with state and local health departments and several community groups (USDHHS, 2005). It is an effective community health planning model that is used by many states and communities and several countries. PATCH aims at increasing the capacity of communities to plan, implement, and evaluate community-based health promotion programs. Thus, capacity building is a very important part of the model. The PATCH model builds on the PRECEDE model (Kreuter, 1992), but is more user friendly and does not use academic terminology. A key strategy of the PATCH model is that it builds linkages within the community and between the community and the state health department, universities, and other regional and national organizations.

> *PATCH was built on the same philosophy as the World Health Organization's Health for All and the Ottawa Charter for Health Promotion which specifies that health promotion is the process of enabling people to increase control over their health and to improve their health.*
>
> —U.S. Department of Health
> and Human Services
> (2005, p. I-H-I)

After its initial development in 1984-1985, a pilot program using the PATCH model was tested in 6 states by the CDC. Based on the feedback received, it was revised and then delivered in 11 additional states. In 1988, evaluation studies were performed by the University of North Carolina, the Research Triangle Institute, and the PATCH National Working Group, and in all three studies the PATCH model was found to be effective. Since 1991, the CDC has not directly delivered the PATCH program in communities; instead, the CDC provides training and consultation to state health departments. Currently, most state health departments have a state coordinator and staff trained in the PATCH model. **Table 2.4** summarizes the five key elements of the PATCH model.

Active participation of community members is vital in the PATCH model. People participate in analyzing community data, setting priorities, planning intervention activities, and making decisions on the health priorities of their communities. Using qualitative and quantitative data to identify a community's health status and needs is also important in the PATCH model. Community members are engaged in analyzing the factors that contribute to a health problem, in linking with *Healthy People 2020* objectives (U.S. Department of Health and Human Services, 2009), and in designing health promotion interventions. Examples of these interventions are educational programs, mass media campaigns, and policy advocacy. These interventions are conducted in various settings, such as schools, health care facilities, community sites, and workplaces. Community members then conduct timely evaluations. Finally, the community becomes empowered and can replicate the process for more than one health condition.

The PATCH model has five distinct phases for planning a health program. The first phase is *mobilizing the community*. In this phase the target community is defined, participants are actively recruited from the community, partnerships are formed, and a demographic profile of the community is completed. Efforts are made to ensure that the participants who have been recruited are representative of the demographic profile of the community. In this phase a steering committee is also formed and community leaders are involved.

TABLE 2.4   Key Elements of the PATCH Model
Community members participate in the process.
Data guides the development of programs.
Participants develop a comprehensive health promotion strategy.
Evaluation emphasizes feedback and program improvement.
Community capacity for health promotion is increased.

The second phase is *collecting and organizing data*. In this phase, community members obtain data on mortality, morbidity, community opinion, and behaviors. The quantitative data is collected from sources such as vital statistics and surveys, and the qualitative data is collected from community leaders and others. The data are analyzed and shared with the community.

The third phase is *choosing health priorities*. In this phase the community group analyzes the social, economic, political, and environmental factors that affect the behaviors that are detrimental for health. As a result of this analysis, they identify priorities and develop objectives.

The fourth phase is *developing a comprehensive intervention plan*. In this phase the community group identifies resources, assesses existing programs, reviews existing policies, and appraises conditions. Then the group develops intervention objectives and an intervention plan. The intervention plan includes details of strategies, a time line, and an activity plan for things such as recruiting volunteers, publicizing activities, evaluating activities, and informing the community about results.

The fifth phase is *evaluation*. The purpose is to monitor and assess progress achieved during the phases of PATCH and to evaluate interventions. The unique feature here is that the community determines the end points of evaluation, and feedback is provided to the community.

Goodman, Steckler, Hoover, and Schwartz (1993) studied PATCH projects to see how communities traversed the various stages of PATCH. They found the approach to be effective, but recommended the following changes to enhance the effectiveness of the PATCH model:

1. Conduct a community capacity assessment prior to initiating a community needs assessment.
2. Do not rely solely on Behavioral Risk Factor Surveys.
3. Analyze needs assessment data quickly and share the assessment with the community as soon as possible.
4. Allow for flexibility and modifications by the community when determining the priority of health objectives.
5. Provide technical assistance throughout the project, not just in the beginning.
6. Fund at least one full-time local coordinator and encourage extensive capacity building.
7. Emphasize multiple interventions around one chronic condition at a time.
8. Emphasize program institutionalization.

Suen, Christenson, Cooper, and Taylor (1995) studied the performance of 2888 local health departments regarding core public health functions. They categorized the core functions of local health departments as follows: (1) health-related data collection, surveillance, and outcomes monitoring; (2) protection of environment, housing, food, and water; (3) investigation and control of diseases and injuries; (4) public information and education; (5) accountability and quality assurance; (6) laboratory services; (7) training and education; and (8) leadership, policy development, and administration. They found that the performance index was greater for all eight functions in those local health departments using health planning models such as the PATCH model. PATCH is indeed a very user-friendly model at the local health department level. For more specific details of this model, see the *Planned Approach to Community Health: Guide for the Local Coordinator* (USDHHS, 2005). The PATCH model has not been reported in the literature in recent years, and it is losing its popularity.

THE MULTILEVEL APPROACH TO COMMUNITY HEALTH MODEL

In the late 1980s, Simons-Morton, Greene, and Gottlieb (1995) introduced the **multilevel approach to community health (MATCH) model**. It is a very practical, yet comprehensive model. It places the health educator at the center of planning and can be implemented without an extensive local needs assessment. Few reports on the use of this model are available other than those by the authors. **Table 2.5** summarizes the five phases in the MATCH model.

The first phase is *goals selection*, and it includes four steps: (1) selecting health status goals by looking at prevalence, perceived and actual importance, changeability, and availability of programmatic resources; (2) selecting the target population by looking at health problem prevalence, accessibility, and programmatic interests; (3) identifying health behavior goals by looking at prevalence, association, and changeability; and (4) identifying environmental goals by looking at access to services, availability of programs and resources, enabling policies, practices, regulations, and barriers.

TABLE 2.5   Phases of the MATCH Model
Phase 1. Goals selection
Phase 2. Intervention planning
Phase 3. Program development
Phase 4. Implementation preparations
Phase 5. Evaluation

The second phase is *intervention planning*, which includes the following four steps: (1) identifying the targets of intervention at the community level, (2) selecting intervention objectives, (3) identifying mediators of the intervention objectives (such as knowledge, skills, attitudes, and practices), and (4) selecting intervention approaches by applying theories.

The third phase is *program development*, and it also includes four steps: (1) creating program units or components that include paying attention to the target population, intervention targets, intervention objectives, structural units, and channels; (2) selecting or developing curricula and creating intervention guides that include learning objectives, content, teaching/learning methods, and materials; (3) developing session plans in which educational objectives are delineated with teaching/learning activities, materials, and specific instructions; and (4) creating or acquiring instructional materials in which existing materials are reviewed and selected and new materials developed after pilot testing.

The fourth phase is *implementation preparation* and comprises two steps. The first step includes facilitating, adopting, implementing, and maintaining a health behavior by developing a specific proposal; developing the need, readiness, and environmental supports for change; providing evidence of the efficacy of the intervention; identifying change agents and opinion leaders; and establishing constructive working relationships with decision makers. The second step in this phase concerns selecting and training implementers.

The fifth and final phase is *evaluation*. There are three levels of evaluation: (1) process evaluation, which assesses recruitment, session, and program implementation, quality of learning activities, and immediate outcomes; (2) impact evaluation, which examines antecedents of behaviors and environments, changes in behaviors and environments, and any side effects of the program; and (3) outcome evaluation, which assesses health outcomes, cost effectiveness, and policy recommendations. For more details on this model, see *Introduction to Health Education and Health Promotion* (Simons-Morton, Greene, & Gottlieb, 1995). In recent years the MATCH model has not been reported in the literature and is losing its popularity.

> *W*hereas PRECEDE-PROCEED emphasizes formal needs assessment, MATCH as formulated by Simons-Morton and associates (1995) is a framework that gives more attention to implementation.
>
> —Simons-Morton, Greene, and Gottlieb (1995, p. 132)

INTERVENTION MAPPING

In the 1990s, Bartholomew and colleagues (2006) proposed a model for health education and health promotion planning called **intervention mapping.** This socioecological approach looks at individual behaviors in an environmental context. Intervention mapping has been used for several types of programs in health promotion and education. Some examples of such programs are breast and cervical cancer screening (Fernandez, Gonzales, Tortolero-Luna, Partida, & Bartholomew, 2005), diet and physical activity promotion (Brug, Oenema, & Ferreira, 2005; van Stralen, de Vries, Mudde, Bolman, & Lechner, 2009), fruit and vegetable promotion (Perez-Rodrigo et al., 2005), HIV and sexually transmitted disease (STD) prevention (Mkumbo et al., 2009; Tortolero et al., 2005), school-based physical activity injury prevention program (Collard, Chinapaw, van Mechelen, & Verhagen, 2009), healthy lifestyles for leg ulcer patients (Heinen, Bartholomew, Wensing, Kerkhof, & Achterberg, 2006), sexual and reproductive health (Aaro et al., 2006), socioeconomic health inequities (Abbema, Van Assema, Kok, De Leeuw, & De Vries, 2004), promoting exercise therapy for urinary incontinence patients (Alewijnse, Mesters, Metsemakers, & van den Borne, 2002), violence prevention (Murray, Kelder, Parcel, Frankowski, & Orpinas, 1999), and weight gain prevention (Kremers et al., 2005; Verweij, Proper, Weel, Hulshof, & van Mechelen, 2009). These applications are summarized in **Table 2.6**.

> *In Intervention Mapping we argued for a social ecological approach in which health is viewed as a function of individuals and of the environments in which individuals live, including family, social networks, organizations, communities, and societies.*
>
> —Batholomew, Parcel, Kok, and Gottlieb (2006, p. 9)

TABLE 2.6   Applications of Intervention Mapping
Breast and cervical cancer screening
Diet and physical activity promotion
Fruit and vegetable promotion
HIV and STD prevention
School-based physical activity injury prevention program
Supporting healthy lifestyles in leg ulcer patients
Sexual and reproductive health
Socioeconomic health inequities
Promoting exercise therapy for urinary incontinence patients
Violence prevention
Weight gain prevention

Intervention mapping is a six-step process:

1. *Performing needs assessment or problem analysis.* An assessment is made of health, quality of life, behavior, and environment, along with an assessment of community capacity. In this step, program outcomes are established.

2. *Creating matrices of change objectives based on the determinants of behavioral and environmental conditions.* In this step, performance objectives are established.

3. *Selecting theory-based intervention methods and practical strategies.* In this step, the program is reviewed with interested participants, theoretical methods are identified, program methods are chosen, and design strategies that match change objectives are chosen.

4. *Translating methods and strategies into an organized program.* In this step, consultation with program participants and implementers is done; program scope, sequence, theme, and materials are listed; protocols are designed; and program materials are prepared and pretested with the target audience.

5. *Planning for the adoption, implementation, and sustainability of the program.* In this step adopters and users are identified; adoption, implementation, and sustainability performance objectives are decided; and interventions are designed to affect program use.

6. *Generating an evaluation plan.* In this step the program is described, along with program outcomes, effect questions, and process questions. Then indicators and measures are developed and evaluation designs are specified.

For complete details on this model, see *Planning Health Promotion Programs: An Intervention Mapping Approach* (Bartholomew, Parcel, Kok, & Gottlieb, 2006).

ASSESSMENT PROTOCOL FOR EXCELLENCE IN PUBLIC HEALTH MODEL

The **assessment protocol for excellence in public health (APEXPH) model** was developed by the National Association of County and City Health Officials (NACCHO) with funding from the CDC in the late 1980s (NACCHO, 1991). The users for this planning model are intended to be local health departments. The model helps in building organizational capacity and establishes a leadership role for local health departments. The unique features of this model are as follows:

- It is a form of self-assessment tool.
- It leads to development of a practical plan of action.

- It focuses on the local health department's capacity and the community's actual and perceived needs.
- It helps the local health department to build its relationships with other local government agencies and community, state, and federal agencies.
- It provides a protocol through which a health department can assess health needs, set priorities, develop policy, and assure that health needs are met.
- It fits local situations and resources.

APEXPH is a three-part process. The first part is an *organizational capacity assessment*. In this part an internal review of the local health department is done to determine the administrative capacity of the department, and a plan of action is created. The second part is the *community process*, in which key members of the community are involved to assess the health of the community. In this part a community advisory committee is established to identify and prioritize key health problems. Then health data are collected and analyzed, followed by setting goals and objectives and identifying local resources. The third part is *completing the cycle*. The organizational action plan and community health plan are monitored and evaluated, and the three core functions of assessment, policy development, and assurance are institutionalized. Some applications of this model have been reported on in Kentucky (Kalos, Kent, & Gates, 2005), Illinois (Turnock, Handler, Hall, Lenihan, & Vaughn, 1995), and Michigan (Vaughn, Richards, Christenson, Taylor, & Eyster, 1994).

> *A*PEXPH is a voluntary process for organizational and community self-assessment, planned improvements, and continuing evaluation and reassessment.
>
> —National Association of County and City Health Officials (1991)

COMPREHENSIVE HEALTH EDUCATION MODEL

One of the earliest planning models is the **comprehensive health education model (CHEM)**, developed in the early 1970s by Sullivan (1973). The chief advantage of this model lies in its simplicity. This model is no longer in use and is included in this discussion mainly for historical reasons. The model comprises six steps:

1. *Involving people.* The target population and the personnel required to carry out the program are identified and a working relationship between the two is established.
2. *Setting goals.* Programmatic goals and objectives are established that mirror health education practices and resources in the target population.
3. *Defining problems.* The planners determine the gaps between what is and what ought to be and prioritize problems.

4. *Designing plans.* The most appropriate approach is identified, program objectives are set, a time line is defined, activities and resources are selected, and a pretest is conducted.
5. *Conducting activities.* The program is implemented.
6. *Evaluating results.* The evaluation results are used for continuing or changing the program.

As the planners move through each of these steps, they must consider the interaction of the health problem with the chosen behaviors, reflect on the available best practices, contemplate the limitations of health education, and identify resources needed to conduct the program.

MODEL FOR HEALTH EDUCATION PLANNING

Another early model in health education planning, developed in the 1960s, is the **model for health education planning (MHEP)** (Ross & Mico, 1980). This model also is not used much in current practice. There are six phases in the model, each of which has three dimensions: the content dimension (subject matter), the method dimension (steps and techniques), and the process dimension (interactions):

1. *Program initiation.* Planners develop an understanding of the target population's problem, develop a relationship with the population, and create awareness of the problem.
2. *Needs assessment.* Planners identify past assessment efforts, collect new data, analyze data, and describe the problem.
3. *Goal setting.* Goals are based on the problems identified in the needs assessment. Goals must be appropriate and realistic. In addition, input from those who will be affected is gathered, and strategies are developed for implementing the identified goals.
4. *Planning/programming.* Planners translate the strategies into a rational implementation plan or program, design systems and tools for managing the activities, and arrange for commitments among all the involved parties.
5. *Implementation.* The activities are initiated, training and technical assistance is provided, problem solving is carried out, and reporting is done.
6. *Evaluation.* Evaluation measures are clarified, data are collected and analyzed, and refinements to the program and process are made.

One application of this model has been for continuing education of occupational health nurses (Moore & Short, 1994). Other than that it has not been applied much in recent years.

MODEL FOR HEALTH EDUCATION PLANNING
AND RESOURCE DEVELOPMENT (MHEPRD)

The **model for health education planning and resource development (MHEPRD)** was proposed by Bates and Winder (1984) in the early 1980s, but it is not among the more popular models and is little used in health education practice today. The hallmarks of this model are that it considers planning a cyclical process, it separates processes from the end products, and it considers evaluation not as a separate step but as an integrated element throughout the model. There are five phases in the model:

1. *Health education plans.* An end result of the needs assessment (which in this model is called a policy analysis process) and an ongoing evaluation process.
2. *Demonstration programs.* Developed through a development process and an ongoing evaluation process.
3. *Operational programs.* The validation process determines which programs should be continued and thus made operational and which ones must be dropped. The ongoing evaluation process continues in this phase. This phase also entails development of an implementation plan.
4. *Research programs.* Implementation of those programs that are based on sound research continues in the implementation process.
5. *Information and statistics.* The data generated once again go through the policy analysis process in phase 1 and guide further planning.

PEN-3 MODEL

The **PEN-3 model** was developed as a child survival program for African countries (Airhihenbuwa, 1993, 1995). Later its use was extended to several other applications with minority populations, such as breast and cervical cancer screening in Latina women (Erwin, Johnson, Feliciano-Libid, Zamora, & Jandorf, 2005; Erwin et al., 2007), cancer screening in African American men (Abernethy et al., 2005), breast cancer education for African American women (Kline, 2007), breast cancer screening promotion in native Hawaiian women (Ka'opua, 2008), dietary behaviors in African Americans (James, 2004; Kannan, Sparks, Webster, Krishnakumar, & Lumeng, 2009), health factors in Latino immigrants (Garces, Scarinci, & Harrison, 2006), and smoking practices in African Americans (Beech & Scarinci, 2003). **Table 2.7** summarizes these applications.

TABLE 2.7   Applications of the PEN-3 Model
Breast and cervical cancer screening in Latina women
Cancer screening in African American men
Breast cancer education for African American women
Breast cancer screening promotion in native Hawaiian women
Child survival in African countries
Dietary behavior in African Americans
Health factors in Latino immigrants
Smoking practices in African Americans

The model consists of three dimensions, each of which contains the acronym PEN. The model is depicted in **Figure 2.2**. The three dimensions are interrelated and interdependent. The first dimension, cultural identity, has the following PEN:

P *Person*. Health education should be committed to improving the health of every person.

E *Extended family*. Health education should be directed toward not just the immediate family but also the extended family or kin group of the person.

FIGURE 2.2   The PEN-3 model.

N *Neighborhood*. Health education should be directed toward improving health in neighborhoods and communities. Involvement of community leaders is vital for culturally appropriate health programming.

The second dimension of the PEN-3 model used to be called educational diagnosis of health behavior, but its new name is "relationships and expectations" (Webster & Airhihenbuwa, 2005). This dimension evolved from the health belief model (Hochbaum, 1958), the theory of reasoned action (Fishbein & Ajzen, 1975), and the PRECEDE-PROCEED model (Green & Kreuter, 2005). In this dimension the PEN acronym is as follows:

P *Perceptions*. These pertain to knowledge, beliefs, attitudes, and values that may facilitate or hinder motivation for changing a given behavior. Here the health programs must start with the perceived perceptions of the person rather than the real needs identified by the planners for the latter to be meaningful and acceptable.

E *Enablers*. These are societal or systemic forces that may augment the health behavior or hinder it by creating barriers. These include available resources, accessibility, referrals, and types of service.

N *Nurturers*. These are reinforcing factors that an individual may receive from significant others. These significant others could be members of the extended family, peers, employers, health personnel, religious leaders, or government officials.

The third dimension of the PEN-3 model used to be called the cultural appropriateness of health beliefs, but is now called "cultural empowerment" (Webster & Airhihenbuwa, 2005). Thus, this model is particularly useful for work with minority populations and yields a culturally appropriate program. The PEN acronym in this dimension is as follows:

P *Positive*. These are the positive perceptions, enablers, and nurturers that help the person, family, or community to engage in positive health practices. These positive health practices lead to empowerment at the individual level, family level, and community level.

E *Existential*. These consist of practices that are neither good nor bad and thus do not need to be changed.

N *Negative*. These are the negative perceptions, enablers, and nurturers that help the person, family, or community to engage in negative practices that impair health.

In planning, this model goes through several phases. The first phase is health education, in which the planners must decide whether the health education effort is directed toward individuals, extended families, or communities. In the second phase, the planners collect data by surveys or interviews and identify the beliefs and practices related to perceptions, enablers, and nurturers. The third phase entails classifying these beliefs into three categories: positive, existential, or negative. In the final phase, the planners classify beliefs into those that are rooted in cultural patterns and those that are newly formed and select culturally appropriate health education strategies.

CDCYNERGY

CDCynergy, created in the 1990s by the Centers for Disease Control and Prevention, is a multimedia CD-ROM used for planning, managing, and evaluating public health communication programs (CDC, 2004). It originated as a planning model for communication programs but has now been expanded and tailored for a variety of public health planning applications. Systematic training for its usage and application is conducted by the Society of Public Health Education (SOPHE). The training curriculum includes a template for creating a health communication plan, examples of real-world public health interventions, a glossary of health communication terminology, and resources useful for developing and evaluating health intervention and communication plans (SOPHE, 2002).

The CDCynergy process is a six-phase process:

1. *Problem definition and description.* The problem is defined and resources are considered.
2. *Problem analysis.* Goals are set.
3. *Communication program planning.* The primary and secondary target audiences are chosen and communication objectives are set.
4. *Program and evaluation development.*
5. *Program implementation and management.*
6. *Feedback.* Feedback is given and used to refine the program.

OTHER MODELS

Some less commonly used models in health promotion and education are the effectiveness-based model from social work (Kettner, Moroney, & Martin, 1999), the evidence-based/risk factor analysis model (Dever, 1997), the social marketing assessment and response tool (SMART) (Neiger, Thackeray, Barnes, & McKenzie, 2003), and total quality improvement (TQI) (Batten, 1992). These models are rarely used in health promotion and health education.

APPLICATION EXERCISE

To learn more about applications, find a full text article of one of the models and analyze how the steps of the model were used in that application. For example, Mkumbo and colleagues (2009) used intervention mapping to develop and implement a school-based sexuality and HIV/AIDS education program in Tanzania. The first step of this model entails performing a needs assessment, which they conducted in a participatory manner, involving the researchers, the curriculum developers, the teachers, and the students. The second step entails creating matrices of change objectives based on the determinants of behavioral and environmental conditions. The third and fourth steps entail choosing theory-based methods and developing a program. They developed a program comprising five lessons, organized around 23 sessions, with the aim of delaying the onset of sexual intercourse and increasing correct and consistent condom use among young people. The fifth step is planning for the adoption, implementation, and sustainability of the program; and sixth step is evaluation. The last two steps in this application are unclear. This is an application of a Western model in a sub-Saharan African country.

Read this article and prepare a critique of 250 words.

SKILL-BUILDING ACTIVITY

Let us take the most popular model for planning health education and health promotion programs, the PRECEDE-PROCEED model, and apply it to a practical situation. Let us assume we are interested in developing a physical activity promotion program for African American women in a midwestern city. **Figure 2.3** depicts each phase of the model and how it can be applied.

In the first phase, you could choose a focus group discussion with the target audience for social assessment. The focus group discussion would identify the target audience's quality of life concerns, common leisure time physical activities, and program expectations. In the first part of the second phase, epidemiological assessment, you could collect local data from the county health department, statewide health data, and national health data about overweight and obesity and a sedentary lifestyle, and compile mortality and morbidity (incidence and prevalence) statistics of diseases associated with a sedentary lifestyle. In the second part of the second phase, only a behavioral

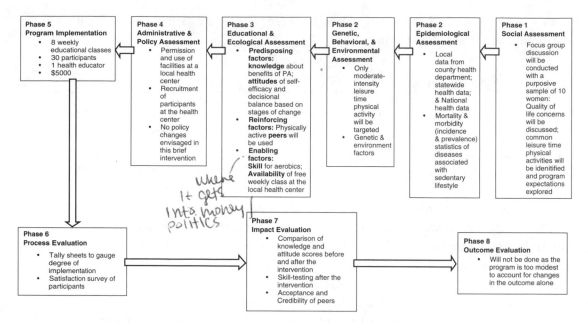

FIGURE 2.3 Application of the PRECEDE-PROCEED model for changing moderate-intensity leisure time physical activity in a small group of African American women in a midwestern city through a brief first-time educational intervention.

factor of moderate-intensity leisure time physical activity can be chosen from the genetic, behavioral, and environmental factors.

In the third phase, educational and ecological assessment, you can select predisposing factors of knowledge about benefits of physical activity, attitudes of self-efficacy, and decisional balance based on the stages of change model (Prochaska & DiClemente, 1983). Physically active peers can be used as reinforcing factors. In the enabling factors category, the program can build skills for aerobics and make a free class available.

In the fourth phase of administrative and policy assessment, permission and use of facilities at a local health center can be obtained, participants can be recruited at the health center, and policy changes would be planned. In the fifth phase, program implementation, one health educator could conduct eight weekly educational sessions with 30 participants at a total cost of $5000.

In the sixth phase, process evaluation, you could use tally sheets to gauge the degree of implementation, and perform a satisfaction survey of participants. In the seventh phase, impact evaluation, you could compare participants' knowledge and attitude scores before and after the intervention, test their skills after the intervention, and assess the acceptance and credibility of peers after the intervention. Since the program is modest and short in duration, the eighth phase of outcome evaluation cannot be done.

Using this approach, plan to work on a health issue of your choice with a target population of your choice. You can apply the PRECEDE-PROCEED model or use another model to plan your program. **Table 2.8** provides a set of questions to assist you in choosing activities that correspond to different phases of the PRECEDE-PROCEED model.

TABLE 2.8 Choosing Activities for Health Education Program Planning Using the PRECEDE-PROCEED Model

1. What will be the best activity to facilitate social assessment?
   - Asset mapping
   - Social reconnaissance
   - Focus group discussion
   - Delphi method
   - Nominal group process
   - Central location intercept interviews
   - Surveys
   - Public service data
   - Other

2. What data will be needed to conduct epidemiological assessment?
   - Mortality data
   - Morbidity data
   - Disability data
   - Behavioral data
   - Environmental data
   - Genetic data
   - Other

3. What factors should be considered in educational and ecological assessment?
   - Predisposing
     - Knowledge
     - Beliefs
     - Attitudes
     - Values
     - Others

(Continued)

TABLE 2.8   *(Continued)*

- Reinforcing
  - Peers
  - Parents
  - Decision makers
  - Employers
  - Others
- Enabling
  - Availability
  - Accessibility
  - Legislation
  - Skills
  - Others

4. What should be considered in administrative and policy assessment?
   - Alignment with priorities
   - Assessment of resources
   - Identification of barriers
   - Assessment of policies
   - Other

5. What should be considered in implementation?
   - Time
   - Personnel
   - Budget
   - Other

6. What should be considered in process evaluation?
   - Degree of fidelity
   - Reception at the site
   - Recipient response
   - Implementer's response
   - Competencies of personnel

7. What should be considered in impact evaluation?
   - Predisposing antecedents
   - Reinforcing antecedents
   - Enabling antecedents
   - Behaviors
   - Environments

8. What should be considered in outcome evaluation?
   - Health status
   - Quality of life

SUMMARY

Planning is an essential responsibility for health educators. Theories from behavioral and social sciences help in micro-level planning (setting objectives and identifying methods), but the macro-level, or overall, planning is done by models. Models are miniaturized and simplified applications of concepts for addressing problems and usually contain inputs from several theories. This chapter discussed several planning models: the PRECEDE-PROCEED model, the planned approach to community health (PATCH) model, the multilevel approach to community health (MATCH) model, the intervention mapping model, the assessment protocol for excellence in public health (APEXPH) model, the comprehensive health education model (CHEM), the model for health education planning (MHEP), the model for health education planning and resource development (MHEPRD), the PEN-3 model, and CDCynergy.

The most popular model is the PRECEDE-PROCEED model, which has been applied in a variety of settings for coalition building, enhancing community participation, planning multiple-channel interventions, developing health instruments, conducting needs assessments, implementing health risk appraisals at worksites, planning disease prevention programs at worksites, planning employee assistance programs at worksites, planning health programs in school settings, training health care staff, and improving self-care and compliance behaviors.

PATCH is a community health planning model that works equally well at state and local levels and builds capacity. MATCH is a model that emphasizes implementation and is feasible in situations where an extensive needs assessment cannot be done. Intervention mapping builds on a socioecological approach that looks at individual behaviors in an environmental context. APEXPH is a useful model at the local level. CHEM, MHEP, and MHEPRD are not commonly used and have been discussed mainly from a historical perspective. The PEN-3 model is culturally sensitive and helps in culturally appropriate planning. CDCynergy is a health communication model that has been tailored to a variety of other applications.

IMPORTANT TERMS

analytical epidemiology
assessment protocol for excellence in
   public health (APEXPH) model
CDCynergy
comprehensive health education model
   (CHEM)

descriptive epidemiology
enabling factors
intervention mapping
model
model for health education planning
   (MHEP)

model for health education planning and resource development (MHEPRD)

multilevel approach to community health (MATCH) model

PEN-3 model

planned approach to community health (PATCH) model

PRECEDE-PROCEED model

predisposing factors

reinforcing factors

REVIEW QUESTIONS

1. Differentiate between a model and a theory.
2. Define the PRECEDE-PROCEED model. How would you design a program to prevent smoking in adolescents using the PRECEDE-PROCEED model?
3. What are the competencies for health educators who are planning health education strategies, interventions, and programs?
4. Describe the essential features of the PATCH model.
5. Discuss the five phases of the MATCH model.
6. Identify the six steps of intervention mapping.
7. What does the acronym APEXPH mean? Briefly discuss this model.
8. Differentiate between the comprehensive health education model and the model for health education planning.
9. Describe the PEN-3 model.
10. Summarize the main features of CDCynergy.

WEBSITES TO EXPLORE

APEXPH PowerPoint Slides

http://www.state.nj.us/health/lh/phpracticestds/apexph.pdf

This website offers a set of 18 PowerPoint slides on the assessment protocol for excellence in public health (APEXPH). *View these slides and identify the benefits of this model for local health departments.*

Centers for Disease Control and Prevention (CDC)

http://www.cdc.gov/

The Centers for Disease Control and Prevention (CDC), founded in 1946, is one of the major components of the United States Department of Health and Human Services.

We have seen in this chapter that the CDC helped in formation of the PATCH model and provided funding for the APEXPH model. This website contains reliable health-related information on almost all important public health topics. *Explore this website to see the numerous activities of the CDC. Type in the word PATCH in its search engine to find historic information about the PATCH model.*

Mississippi State University Extension Service: Health Education Planning Models

http://msucares.com/health/health/appa2.htm

The website presents a summary of 10 health education planning models: the comprehensive health education model (CHEM), model for health education planning (MHEP), the PRECEDE framework, generic health/fitness delivery system, community wellness model, PRECEDE-PROCEED model, the PEN-3 model, APEXPH, PATCH, and formative evaluation, consultation, and systems technique (FORECAST) model. *Visit this website and read about models that have not been discussed in this chapter.*

National Association of County and City Health Officials (NACCHO)

http://www.naccho.org/

NACCHO is the national organization representing local public health agencies. The assessment protocol for excellence in public health (APEXPH) model was developed by NACCHO. The website provides news and information about events pertaining to local health departments, programs and activities, publications and tools, public health advocacy, press room, and membership. *In the publications and tools section, locate the information on how to order the APEXPH workbook.*

PRECEDE-PROCEED Model

http://www.lgreen.net/precede.htm

The PRECEDE-PROCEED model has evolved since 1970s, using inputs from several professionals around the country. This website includes a brief history of the genesis and evolution of the model. *Explore this website to find out about the new features in the current edition of the book that describes this model.*

REFERENCES

Aaro, L. E., Flisher, A. J., Kaaya, S., Onya, H., Fuglesang, M., Klepp, K. I., et al. (2006). Promoting sexual and reproductive health in early adolescence in South Africa and Tanzania: Development of a theory- and evidence-based intervention programme. *Scandinavian Journal of Public Health, 34*(2), 150–158.

Abbema, E. A., Van Assema, P., Kok, G. J., De Leeuw, E., & De Vries, N. K. (2004). Effect evaluation of a comprehensive community intervention aimed at reducing socioeconomic health inequalities in The Netherlands. *Health Promotion International, 19*(2), 141–156.

Abernethy, A. D., Magat, M. M., Houston, T. R., Arnold, H. L., Jr., Bjorck, J. P., & Gorsuch, R. L. (2005). Recruiting African American men for cancer screening studies: Applying a culturally based model. *Health Education and Behavior, 32*(4), 441–451.

Airhihenbuwa, C. O. (1993). Health promotion for child survival in Africa: Implications for cultural appropriateness. *Hygie, 12*(3), 10–15.

Airhihenbuwa, C. O. (1995). *Health and culture: Beyond the Western paradigm.* Thousand Oaks, CA: Sage Publications.

Alewijnse, D., Mesters, I. E., Metsemakers, J. F., & van den Borne, B. H. (2002). Program development for promoting adherence during and after exercise therapy for urinary incontinence. *Patient Education and Counseling, 48*(2), 147–160.

Bailey, P. H., Rukholm, E. E., Vanderlee, R., & Hyland, J. (1994). A heart health survey at the worksite: The first step to effective programming. *AAOHN Journal, 42,* 9–14.

Bartholomew, L. K., Parcel, G. S., Kok, G., & Gottlieb, N. H. (2006). *Planning health promotion programs: An intervention mapping approach.* San Francisco: Jossey-Bass.

Bates, I. J., & Winder, A. E. (1984). *Introduction to health education.* Mountain View, CA: Mayfield.

Batten, J. D. (1992). *Building a total quality culture.* Menlo Park, CA: Crisp.

Beech, B. M., & Scarinci, I. C. (2003). Smoking attitudes and practices among low-income African-Americans: Qualitative assessment of contributing factors. *American Journal of Health Promotion, 17*(4), 240–248.

Brouse, C. H., Basch, C. E., Wolf, R. L., & Shmukler, C. (2004). Barriers to colorectal cancer screening: An educational diagnosis. *Journal of Cancer Education, 19*(3), 170–173.

Brug, J., Oenema, A., & Ferreira, I. (2005). Theory, evidence and intervention mapping to improve behavior nutrition and physical activity interventions. *International Journal of Behavioral and Nutrition and Physical Activity, 2*(1), 2.

Centers for Disease Control and Prevention. (2004). *CDCynergy overview.* Retrieved May 31, 2006, from http://www.cdc.gov/communication/cdcynergy.htm

Chang, M. W., Brown, R. L., Nitzke, S., & Baumann, L. C. (2004). Development of an instrument to assess predisposing, enabling, and reinforcing constructs associated with fat intake behaviors of low-income mothers. *Journal of Nutrition, Education and Behavior, 36,* 27–34.

Chiang, L. C., Huang, J. L., Yeh, K. W., & Lu, C. M. (2004). Effects of a self management asthma educational program in Taiwan based on PRECEDE PROCEED model for parents with asthmatic children. *Journal of Asthma, 41*(2), 205–215.

Cole, R. E., & Horacek, T. (2009). Applying precede-proceed to develop an intuitive eating nondieting approach to weight management pilot program. *Journal of Nutrition Education & Behavior, 41*(2), 120–126.

Cole, R. E., & Horacek, T. (2010). Effectiveness of the "My Body Knows When" intuitive-eating pilot program. *American Journal of Health Behavior, 34*(3), 286–297.

Collard, D. C., Chinapaw, M. J., van Mechelen, W., & Verhagen, E. A. (2009). Design of the iPlay study: Systematic development of a physical activity injury prevention programme for primary school children. *Sports Medicine, 39*(11), 889–901. doi: 10.2165/11317880-000000000-00000

Dever, G. E. (1997). *Improving outcomes in public health practice: Strategy and methods.* Gaithersburg, MD: Aspen.

Dille, J. H. (1999). Worksite influenza immunization. Successful program. *AAOHN Journal, 47*(7), 292–300.

Erwin, D. O., Johnson, V. A., Feliciano-Libid, L., Zamora, D., & Jandorf, L. (2005). Incorporating cultural constructs and demographic diversity in the research and development of a Latina breast and cervical cancer education program. *Journal of Cancer Education, 20*(1), 39–44.

Erwin, D. O., Johnson, V. A., Trevino, M., Duke, K., Feliciano, L., & Jandorf, L. (2007). A comparison of African American and Latina social networks as indicators for culturally tailoring a breast and cervical cancer education intervention. *Cancer, 109*(2 Suppl), 368–377.

Fernandez, M. E., Gonzales, A., Tortolero-Luna, G., Partida, S., & Bartholomew, L. K. (2005). Using intervention mapping to develop a breast and cervical cancer screening program for Hispanic farmworkers: Cultivando La Salud. *Health Promotion Practice, 6*(4), 394–404.

Fishbein, M., & Ajzen, I. (1975). *Belief, attitude, intention, and behavior: An introduction to theory and research.* Reading, MA: Addison Wesley.

Fisher, E. B., Jr., Strunk, R. C., Sussman, L. K., Arfken, C., Sykes, R. K., Munro, J. M., et al. (1996). Acceptability and feasibility of a community approach to asthma management: The Neighborhood Asthma Coalition (NAC). *Journal of Asthma, 33*(6), 367–383.

Garces, I. C., Scarinci, I. C., & Harrison, L. (2006). An examination of sociocultural factors associated with health and health care seeking among Latina immigrants. *Journal of Immigrant and Minority Health, 8*(4), 377–385.

Gold, R. S., Green, L. W., & Kreuter, M. W. (1998). *EMPOWER: Enabling methods of planning and organizing within everyone's reach.* Sudbury, MA: Jones and Bartlett.

Goodman, R. M., Steckler, A., Hoover, S., & Schwartz, R. (1993). A critique of contemporary community health promotion approaches: Based on a qualitative review of six programs in Maine. *American Journal of Health Promotion, 7*(3), 208–220.

Green, L. W. (1970). Identifying and overcoming barriers to the diffusion of knowledge about family planning. *Advances in Fertility Control, 5,* 21–29.

Green, L. W. (1974). Toward cost-benefit evaluations of health education: Some concepts, methods and examples. *Health Education Monographs, 2*(Suppl. 1) 34–64.

Green, L. W., & Kreuter, M. W. (2005). *Health program planning: An educational and ecological approach* (4th ed.). Boston: McGraw-Hill.

Green, L. W., Kreuter, M. W., Deeds, S. G., & Partridge, K. B. (1980). *Health education planning: A diagnostic approach.* Palo Alto, CA: Mayfield.

Green, L. W., Levine, D. M., & Deeds, S. G. (1975). Clinical trials of health education for hypertensive outpatients: Design and baseline data. *Preventive Medicine, 4,* 417–425.

Green, L. W., Levine, D. M., Wolle, J., & Deeds, S. G. (1979). Development of randomized patient education experiments with urban poor hypertensives. *Patient Counseling and Health Education, 1,* 106–111.

Hall, N., & Best, J. A. (1997). Health promotion practice and public health: Challenge for the 1990s. Heart Health Think Tank Group. *Canadian Journal of Public Health, 88*, 409–415.

Heinen, M. M., Bartholomew, L. K., Wensing, M., Kerkhof, P., & Achterberg, T. (2006). Supporting adherence and healthy lifestyles in leg ulcer patients: Systematic development of the Lively Legs program for dermatology outpatient clinics. *Patient Education and Counseling, 61*(2), 279–291.

Hochbaum, G. M. (1958). *Public participation in medical screening programs: A sociopsychological study* (PHS Publication No. 572). Washington, DC: U.S. Government Printing Office.

Hu, J., Wallace, D. C., Jones, E., & Liu, H. (2009). Cardiometabolic health of Chinese older adults with diabetes living in Beijing, China. *Public Health Nursing, 26*(6), 500–511.

James, D. C. (2004). Factors influencing food choices, dietary intake, and nutrition-related attitudes among African Americans: Application of a culturally sensitive model. *Ethnicity and Health, 9*(4), 349–367.

Kalos, A., Kent, L., & Gates, D. (2005). Integrating MAPP, APEXPH, PACE-EH, and other planning initiatives in Northern Kentucky. *Journal of Public Health Management and Practice,* 11(5), 401–406.

Kang, J. H., Han, H. R., Kim, K. B., & Kim, M. T. (2006). Barriers to care and control of high blood pressure in Korean-American elderly. *Ethnicity and Disease, 16*(1), 145–151.

Kannan, S., Sparks, A. V., Webster, J. D., Krishnakumar, A., & Lumeng, J. (2009). Healthy eating and Harambee: Curriculum development for a culturally-centered bio-medically oriented nutrition education program to reach African American women of childbearing age. Maternal and *Child Health Journal*, Epub ahead of print PMID: 19655237

Ka'opua, L. S. (2008). Developing a culturally responsive breast cancer screening promotion with Native Hawaiian women in churches. *Health & Social Work,* 33(3), 169–177.

Kettner, P., Moroney, R., & Martin, L. (1999). *Designing and managing programs: An effectiveness based approach* (2nd ed.). Thousand Oaks, CA: Sage.

Kline, K. N. (2007). Cultural sensitivity and health promotion: Assessing breast cancer education pamphlets designed for African American women. *Health Communication, 21*(1), 85–96.

Kremers, S. P., Visscher, T. L., Brug, J., Chin, A.P.M.J., Schouten, E. G., Schuit, A. J., et al. (2005). Netherlands research programme weight gain prevention (NHF-NRG): Rationale, objectives and strategies. *European Journal of Clinical Nutrition, 59*(4), 498–507.

Kreuter, M. W. (1992). PATCH: Its origin, basic concepts, and links to contemporary public health policy. *Journal of Health Education, 23*(3), 135–139.

Larson, E. L., Cohn, E. G., Meyer, D. D., & Boden-Albala, B. (2009). Consent administrator training to reduce disparities in research participation. *Journal of Nursing Scholarship, 41*(1), 95–103.

Lengerich, E. J., Kluhsman, B. C., Bencivenga, M., Allen, R., Miele, M. B., & Farace, E. (2007). Development of community plans to enhance survivorship from colorectal cancer: Community-based participatory research in rural communities. *Journal of Cancer Survivorship, 1*(3), 205–211.

Li, Y., Cao, J., Lin, H., Li, D., Wang, Y., & He, J. (2009). Community health needs assessment with precede-proceed model: A mixed methods study. *BMC Health Services Research,* 9, 181.

Linnan, L. A., Sterba, K. R., Lee, A. M., Bontempi, J. B., Yang, J., & Crump, C. (2005). Planning and the professional preparation of health educators: Implications for teaching, research, and practice. *Health Promotion Practice, 6*, 308–319.

MacDonald, M. A., & Green, L. W. (2001). Reconciling concept and context: The dilemma of implementation in school-based health promotion. *Health Education and Behavior, 28*(6), 749–768.

Macrina, D., Macrina, N., Horvath, C., Gallaspy, J., & Fine, P. R. (1996). An educational intervention to increase use of the Glasgow Coma Scale by emergency department personnel. *International Journal of Trauma Nursing, 2*(1), 7–12.

Mkumbo, K., Schaalma, H., Kaaya, S., Leerlooijer, J., Mbwambo, J., & Kilonzo G. (2009). The application of intervention mapping in developing and implementing school-based sexuality and HIV/AIDS education in a developing country context: The case of Tanzania. *Scandinavian Journal of Public Health, 37*(Suppl. 2), 28–36.

Moore, P. V., & Short, J. (1994). Planning a continuing education program: The model for health education planning. *AAOHN Journal, 42*(9), 430–434.

Murray, N. G., Kelder, S. H., Parcel, G. S., Frankowski, R., & Orpinas, P. (1999). Padres Trabajando por la Paz: A randomized trial of a parent education intervention to prevent violence among middle school children. *Health Education Research, 14*(3), 421–426.

National Association of County and City Health Officials. (1991). *Assessment Protocol for Excellence in Public Health (APEXPH) workbook*. Washington, DC: Author.

Neiger, B. L., Thackeray, R., Barnes, M. D., & McKenzie J. F. (2003). Positioning social marketing as a planning process for health education. *American Journal of Health Studies, 18*(2/3), 75–81.

Perez-Rodrigo, C., Wind, M., Hildonen, C., Bjelland, M., Aranceta, J., Klepp, K. I., et al. (2005). The pro children intervention: Applying the intervention mapping protocol to develop a school-based fruit and vegetable promotion programme. *Annals of Nutrition and Metabolism, 49*(4), 267–277.

Prochaska, J. O., & DiClemente, C. C. (1983). Stages and processes of self change of smoking: Toward an integrative model of change. *Journal of Consulting and Clinical Psychology, 51*, 390–395.

Rosenstock, I. M., Derryberry, M., & Carriger, B. (1959). Why people fail to seek poliomyelitis vaccination. *Public Health Reports, 74*, 98–103.

Ross, H., & Mico, P. (1980). *Theory and practice in health education*. Palo Alto, CA: Mayfield.

Simons-Morton, B. G., Greene, W. H., & Gottlieb, N. H. (1995). *Introduction to health education and health promotion* (2nd ed.). Prospect Heights, IL: Waveland.

Society for Public Health Education. (2002). *CDCynergy training*. Retrieved May 30, 2006, from http://www.sophe.org/public/cdcynergy/cdc_description.html

Suen, J., Christenson, G. M., Cooper, A., & Taylor, M. (1995). Analysis of the current status of public health practice in local health departments. *American Journal of Preventive Medicine, 11*(Suppl. 6), 51–54.

Sullivan, D. (1973). Model for comprehensive, systematic program development in health education. *Health Education Report, 1*(1), 4–5.

Tortolero, S. R., Markham, C. M., Parcel, G. S., Peters, R. J., Jr., Escobar-Chaves, S. L., Basen-Engquist, K., et al. (2005). Using intervention mapping to adapt an effective HIV, sexually transmitted disease, and pregnancy prevention program for high-risk minority youth. *Health Promotion Practice, 6*(3), 286–298.

Turnock, B. J., Handler, A., Hall, W., Lenihan, D. P., & Vaughn, E. (1995). Capacity-building influences on Illinois local health departments. *Journal of Public Health Management and Practice, 1*(3), 50–58.

U.S. Department of Health and Human Services. (2005). *Planned Approach to Community Health: Guide for the local coordinator*. Atlanta, GA: U.S. Department of Health and Human Services, Centers for Disease Control and Prevention, National Center for Chronic Disease Prevention and Health Promotion. Retrieved May 23, 2006, from http://www.cdc.gov/nccdphp/publications/PATCH/index.htm

U.S. Department of Health and Human Services. (2009). *Healthy People 2020: The road ahead*. Retrieved from http://www.healthypeople.gov/HP2020/default.asp

van Stralen, M. M., de Vries, H., Mudde, A. N., Bolman, C., & Lechner, L. (2009). The working mechanisms of an environmentally tailored physical activity intervention for older adults: A randomized controlled trial. *International Journal of Behavioral Nutrition and Physical Activity*, *6*, 83.

Vaughn, E. H., Richards, T. B., Christenson, G. M., Taylor, M. S., & Eyster, J. (1994). An information manager for the Assessment Protocol for Excellence in Public Health. *Public Health Nursing*, *11*(6), 399–405.

Verweij, L. M., Proper, K. I., Weel, A. N., Hulshof, C. T., & van Mechelen, W. (2009). Design of the Balance Systematic development, evaluation and implementation of an occupational health guideline aimed at the prevention of weight gain among employees. *BMC Public Health*, *9*, 461.

Watson, M. R., Horowitz, A. M., Garcia, I., & Canto, M. T. (2001). A community participatory oral health promotion program in an inner-city Latino community. *Journal of Public Health Dentistry*, *61*, 34–41.

Webster, J. D., & Airhihenbuwa, C. O. (2005). *PEN-3 model: A cultural framework for organizing CBPR principles and practice*. Paper presented at 133rd Annual Meeting of American Public Health Association. Abstract retrieved from http://apha.confex.com/apha/133am/techprogram/paper_107991.htm

Wilkens, P. M. (2003). Preventing work-related musculoskeletal disorders in VDT users: A comprehensive health promotion program. *Work*, *20*(3), 171–178.

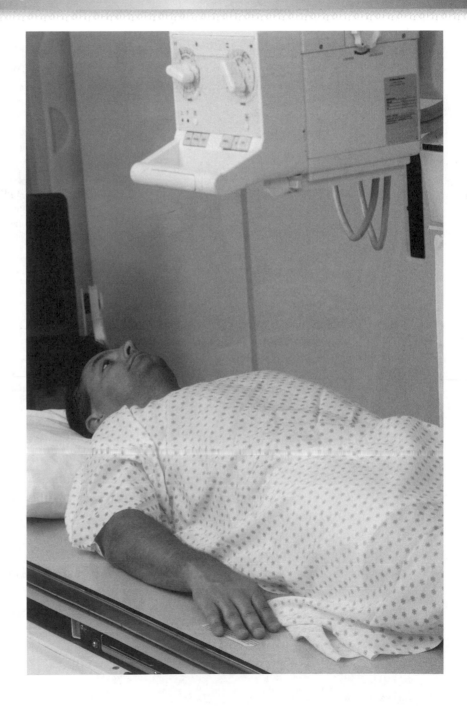

CHAPTER 3

The Health Belief Model

KEY CONCEPTS

- cues to action
- health belief model (HBM)
- illness behaviors
- perceived barriers
- perceived benefits
- perceived severity

- perceived susceptibility
- perceived threat
- preventive or health behaviors
- self-efficacy
- sick role behaviors
- value expectancy theories

AFTER READING THIS CHAPTER YOU SHOULD BE ABLE TO

- Describe the historical genesis of the health belief model (HBM)
- List six constructs of the HBM
- Summarize the applications of the HBM in health education and health promotion
- Identify educational methods and match these to modify each construct from the HBM
- Apply the HBM in changing a health behavior of your choice

The **health belief model (HBM)** is one of the first theories developed exclusively for health-related behaviors. Although labeled a "model," the HBM meets all the criteria for a theory (see Chapter 2 for a discussion of the differences between a model and a theory). The HBM originated in the 1950s and has been thoroughly tested in a variety of situations since that time. Today it is one of the most popular models as it provides specific guidance at the micro level for planning the "how to" part of interventions. Based on experimentation over the years, the HBM has expanded and borrowed from other theories to strengthen its predictive and explanatory potential.

This chapter begins with a description of the historical aspects of the genesis of the health belief model. Next we describe the various constructs that make up the model. Then we discuss the applications of the HBM in behavioral research, primary prevention, and secondary prevention. Finally, the limitations of the model are discussed, and a skill-building application using the HBM is presented.

HISTORICAL PERSPECTIVE

The HBM originated from the work of a group of social psychologists in the U.S. Public Health Service in the 1950s. Godfrey Hochbaum, Stephen Kegels, and Irwin Rosenstock (Rosenstock, 1974a). These social psychologists were confronted with the problem that very few people were participating in preventive and disease detection programs. The Public Health Service sent out chest x-ray units to neighborhoods to conduct free screening for tuberculosis, yet few people took advantage of the service. To explain this phenomenon and to help recruit more participation from people, the group looked at the existing theories and then developed the HBM.

Development of the health belief model was influenced by the theory of Kurt Lewin and his colleagues (Lewin, 1935; Lewin, Dembo, Festinger, & Sears, 1944) that behavior depends on two variables: (1) the value placed by an individual on an outcome (value) and (2) the individual's estimate of the likelihood that a given action will result in that outcome (expectancy). It is a goal-setting theory based on level of aspiration, in which the individual sets the target of future performance based on past performance (Maiman & Becker, 1974). Such theories are called **value expectancy theories**, and the HBM falls into this category. Maiman and Becker (1974) noted that the HBM was conceptually similar to five other theories of decision making prominent in the 1950s: Atkinson's (1957) risk-taking model, Edwards's (1954) subjective expected utility model, Feather's (1959) decision making under uncertainty model, Rotter's (1954) reinforcement model, and Tolman's (1955) performance behavior theory.

Atkinson's (1957) risk-taking model described behavior as a multiplicative relationship among expectancy, incentive, and motive. Expectancy is the person's anticipation of outcomes from an action, which can be positive or negative. Incentives are rewards that will accrue when the person performs the behavior. Motives are characteristics that encourage the person to pursue positive incentives and avoid negative incentives. Edwards's (1954) subjective expected utility model purports that action is based on the subjective value (or utility) of attaining the goal and the subjective probability (or likelihood) of attaining that goal.

Feather's (1959) decision making under uncertainty model utilizes three constructs: (1) attainment attractiveness, which is the individual's preference to pursue a goal; (2) success probability, which is the likelihood that a given goal is attainable; and (3) choice potential, which is the behavior to be done. Rotter's (1954) reinforcement model purports that behavior is based on the expectancy that a certain action will lead to a certain outcome and on reinforcement from previous learning.

Finally, Tolman's (1955) theory describes six variables (three positive and three negative) that influence the performance of any behavior: (1) need-push for food,

(2) positive valence of expected food, (3) expectation of food, (4) need-push against work, (5) negative valence of expected work, and (6) expectation of work.

Maiman and Becker (1974) noted that these models all predict behavior based on two variables: the value the individual placed on a particular goal (attractiveness of the goal) and the individual's estimate regarding the likelihood of attaining that goal (subjective probability). Thus all these theories are value expectancy theories.

> *The Health Belief Model relates psychological theories of decision making (which attempt to explain action in a choice situation) to an individual's decision about alternative health behaviors.*
>
> —Maiman and Becker (1974, p. 9)

Kasl and Cobb (1966) classified three kinds of behaviors regarding health. The first are **preventive (or health) behaviors**, which consist of actions taken for the purpose of preventing disease or detecting disease in an asymptomatic phase by a person who believes him- or herself to be healthy. Initially, the HBM was developed mainly to address these preventive behaviors (Rosenstock, 1974b). The second group are **illness behaviors**, which consist of actions taken by a person who feels sick and indulges in the behavior for the purpose of defining the state of his or her health and for discovering suitable remedies. The third group are **sick role behaviors**, which consist of actions taken by people who are sick for the purpose of getting well. The HBM also has been applied to illness behaviors (Kirscht, 1974), sick role behaviors (Becker, 1974), and behaviors related to chronic illness (Kasl, 1974).

In the 1970s a review measured the various dimensions of the HBM on standardized scales (Maiman, Becker, Kirscht, Haefner, & Drachman, 1977), and in the 1980s the model was strengthened further, mostly by the work of Marshall Becker and colleagues (Janz & Becker, 1984). In the late 1980s the model was expanded to include self-efficacy (Rosenstock, Strecher, & Becker, 1988). Since then the model has been applied to a variety of health behaviors.

CONSTRUCTS OF THE HEALTH BELIEF MODEL

Theories from behavioral and social sciences have what are known as "constructs," and these building blocks can be distinctly identified. The constructs of HBM are depicted in **Figure 3.1**. The HBM has six constructs, the first of which is **perceived susceptibility**. This refers to the subjective belief that a person has with regard to acquiring a disease or reaching a harmful state as a result of indulging in a particular behavior. Individuals vary considerably with regard to their perception of susceptibility to any given illness or harmful condition. On one extreme are individuals who completely deny any possibility of their acquiring the disease. In the middle are people who may admit to the possibility of acquiring the disease, but believe it is not likely to

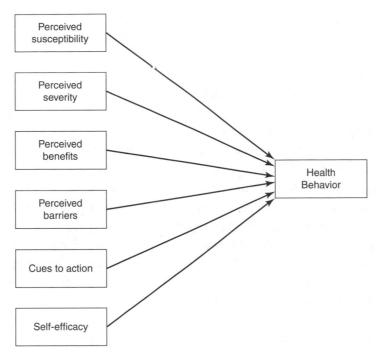

FIGURE 3.1   Constructs of the health belief model.

happen to them. At the other extreme are people who are so fearful of acquiring the disease that they believe they will in all probability acquire it. The more susceptible a person feels, the greater the likelihood of his or her taking preventive measures.

Perceived susceptibility has a strong cognitive component and is partly dependent on knowledge (Rosenstock, 1974a). According to the HBM, health educators need to build perceived susceptibility by elaborating on the possibility of negative consequences and personalizing those risks for their participants. For example, in a smoking prevention program, health educators might mention that smoking causes lung cancer and, based on the relative risk calculated from epidemiological studies, mention that this risk is 22 times higher for a smoker than for a nonsmoker. A word of caution needs to be kept in mind: in building perceived susceptibility, one should not create unrealistic or exaggerated fears about the condition.

The second construct of HBM is **perceived severity**, which refers to a person's subjective belief in the extent of harm that can result from the disease or harmful state as a result of a particular behavior. This perception also varies from person to person. One person might perceive the disease from a purely medical perspective and thus be concerned with signs, symptoms, any limitations arising out of the condition, the temporary or permanent nature of the condition, its potential for causing death, and so on; whereas another individual might look at the disease from a broader perspective, such as the adverse effects it might have on his or her family, job, and relationships.

Perceived severity also has a strong cognitive component, which is dependent on knowledge (Rosenstock, 1974a). According to the HBM, health educators need to build perceived severity by describing the serious negative consequences and personalizing them for participants. For example, in a nutrition education class, health educators might mention that consuming large amounts of saturated fats may lead to development of heart disease and share a story about a member of the community who suffered a heart attack. In addition to describing the clinical consequences, the effects on family, job, and relationships would also be shared. The constructs of perceived severity and perceived susceptibility are often grouped together and called **perceived threat**.

The third construct of the HBM is **perceived benefits**, which refers to belief in the advantages of the methods suggested for reducing the risk or seriousness of the disease or harmful state resulting from a particular behavior. The relative effectiveness of known available alternatives plays a role in shaping actions. An alternative is likely to be seen as beneficial if it reduces the perceived susceptibility or perceived severity of the disease (Rosenstock, 1974a). In facilitating the construct of perceived benefits, health educators need to specify the exact action to be taken and specify the advantages or benefits that would result from that course of action. For example, health educators teaching about breast self-examination would describe the exact technique and the benefits, such as the ability to detect cancer or other diseases early, feeling good about oneself, feeling in control of one's health, and feeling more responsible toward oneself and one's family.

The fourth construct, which goes hand-in-hand with the construct of perceived benefits, is **perceived barriers**. Perceived barriers refer to beliefs concerning the actual and imagined costs of following the new behavior. An individual may believe that a new action is effective in reducing perceived susceptibility or perceived severity of the disease but may consider the action to be expensive, inconvenient, unpleasant, painful, or upsetting (Rosenstock, 1974a). Health educators need to reduce such barriers so the person will take the recommended actions. They may do so by giving reassurance, correcting misperceptions, and providing incentives. For example, in a smoking cessation class, health educators might continually reassure participants that they can overcome the habit of smoking, correct the misperception that tobacco addiction is impossible to break by giving examples of persons who have broken the habit, and provide monetary incentives for participants to continue in the smoking cessation class.

The fifth construct in the HBM is **cues to action**, which are the precipitating forces that make a person feel the need to take action. Such cues may be internal (e.g., perception of a bodily state) or external (e.g., interpersonal interactions, media communication, or receiving a postcard from the doctor for a follow-up examination) (Rosenstock, 1974a). If the perceived susceptibility or perceived severity is low, then a very intense stimulus is needed as a cue to action. When the perceived susceptibility or perceived severity is high, then even a slight stimulus is adequate.

The final construct, **self-efficacy**, was added to the model in the 1980s (Rosenstock et al., 1988). We will learn more about this construct in Chapter 7 in the discussion of social cognitive theory, from which it was borrowed. Self-efficacy is the confidence that a person has in his or her ability to pursue a behavior. It is behavior specific and is in the present. It is not about the past or future. Four strategies can be used to build self-efficacy:

1. *Breaking down the complex behavior into practical and doable small steps.* For example, instead of telling women to perform breast self-examination, the women could be taught the entire procedure in small steps.

2. *Using a demonstration from a credible role model.* For example, in facilitating an educational program about quitting alcohol, a popular movie star (with whom the participants identify) who has successfully gone through the rehabilitation process could share his or her story to help enhance the self-efficacy of the participants.

3. *Using persuasion and reassurance.* If a person has failed in the past to make a behavior change, those failures can be attributed to external reasons. For example, in a smoking cessation program, a health educator could ask participants to identify their past failures with smoking cessation and then mention that they could have failed because of bad timing, having too many tasks at hand at that time, the season in which they were attempting the change, and so on.

4. *Reducing stress.* Any behavior change is associated with some amount of stress, which hinders the change process. When this stress is negative, or distress, it hinders the learning process. Reducing distress is an effective means of building self-efficacy. For example, if participants find breast self-examination to be stressful, they can be encouraged to relax by taking a shower or listening to music or practicing progressive muscle relaxation before performing the behavior.

Table 3.1 summarizes the key constructs of the health belief model.

The Health Belief Model (HBM) hypothesizes that health-related action depends upon the simultaneous occurrences of three classes of factors:

1. *The existence of sufficient motivation (or health concern) to make health issues salient or relevant.*
2. *The belief that one is susceptible (vulnerable) to a serious health problem or to the sequelae of that illness or condition. This is often termed perceived threat.*
3. *The belief that following a particular health recommendation would be beneficial in reducing the perceived threat, and at a subjectivity-acceptable cost.*

—Rosenstock, Strecher, and Becker (1988, p. 177)

TABLE 3.1	Key Constructs of the Health Belief Model	
Construct	**Definition**	**How to Modify?**
Perceived susceptibility	Subjective belief that a person may acquire a disease or enter a harmful state as a result of a particular behavior	• Mention negative consequences (e.g., smoking causes lung cancer) • Personalize the risks for participants (e.g., the chances of developing lung cancer if you are a smoker are 22 times more than a nonsmoker, based on a relative risk computed by epidemiological studies)
Perceived severity	Belief in the extent of harm that can result from the acquired disease or harmful state as a result of a particular behavior	• Mention serious negative consequences (e.g., eating saturated fats causes heart disease) • Personalize the seriousness for the education participants (e.g., share a story about a person who died from a heart attack in the community)
Perceived benefits	Belief in the advantages of the methods suggested for reducing the risk or seriousness of the disease or harmful state resulting from a particular behavior	• Specify the exact action (e.g., the individual will carry out breast self-examination in every quadrant every month after taking a shower) • Specify the positive benefits that will accrue from the behavior (e.g., doing breast self-examination monthly will allow you to detect cancer or other diseases early, to feel good about yourself, to feel in control of your health, and to feel more responsible toward yourself and your family)
Perceived barriers	Belief concerning actual and imagined costs of performing the suggested behavior	• Reassure the education recipients that the behavior has minimal cost (e.g., for breast self-examination, state that it would only mean spending another 15 minutes while taking a shower) • Correct any misperceptions that education participants may have (e.g., a person may think a gall bladder ultrasound is an invasive procedure; correcting that misperception may increase the likelihood of the person getting that test)

TABLE 3.1	*(continued)*		
Construct	Definition		How to Modify?
			• Provide incentives for indulging in the behavior (e.g., free cholesterol testing may be offered to increase the chances that more people will get tested)
Cues to action	Precipitating force that makes a person feel the need to take action		• Implement a reminder system to encourage the behavior (e.g., post a note or call the person on the phone)
Self-efficacy	Confidence in one's ability to acquire the new behavior		• Practice in small steps (e.g., breaking down complex behavior of self-examination into doable small steps)
			• Have a role model demonstrate the behavior (e.g., show a video of a well-known movie star with whom the target audience can identify performing the same behavior)
			• Use persuasion and reinforcement (e.g., tell participants that they have what it takes to perform the behavior, and attribute failures to external forces)
			• Reduce stress associated with implementing a new behavior (e.g., have participants take a relaxing shower before doing a breast self-examination)

APPLICATIONS OF THE HEALTH BELIEF MODEL

It is not possible to summarize all the applications of the HBM since the 1950s because so many practitioners and researchers have used it. However, the applications can be divided into three general categories:

The Health Belief Model was originally formulated to explain (preventive) health behavior.

—Rosenstock (1974b, p. 27)

1. Behavioral research model building and instrument development
2. Primary prevention through health education regarding prevention of diseases or for specific protection against diseases, such as immunization
3. Screening for diseases, compliance with treatment, and other secondary prevention tasks

Examples of behavioral research in which the HBM was used include developing an AIDS health belief scale (Zagumny & Brady, 1998), identifying factors associated with infant mortality (Eshleman, Poole, & Davidhizar, 2005), refining an instrument for breast cancer screening (Champion, 1993; Medina-Shepherd & Kleier, 2010), involvement of dental practitioners in the prevention of eating disorders (DiGioacchino, Keenan, & Sargent, 2000), modeling for physical activity behavior (Juniper, Oman, Hamm, & Kerby, 2004), predictive modeling to prevent severe acute respiratory syndrome (SARS) (Wong & Tang, 2005), predictors of health behaviors in college students (Von Ah, Ebert, Ngamvitroj, Park, & Kang, 2004), modeling of sexual behavior (Lin, Simoni, & Zemon, 2005), smoking in college students (Kofahi & Haddad, 2005), sociopsychological modeling for diabetes (Gillibrand & Stevenson, 2006), and using a sodium adherence dietary scale (Welch, Bennett, Delp, & Agarwal, 2006). **Table 3.2** summarizes these applications.

TABLE 3.2   Applications of the Health Belief Model in Behavioral Research

AIDS health belief scale

Factors associated with infant mortality

Instrument for breast cancer screening

Involvement of dental practitioners in the prevention of eating disorders

Modeling for physical activity behavior

Predictive modeling to prevent severe acute respiratory syndrome (SARS)

Predictors of health behaviors in college students

Modeling of sexual behavior

Smoking in college students

Sociopsychological modeling for diabetes

Sodium adherence dietary scale

The HBM has been used for primary prevention for promoting bicycle helmet use (Lajunen & Rasanen, 2004), promoting condom use in female sex workers (Buckingham, Moraros, Bird, Meister, & Webb, 2005), decreasing tanning bed use (Greene & Brinn, 2003), promoting healthy dietary behavior (Chew, Palmer, & Kim, 1998), genetic testing (Raz, Atar, Rodnay, Shoham-Vardi, & Carmi, 2003), promoting hepatitis B vaccination (Bigham et al., 2006), promoting influenza vaccination (Lau, Yang, Tsui, & Kim, 2006), promoting measles immunization (Pielak & Hilton, 2003), osteoporosis prevention (Nieto-Vázquez, Tejeda, Colin, & Matos, 2009), pesticide safety (Martinez, Gratton, Coggin, Rene, & Waller, 2004), prevention of periodontal disease (Ndiokwelu, 2004), solar disinfection of drinking water (Rainey & Harding, 2005), and tuberculosis prevention (Rodriguez-Reimann, Nicassio, Reimann, Gallegos, & Olmedo, 2004). **Table 3.3** summarizes these applications.

Some examples in which the HBM has been used for secondary prevention are for adherence to malaria chemoprophylaxis (Farquharson, Noble, Barker, & Behrens, 2004), breast self-examination and mammography (Dundar et al., 2006; Tavafian, Hasani, Aghamolaei, Zare, & Gregory, 2009), cervical cancer screening (Ben-Natan & Adir, 2009; Park, Chang, & Chung, 2005), cognitive status examination for Alzheimer's disease (Werner, 2003), colorectal cancer screening (Austin et al., 2009; Greenwald, 2006; Omran & Ismail, 2010), compliance with anticoagulant warfarin

TABLE 3.3   Applications of the Health Belief Model in Primary Prevention

Bicycle helmet use

Condom use in female sex workers

Decreasing tanning bed use

Dietary behavior

Genetic testing

Hepatitis B vaccination

Influenza vaccination

Measles immunization

Osteoporosis prevention

Pesticide safety

Prevention of periodontal disease

Solar disinfection of drinking water

Tuberculosis prevention

TABLE 3.4   Applications of the Health Belief Model in Secondary Prevention
Adherence to malaria chemoprophylaxis
Breast self-examination and mammography
Cervical cancer screening
Cognitive status examination for Alzheimer's disease
Colorectal cancer screening
Compliance with anticoagulant warfarin therapy
Compliance with antiviral therapy in hepatitis B patients
HIV testing
Medication compliance in schizophrenia
Medication adherence in AIDS
Medication use in osteoporosis
Patient acceptance of continuous positive airway pressure (CPAP) therapy in sleep apnea
Prostate cancer screening
Recurrent injury prevention in trauma patients
Screening for bone loss in epileptic patients
Tuberculosis screening

therapy (Orensky & Holdford, 2005), compliance with antiviral therapy in hepatitis B patients (Wai et al., 2005), HIV testing (de Paoli, Manongi, & Klepp, 2004), medication compliance in schizophrenia (Seo & Min, 2005), medication adherence in AIDS (Cox, 2009), medication use in osteoporosis (Unson, Fortinsky, Prestwood, & Reisine, 2005), patient acceptance of continuous positive airway pressure (CPAP) therapy in sleep apnea (Tyrrell, Poulet, Pe Pin, & Veale, 2006), prostate cancer screening (Doukas, Localio, & Li, 2004), recurrent injury prevention in trauma patients (Van Horn, 2005), screening for bone loss in epileptic patients (Elliott & Jacobson, 2006), and tuberculosis screening (Poss, 1999). **Table 3.4** summarizes these applications.

LIMITATIONS OF THE HEALTH BELIEF MODEL

The health belief model is particularly useful for planning programs for disease avoidance and injury avoidance, but it does not lend itself very well to promotion of behaviors, particularly long-term behavior change. Harrison, Mullen, and Green (1992) conducted a meta-analysis of the relationships among four HBM dimensions (perceived suscep-tibility, perceived severity, perceived benefits, and perceived costs) and health behav-iors in 16 studies. They computed mean effect sizes for all studies and found weak ef-fect sizes and lack of homogeneity in a majority of the studies. They concluded that the model lacked consistent predictive power mainly because it focuses on a limited number of factors. Cultural factors, socioeconomic status, and previous experiences also shape health behaviors, and those factors are not accounted for in the model. A study by Mullen, Hersey, and Iverson (1987) found less predictive power for the HBM when compared with the theory of reasoned action, the theory of planned be-havior, and the PRECEDE-PROCEED model. This conclusion once again under-scores the need for the HBM to expand its predictors. To some extent, that has been done by adding the construct of self-efficacy.

Another problem with the HBM (which is also true for other models) is that different questions are used in different studies to determine the same beliefs, thereby making it difficult to compare studies. Janz, Champion, and Strecher (2002) noted that the constructs of the HBM do not all carry equal value. For example, perceived barriers are the single most important predictors of behaviors in the HBM. Often it is not possible to easily influence the barriers, and thus the model will not work.

Ogden (2003) noted that the HBM is a pragmatic model but has criticized its conceptual basis. First, she noted that some studies of the HBM have found no role of perceived susceptibility, indicating that its constructs are not specific and cannot be tested. Second, she described two types of truth in the philosophy of science: syn-thetic truth, which can be known through exploration and testing; and analytic truth, which is known by definition. She contended that the HBM focuses on analytic truth; thus its conclusions are not supported by observation. Finally, she noted that com-pleting questions about an individual's cognition in the operationalization of the HBM may change that person's thinking rather than tap into how the individual was originally thinking. In a rejoinder to Ogden's article, Ajzen and Fishbein (2004) refuted all these assertions.

APPLICATION EXERCISE

Applications of the health belief model in behavioral research, primary prevention, and secondary prevention have been cited throughout the chapter. Choose one study in an area that interests you and obtain the full text article to see how this model has been applied.

One example is the development of an instrument for breast cancer screening behaviors by Champion (1993). She delimited her instrument development parameters to the constructs of the health belief model; namely, perceived susceptibility, perceived severity, perceived benefits, perceived barriers, cues to action, and self-efficacy. She developed items for each construct and used a Likert scale. She established construct validity of the scale through a panel of national experts and performed a factor analysis. Cronbach's alpha reliability coefficients for various construct scales ranged from .80 to .93. Test-retest correlations ranged from .45 to .70.

Locate the full text article for this study and prepare a 250 word critique.

SKILL-BUILDING ACTIVITY

Let us see how we can apply the HBM to the issue of safer sex practices among college students. **Figure 3.2** depicts each of the constructs from the HBM and links these with the educational processes and behavior objectives in this example.

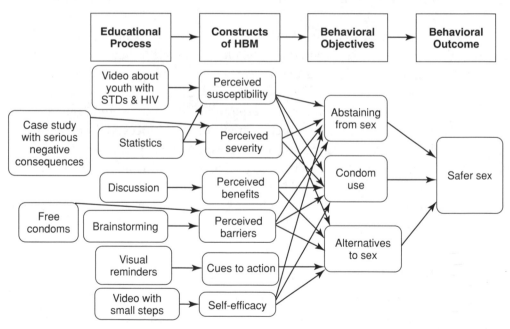

FIGURE 3.2   How the health belief model can be used to modify sexual behavior in youth to promote safer sex.

The health education intervention would start with modifying the construct of perceived susceptibility, which can be done by showing a video about college students suffering from HIV/AIDS and STDs. The video must show people who are similar to the target audience in their characteristics. The construct of perceived severity can be built by making a presentation using statistics and a case study that underscores the serious negative consequences. These consequences can be medical as well as involving school, work, family, and relationships. To influence perceived benefits, make sure students have all the information they need to take the action: for example, where to get condoms, how to choose them, how to store them, when to use them, how to put them on, how to remove them, and how to dispose of them. To modify perceived barriers, have the students brainstorm all real and imagined barriers. Then discuss in a large group how each of these barriers can be overcome to abstain from sex, use condoms, or use alternatives to sex. In addition, as an incentive, the students could be provided with a small supply of free condoms. To influence cues to action, visual reminders would be used. Youth would be provided with key chains with the messages so that they could remember to perform the chosen healthy behaviors. To build self-efficacy, a video with a credible role model could be shown that depicts the behaviors in small steps; reinforces the messages about abstinence, condom use, and alternatives to sex; and provides practical advice to reduce stress and anxiety in times of making love.

Using this approach, apply the HBM to a health behavior issue for a target group of your choice. **Table 3.5** provides a set of questions to assist you in choosing an appropriate educational method that corresponds to different constructs of the HBM.

SUMMARY

The health belief model is the first theory that was developed exclusively for health-related behaviors. It had its start in an exploration of the reasons people were not accessing free screening for tuberculosis. The HBM predicts behavior based on the constructs of perceived susceptibility, perceived severity, perceived benefits, perceived costs, cues to action, and self-efficacy. Perceived susceptibility refers to the subjective belief a person has regarding the likelihood of acquiring a disease or harmful state as a result of indulging in a particular behavior. Perceived severity refers to the subjective belief in the extent of harm that can result from the acquired disease or harmful state as a result of a particular behavior. Perceived susceptibility and perceived severity are together called perceived threat. Perceived benefits are beliefs in the advantages of the methods suggested for reducing the risk or seriousness of the disease or harmful state resulting from a particular behavior. Perceived barriers are beliefs concerning the actual

TABLE 3.5	**Choosing the Educational Methods for Health Education Program Planning Using the Health Belief Model**

1. What is the best educational method to facilitate perceived susceptibility?
   - Lecture underscoring negative consequences
   - Presenting statistics
   - Case study with negative consequences
   - Video film highlighting negative consequences
   - Other
2. What is the best educational method to facilitate perceived severity?
   - Lecture
   - Presenting statistics
   - Case study
   - Video film
   - Other
3. What is the best educational method to facilitate perceived benefits?
   - Lecture
   - Small group discussion
   - Large group discussion
   - Other
4. What is the best educational method to facilitate perceived barriers?
   - Brainstorming
   - Small group discussion
   - Large group discussion
   - Incentives
   - Other
5. What is the best educational method to facilitate cues to action?
   - Visual reminders
   - Phone call
   - Personal reminder
   - Other
6. What is the best educational method to facilitate self-efficacy?
   - Demonstration
   - Role play
   - Video with a credible role model
   - Stress reduction techniques
     - Progressive muscle relaxation
     - Visual imagery
     - Autogenic training
     - Yoga
     - Other
   - Other

and imagined costs of following the new behavior. Cues to action are the precipitating forces that make a person feel the need to take action. Self-efficacy is the confidence that a person has in his or her ability to pursue a behavior. The HBM has been widely used in behavioral research, primary prevention, and secondary prevention.

IMPORTANT TERMS

cues to action	perceived susceptibility
health belief model (HBM)	perceived threat
illness behaviors	preventive (or health) behaviors
perceived barriers	self-efficacy
perceived benefits	sick role behaviors
perceived severity	value expectancy theories

REVIEW QUESTIONS

1. Discuss the historical genesis of the health belief model.
2. Describe the constructs of the health belief model.
3. Define self-efficacy. How is self-efficacy built?
4. Differentiate between perceived severity and perceived susceptibility.
5. How can the construct of perceived barriers be modified?
6. Discuss the limitations of the health belief model.

WEBSITES TO EXPLORE

Centers for Disease Control and Prevention: Summary of HBM

http://www.cdc.gov/std/program/community/9-PGcommunity.htm

Visit this website from the Centers for Disease Control and Prevention. It has a summary of various models from individual and community level behavior change interventions. The descriptions of the constructs of the health belief model are summarized by one sentence depictions. *Read these depictions and explain how these add to your understanding of the HBM.*

Health Belief Model

http://std.about.com/od/education/a/healthbelief.htm

This website describes HBM and gives examples of applications of its constructs. *Review this website and develop a program that applies HBM to promote condom use.*

Meta-Analysis of HBM

http://her.oxfordjournals.org/cgi/content/abstract/7/1/107

This website presents an abstract of a study that included a meta-analysis of the relationships between four HBM constructs (perceived susceptibility, perceived severity, perceived benefits, and perceived barriers) and health behavior involving 16 studies. *Locate the full text article from your library and read it. Comment on the usefulness of the HBM based on this article.*

University of Twente: Health Belief Model

http://www.cw.utwente.nl/

Visit this website of University of Twente in Netherlands. Translate the page in English if needed. On the left side is the website's search engine. In that type the words Health Belief Model, and it will take you to a page that describes the model. It discusses the application of HBM to sexuality education. *Review the application and comment on its strengths and weaknesses.*

REFERENCES

Ajzen, I., & Fishbein, M. (2004). Questions raised by a reasoned action approach: Comment on Ogden (2003). *Health Psychology, 23*, 431–434.

Atkinson, J. W. (1957). Motivational determinants of risk taking behavior. *Psychological Review, 64*, 359–372.

Austin, K. L., Power, E., Solarin, I., Atkin, W. S., Wardle, J., & Robb, K. A. (2009). Perceived barriers to flexible sigmoidoscopy screening for colorectal cancer among UK ethnic minority groups: A qualitative study. *Journal of Medical Screening, 16*(4), 174–179.

Becker, M. H. (1974). The health belief model and sick role behavior. In M. H. Becker (Ed.), *The health belief model and personal health behavior* (pp. 82–92). Thorofare, NJ: Charles B. Slack.

Ben-Natan, M., & Adir, O. (2009). Screening for cervical cancer among Israeli lesbian women. *International Nursing Review, 56*(4), 433–441.

Bigham, M., Remple, V. P., Pielak, K., McIntyre, C., White, R., & Wu, W. (2006). Uptake and behavioural and attitudinal determinants of immunization in an expanded routine infant hepatitis B vaccination program in British Columbia. *Canadian Journal of Public Health, 97*(2), 90–95.

Buckingham, R. W., Moraros, J., Bird, Y., Meister, E., & Webb, N. C. (2005). Factors associated with condom use among brothel-based female sex workers in Thailand. *AIDS Care, 17*(5), 640–647.

Butraporn, P., Pach, A., Pack, R. P., Masngarmmeung, R., Maton, T., Sri-aroon, P., et al. (2004). The health belief model and factors relating to potential use of a vaccine for shigellosis in Kaeng Koi district, Saraburi province, Thailand. *Journal of Health, Population, and Nutrition, 22*, 170–181.

Champion, V. L. (1993). Instrument refinement for breast cancer screening behaviors. *Nursing Research, 42*,139–143.

Chew, F., Palmer, S., & Kim, S. (1998). Testing the influence of the health belief model and a television program on nutrition behavior. *Health Communication, 10*(3), 227–245.

Cox, L. E. (2009). Predictors of medication adherence in an AIDS clinical trial: Patient and clinician perceptions. *Health and Social Work, 34*(4), 257–264.

de Paoli, M. M., Manongi, R., & Klepp, K. I. (2004). Factors influencing acceptability of voluntary counselling and HIV-testing among pregnant women in northern Tanzania. *AIDS Care, 16*(4), 411–425.

DiGioacchino, R. F., Keenan, M. F., & Sargent, R. (2000). Assessment of dental practitioners in the secondary and tertiary prevention of eating disorders. *Eating Behaviors, 1*(1), 79–91.

Doukas, D. J., Localio, A. R., & Li, Y. (2004). Attitudes and beliefs concerning prostate cancer genetic screening. *Clinical Genetics, 66*(5), 445–451.

Dundar, P. E, Ozmen, D., Ozturk, B., Haspolat, G., Akyildiz, F., Coban, S., et al. (2006). The knowledge and attitudes of breast self-examination and mammography in a group of women in a rural area in western Turkey. *BMC Cancer, 6*, 43.

Edwards, W. (1954). The theory of decision making. *Psychological Bulletin, 51*, 380–417.

Elliott, J. O., & Jacobson, M. P. (2006). Bone loss in epilepsy: Barriers to prevention, diagnosis, and treatment. *Epilepsy and Behavior, 8*(1), 169–175.

Eshleman, M. J., Poole, V., & Davidhizar, R. (2005). An investigation of factors associated with infant mortality in two midwest counties. *Journal of Practical Nursing, 55*(3), 5–10.

Farquharson, L., Noble, L. M., Barker, C., & Behrens, R. H. (2004). Health beliefs and communication in the travel clinic consultation as predictors of adherence to malaria chemoprophylaxis. *British Journal of Health Psychology, 9*(Pt. 2), 201–217.

Feather, N. T. (1959). Subjective probability and decision under uncertainty. *Psychological Review, 66*, 150–164.

Gillibrand, R., & Stevenson, J. (2006). The extended health belief model applied to the experience of diabetes in young people. *British Journal of Health Psychology, 11*, 155–169.

Greene, K., & Brinn, L. S. (2003). Messages influencing college women's tanning bed use: Statistical versus narrative evidence format and a self-assessment to increase perceived susceptibility. *Journal of Health Communication, 8*(5), 443–461.

Greenwald, B. (2006). Promoting community awareness of the need for colorectal cancer screening: A pilot study. *Cancer Nursing, 29*(2),134–141.

Harrison, J. A., Mullen, P. D., & Green, L. W. (1992). A meta-analysis of studies of the health belief model with adults. *Health Education Research, 7*(1), 107–116.

Janz, N. K., & Becker, M. H. (1984). The health belief model: A decade later. *Health Education Quarterly, 11*, 1–47.

Janz, N. K., Champion, V. L., & Strecher, V. J. (2002). The health belief model. In K. Glanz, B. K. Rimer, & F. M. Lewis (Eds.), *Health behavior and health education: Theory, research, and practice* (3rd ed., pp. 45–66). San Francisco: Jossey-Bass.

Juniper, K. C., Oman, R. F., Hamm, R. M., & Kerby, D. S. (2004). The relationships among constructs in the health belief model and the transtheoretical model among African-American college women for physical activity. *American Journal of Health Promotion, 18*(5), 354–357.

Kasl, S. V. (1974). The health belief model and behavior related to chronic illness. In M. H. Becker (Ed.), *The health belief model and personal health behavior* (pp. 106–127). Thorofare, NJ: Charles B. Slack.

Kasl, S. V., & Cobb, S. (1966). Health behavior, illness behavior, and sick role behavior. I. Health and illness behavior. *Archives of Environmental Health, 12*(2), 246–266.

Kirscht, J. P. (1974). The health belief model and illness behavior. In M. H. Becker (Ed.), *The health belief model and personal health behavior* (pp. 60–81). Thorofare, NJ: Charles B. Slack.

Kofahi, M. M., & Haddad, L. G. (2005). Perceptions of lung cancer and smoking among college students in Jordan. *Journal of Transcultural Nursing, 16*(3), 245–254.

Lajunen, T., & Rasanen, M. (2004). Can social psychological models be used to promote bicycle helmet use among teenagers? A comparison of the health belief model, theory of planned behavior and the locus of control. *Journal of Safety Research, 35*(1), 115–123.

Lau, J. T., Yang, X., Tsui, H. Y., & Kim, J. H. (2006). Prevalence of influenza vaccination and associated factors among community-dwelling Hong Kong residents of age 65 or above. *Vaccine, 24*(26), 5526–5534.

Lewin, K. (1935). *A dynamic theory of personality: Selected papers.* New York: McGraw-Hill.

Lewin, K., Dembo, T., Festinger, L., & Sears, P. S. (1944). Level of aspiration. In J. M. Hunt (Ed.), *Personality and the behavior disorders: A handbook based on experimental and clinical research* (pp. 333–378). New York: The Ronald Press.

Lin, P., Simoni, J. M., & Zemon, V. (2005). The health belief model, sexual behaviors, and HIV risk among Taiwanese immigrants. *AIDS Education & Prevention, 17*(5), 469–483.

Maiman, L. A., & Becker, M. H. (1974). The health belief model: Origins and correlates in psychological theory. In M. H. Becker (Ed.), *The health belief model and personal health behavior* (pp. 9–26). Thorofare, NJ: Charles B. Slack.

Maiman, L. A., Becker, M. H., Kirscht, J. P., Haefner, D. P., & Drachman, R. H. (1977). Scales for measuring health belief model dimensions: A test of predictive value, internal consistency, and relationships among beliefs. *Health Education Monographs, 5*, 215–230.

Martinez, R., Gratton, T. B., Coggin, C., Rene, A., & Waller, W. (2004). A study of pesticide safety and health perceptions among pesticide applicators in Tarrant County, Texas. *Journal of Environmental Health, 66*(6), 34–37, 43.

Medina-Shepherd, R., & Kleier, J. A. (2010). Spanish translation and adaptation of Victoria Champion's Health Belief Model Scales for breast cancer screening-mammography. *Cancer Nursing, 33*(2), 93–101.

Mullen, P. D., Hersey, J. C., & Iverson, D. C. (1987). Health behavior models compared. *Social Science and Medicine, 24*, 973–981.

Ndiokwelu, E. (2004). Applicability of Rosenstock-Hochbaum health behaviour model to prevention of periodontal disease in Enugu students. *Odontostomatologie Tropicale, 27*(106), 4–8.

Nieto-Vázquez, M., Tejeda, M. J., Colin, J., & Matos, A. (2009). Results of an osteoporosis educational intervention randomized trial in a sample of Puerto-Rican women. *Journal of Cultural Diversity, 16*(4), 171–177.

Ogden, J. (2003). Some problems with social cognition models: A pragmatic and conceptual analysis. *Health Psychology, 22*, 424–428.

Omran, S., & Ismail, A. A. (2010). Knowledge and beliefs of Jordanians toward colorectal cancer screening. *Cancer Nursing, 33*(2), 141–148.

Orensky, I. A., & Holdford, D. A. (2005). Predictors of noncompliance with warfarin therapy in an outpatient anticoagulation clinic. *Pharmacotherapy, 25*(12), 1801–1808.

Park, S., Chang, S., & Chung, C. (2005). Effects of a cognition-emotion focused program to increase public participation in Papanicolaou smear screening. *Public Health Nursing, 22*(4), 289–298.

Pielak, K. L., & Hilton, A. (2003). University students immunized and not immunized for measles: A comparison of beliefs, attitudes, and perceived barriers and benefits. *Canadian Journal of Public Health, 94*(3), 193–196.

Poss, J. E. (1999). Developing an instrument to study the tuberculosis screening behaviors of Mexican migrant farmworkers. *Journal of Transcultural Nursing, 10*(4), 306–319.

Rainey, R. C., & Harding, A. K. (2005). Acceptability of solar disinfection of drinking water treatment in Kathmandu Valley, Nepal. *International Journal of Environmental Health Research, 15*(5), 361–372.

Raz, A. E., Atar, M., Rodnay, M., Shoham-Vardi, I., & Carmi, R. (2003). Between acculturation and ambivalence: Knowledge of genetics and attitudes towards genetic testing in a consanguineous Bedouin community. *Community Genetics, 6*(2), 88–95.

Rodriguez-Reimann, D. I., Nicassio, P., Reimann, J. O., Gallegos, P. I., & Olmedo, E. L. (2004). Acculturation and health beliefs of Mexican Americans regarding tuberculosis prevention. *Journal of Immigrant Health, 6*(2), 51–62.

Rosenstock, I. M. (1974a). Historical origins of the health belief model. In M. H. Becker (Ed.), *The health belief model and personal health behavior* (pp. 1–8). Thorofare, NJ: Charles B. Slack.

Rosenstock, I. M. (1974b). The health belief model and preventive health behavior. In M. H. Becker (Ed.), *The health belief model and personal health behavior* (pp. 27–59). Thorofare, NJ: Charles B. Slack.

Rosenstock, I. M., Strecher, V. J., & Becker, M. H. (1988). Social learning theory and the health belief model. *Health Education Quarterly, 15*, 175–183.

Rotter, J. B. (1954). *Social learning and clinical psychology.* New York: Prentice-Hall.

Seo, M. A., & Min, S. K. (2005). Development of a structural model explaining medication compliance of persons with schizophrenia. *Yonsei Medical Journal, 46*(3), 331–340.

Tavafian, S. S., Hasani, L., Aghamolaei, T., Zare, S., & Gregory, D. (2009). Prediction of breast self-examination in a sample of Iranian women: An application of the Health Belief Model. *BMC Womens Health, 9*, 37.

Tolman, E. C. (1955). Principles of performance. *Psychological Review, 62*, 315–326.

Tyrrell, J., Poulet, C., Pe Pin, J. L., & Veale, D. (2006). A preliminary study of psychological factors affecting patients' acceptance of CPAP therapy for sleep apnoea syndrome. *Sleep Medicine, 7*(4), 375–379.

Unson, C. G., Fortinsky, R., Prestwood, K., & Reisine, S. (2005). Osteoporosis medications used by older African-American women: Effects of socioeconomic status and psychosocial factors. *Journal of Community Health, 30*(4), 281–297.

Van Horn, E. (2005). An exploration of recurrent injury prevention in patients with trauma. *Orthopaedic Nursing, 24*(4), 249–258.

Von Ah, D., Ebert, S., Ngamvitroj, A., Park, N., & Kang, D. H. (2004). Predictors of health behaviours in college students. *Journal of Advanced Nursing, 48*(5), 463–474.

Wai, C. T., Wong, M. L., Ng, S., Cheok, A., Tan, M. H., Chua, W., et al. (2005). Utility of the health belief model in predicting compliance of screening in patients with chronic hepatitis B. *Alimentary Pharmacology and Therapeutics, 21*(10), 1255–1262.

Welch, J. L., Bennett, S. J., Delp, R. L., & Agarwal, R. (2006). Benefits of and barriers to dietary sodium adherence. *Western Journal of Nursing Research 28*(2), 162–180.

Werner, P. (2003). Factors influencing intentions to seek a cognitive status examination: A study based on the health belief model. *International Journal of Geriatric Psychiatry, 18*(9), 787–794.

Wong, C. Y., & Tang, C. S. (2005). Practice of habitual and volitional health behaviors to prevent severe acute respiratory syndrome among Chinese adolescents in Hong Kong. *Journal of Adolescent Health, 36*(3), 193–200.

Zagumny, M. J., & Brady, D. B. (1998). Development of the AIDS Health Belief Scale (AHBS). *AIDS Education and Prevention, 10*(2), 173–179.

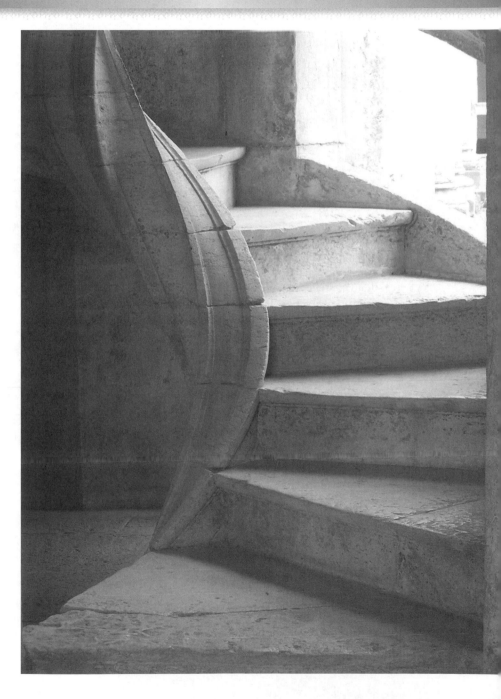

The Transtheoretical Model

AFTER READING THIS CHAPTER YOU SHOULD BE ABLE TO

- Describe the historical genesis of the transtheoretical model
- List 10 processes of the transtheoretical model
- Summarize the applications of the transtheoretical model in health education and health promotion
- Identify educational methods for modifying each process from the transtheoretical model
- Apply the transtheoretical model in changing a health behavior of your choice

The **transtheoretical model (TTM)** has had various names over the years and has been tested and expanded in accordance with various theories. It is currently one of the most popular models in the field of behavior change. This model focuses on explaining behavior change, whereas many other models focus just on the behavior. The TTM is unique in that it specifies a time dimension in behavior change. It proposes that people move through various stages while making a behavior change and that the whole process can take anywhere from 6 months to 5 years. Due to its emphasis on stages, the model is also known as the stages of change (SOC) model. More than 1000 publications have cited this model since its origin in the late 1970s.

This chapter begins with a discussion of the historical aspects of the genesis of this model. Next we describe the various constructs or processes that make up the model. Applications of the TTM in behavioral research, primary prevention, and secondary prevention are discussed next. Finally, we discuss the limitations of the model and presents a skill-building application using the TTM.

HISTORICAL PERSPECTIVE

In the late 1970s, James Prochaska from the University of Rhode Island undertook to review the various theories of psychotherapy. In this process he laid the foundations for the transtheoretical model (Prochaska, 1979). Prochaska is currently the director of the Cancer Prevention Research Consortium and professor of clinical and health psychology at the University of Rhode Island. He completed his doctorate in clinical psychology in 1969 at Wayne State University. He has won several awards, including the Top Five Most Cited Authors in Psychology award from the American Psychology Society. In his book *Systems of Psychotherapy: A Transtheoretical Analysis*, published in 1979, Prochaska reviewed 18 theories of psychotherapy, among them Adlerian therapy (Adler, 1929), behavior therapy (Wolpe, 1973), emotional flooding therapies (Olsen, 1976), existential analysis (Binswanger, 1958), Freud's psychoanalysis (1959), gestalt therapy (Perls, 1969), rational emotive therapy (Ellis, 1973), Rogers's client-centered therapy (1951), and transactional analysis (Berne, 1966). Although these psychotherapies were quite different from each other, Prochaska saw that they shared certain commonalities in how they looked at the process of change (Prochaska, 1999). During the same time he teamed with Carlo DiClemente, who did his doctoral work at the University of Rhode Island and is now a professor of psychology at the University of Maryland, to develop and refine the TTM (Prochaska & DiClemente, 1983).

In the 1980s, the University of Rhode Island Change Assessment (URICA) scale was developed for problems leading individuals to psychotherapy (McConnaughy, DiClemente, Prochaska, & Velicer, 1989). This is a 32-item self-report using the TTM that measures attitudes toward behavior change for different problems. A version of URICA for alcohol use has also been developed called URICA-A (Migneault, Velicer, Prochaska, & Stevenson, 1999).

> *TTM has been a major force in helping the field progress to more inclusive approaches to research and practice that complement old paradigms with new ones. It does not put old paradigms to rest, but rather complements these with more comprehensive approaches.*
>
> —James O. Prochaska (2006, p. 772)

In the 1990s, two scales were developed using the TTM. The first is the Readiness to Change Questionnaire (RCQ), developed by Rollnick, Heather, Gold, and Hall (1992). The RCQ consists of three 4-item scales: precontemplation, contemplation, and action. Items pertaining to maintenance were included in the original scale, but the factor was not found to be empirically valid and was later excluded. The second scale is the Stages of Change Readiness and Treatment Eagerness Scale (SOCRATES), which was developed by Miller and Tonigan (1996). Originally this was a 40-item instrument, but it has now been reduced to 19 items. The transtheoretical model at present enjoys the status of being the most popular model. Studies using this model continue to be reported every year.

CONSTRUCTS OF THE TRANSTHEORETICAL MODEL

The first construct of the TTM is **stages of change**. The stages of change are depicted in **Figure 4.1**. The construct of stages provides a temporal or time dimension and implies that change occurs over time (Prochaska, 2000). The construct also offers a middle level of abstraction between psychological states and personality traits. Stages are dynamic like psychological states and yet have stable characteristics like personality traits. This enables a person to move from one stage to another while making a behavior change. A person transits through five stages when considering changing a behavior (**Table 4.1**).

The first stage is the **precontemplation stage**, when a person is not considering change in the foreseeable future, usually defined as the next 6 months. There are two categories of people in this stage. First are uninformed or less informed people who are unaware of the consequences of their behavior. Second are people who have experimented with change but have failed in the past so that they are no longer seeking to change. Usually this second category is resistant or unmotivated to change.

The second stage is the **contemplation stage**, when one is considering change in the foreseeable future but not immediately, usually defined as between 1 and 6 months.

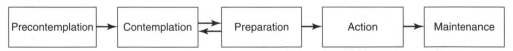

FIGURE 4.1   Stages of change in the transtheoretical model. The progression through the stages is not linear but cyclical or spiral; one might progress from precontemplation to action and then regress to contemplation and then again progress to action and so on.

TABLE 4.1	Stages of Behavior Change in the Transtheoretical Model
Precontemplation	One is not considering change in the foreseeable future, usually defined as the next 6 months.
Contemplation	One is considering change in the foreseeable future but not immediately, usually defined as between 1 and 6 months.
Preparation	One is planning for change in the immediate future, usually defined as in the next month.
Action	One has made meaningful change in the past 6 months.
Maintenance	One has maintained change for a period of time, usually considered as 6 or more months.

These people have considered the benefits (or pros) and costs (or cons) of changing their behavior. The third stage is the **preparation stage**, when one is planning for change in the immediate future, usually defined as in the next month. The people in this stage have taken some significant steps, such as going to a recovery group, buying some exercise equipment, consulting a counselor, buying self-help materials, and so on.

The fourth stage is the **action stage**, in which the person has made meaningful change in the past 6 months. Behaviors are actions, and the new actions can be observed clearly in this stage. The person is making conscious efforts to perform the new actions. The fifth stage is the **maintenance stage**, in which the person has maintained the change for a period of time, usually considered as 6 or more months. Prochaska (2000) estimates that the maintenance stage can range in duration from 6 months to up to 5 years. When changing negative habits, the term **termination** is used when the person has completely quit the habit, has no temptation to relapse, and is fully self-efficacious to continue with the change.

The progression through these stages is not linear but cyclical or spiral; one might progress from precontemplation to action and then regress to contemplation, and then again progress to action, and so on (Prochaska, DiClemente, & Norcross, 1992).

The second construct of the TTM pertains to the 10 processes of change, summarized in **Table 4.2**. The first process of change, which is borrowed from the Freudian school of psychotherapy (Freud, 1960), is the process of **consciousness raising**. Consciousness raising is an experiential process that entails raising awareness about the causes, consequences, and cures for a particular problem. This can be achieved

TABLE 4.2	Key Processes of the Transtheoretical Model	
Construct	**Definition**	**How to Modify?**
Consciousness raising	Experiential process that entails raising awareness about causes and cures for a particular problem	• Discussion sharing observations • Discussion with confrontations • Discussion sharing interpretations • Discussion with feedback • Lecture
Dramatic relief	Experiential process that enhances emotional arousal about one's behavior and the relief that can come from changing it	• Psychodrama • Role playing • Personal testimony • Grieving
Environmental reevaluation	Experiential process that involves both affective and cognitive components on how the behavior affects one's environment and how changing the behavior would influence the environment	• Empathy training • Discussion with value clarification • Family or network interventions
Self-reevaluation	Experiential process that involves both affective and cognitive components and includes one's assessment of self-image with the new behavior	• Imagery • Healthier role models • Discussion with values clarification
Self-liberation	Behavioral process that entails belief that one can change and a commitment and recommitment to act on that change	• Making public commitments • Making resolutions • Providing multiple alternatives to choose from
Counterconditioning	Behavioral process that requires learning new, healthier behavior to replace old, unhealthy behavior	• Desensitization • Assertion • Practicing relaxation • Cognitive counters to irrational self-statements
Reinforcement management	Behavioral process that utilizes reinforcements and punishments for taking steps in a particular direction	• Self-reinforcements • Contracting • Group recognition

TABLE 4.2 *(Continued)*		
Construct	**Definition**	**How to Modify?**
Stimulus control	Behavioral process that involves modifying the environment to increase cues for healthy behavior and decrease cues for unhealthy behavior	• Avoidance • Environmental reengineering by removing cues for unhealthy behavior • Self-help groups that provide cues for healthier behavior
Helping relationships	Behavioral process that entails developing caring, open, trusting, and accepting relationships to adhere to the healthy behavior	• Rapport building • Health educator calls • Buddy systems • Self-help groups
Social liberation	Experiential process that results in an increase in social opportunities or alternatives	• Advocacy • Empowerment methods • Policies

by arranging for observation sessions, confronting the participants on the issue, providing interpretations from the literature, providing feedback to the participants, or giving an informational lecture or talk. This process is important in the precontemplation and contemplation stages in helping people move forward.

The second process of change is **dramatic relief**, which is an experiential process that enhances emotional arousal about one's behavior and emphasizes the relief that can come from changing it. This can be facilitated through methods such as enacting a psychodrama, having the participants partake in a role play, sharing personal testimony from people in similar situations, or allowing the participants to grieve over their situation so that their emotions are brought forward. This process is important in the precontemplation and contemplation stages in helping people move forward.

The third process of change is **environmental reevaluation**, which is the experiential process that involves both affective and cognitive components regarding how the behavior affects one's environment and how changing the behavior would influence the environment. It can be influenced by empathy training, values clarification, or family or network interventions. It is also important in the precontemplation and contemplation stages.

The fourth process of change is **self-reevaluation**, an experiential process that involves both affective and cognitive components and includes a person's assessment of his or her self-image with the new behavior. The self-image can be changed by using imagery, healthier role models, and values clarification. Self-reevaluation is important in the contemplation and preparation stages.

The fifth process of change is **self-liberation**, a behavioral process that entails belief that one can change and a commitment and recommitment to act on that change. It can be facilitated by making public commitments as opposed to private commitments, making resolutions, or having multiple alternatives to choose from. Prochaska (2000) noted that whenever possible we should try to provide people with the three best possible choices. Having fewer than or more than three choices is less effective. This process is important in the preparation and action stages and helps to confirm the person's commitment toward behavior change.

The sixth process of change is **counterconditioning**, which refers to a behavioral process that requires learning a new, healthier behavior to replace the unhealthy behavior. Methods such as desensitization, assertion, practicing relaxation, or using cognitive counters to irrational self-statements can be utilized to facilitate this process. This process is important in the action stage.

The seventh process of change is borrowed from the Skinnerian tradition (Skinner, 1953) and is called **contingency management** or **reinforcement management**. This is a behavioral process that utilizes reinforcements and punishments for taking steps in a particular direction. The process can be fostered by developing self-reinforcements, using contracts, and providing group recognition for achievements with regard to behavior acquisition. This process is important in the action and maintenance stages.

The eighth process of change is **stimulus control**, a behavioral process that involves modifying the environment to increase cues for healthy behavior and decrease cues for unhealthy behavior. Behavior can be modified by avoidance of the cues for unhealthy behavior, environmental reengineering that removes cues for unhealthy behaviors, and participation in self-help groups that provide cues for healthy behaviors. This process is important in the action and maintenance stages.

The ninth process of change is borrowed from the Rogerian school of psychotherapy (Rogers, 1961) and is called **helping relationships**. This is a behavioral process that entails developing caring, open, trusting, and accepting relationships to help the person adhere to the healthy behavior. These can be developed through rapport building, health educator calls, formation of buddy systems, and participation in self-help groups. This process is important in the action and maintenance stages.

The final process of change is **social liberation**, which refers to an experiential process that increases social opportunities or alternatives. Social liberation can be enhanced through advocacy, empowerment-building methods, and policies that increase social opportunities. The relationship of this process to specific stages is unclear (Prochaska, Redding, & Evers, 2008), but it probably helps in the preparation and action stages.

The third construct of the TTM is **decisional balance**, or pros and cons. This construct has been taken from the work of Janis and Mann (1977) with decision making. It addresses the relative importance placed by an individual on the advantages (pros) of behavior change as opposed to the disadvantages (cons). According to this model, behavior change occurs when the pros of the behavior change are viewed as more important than the cons of change. Hence, educators must make an attempt to enhance the pros while reducing the cons. This construct is especially important in the precontemplation and contemplation stages of change.

The fourth construct of the TTM is **self-efficacy**. This construct, taken from Bandura's social cognitive theory (1986), is discussed in Chapter 3 in connection with the health belief model and is discussed in detail in Chapter 7. Self-efficacy is the confidence that a person has in his or her ability to pursue a given behavior. It is specific to the behavior and is in the present. It is not about the past or future.

The fifth construct of the TTM, which goes hand in hand with self-efficacy, is **temptation**. Temptation refers to the urge to engage in unhealthy behavior when confronted with a difficult situation (Prochaska et al., 2008). It is, in essence, the converse of self-efficacy. In research, the same set of items using different response formats is used to measure both self-efficacy and temptation. Temptation is represented by three factors that denote the most common types of tempting situations: negative affect or emotional distress, positive social situations, and craving.

The sixth construct of TTM that is usually considered in psychotherapy is **levels of change** (Prochaska, 1995). Five distinct but interrelated levels of psychological problems can be addressed in psychotherapy: symptom/situational problems, maladaptive cognitions, current interpersonal conflicts, family/system conflicts, and intrapersonal conflicts. These levels have limited utility for designing health behavior change interventions and have been included in this chapter mainly to provide a sense of completeness.

> *While research results to date are encouraging, much still needs to be done to advance the Transtheoretical Model. Research should explore relationships of TTM variables with constructs from other established health behavior theories including perceived risk, subjective norms, and problem severity.*
>
> —Prochaska, Redding, and Evers (2008, p .115)

PHASES OF INTERVENTIONS BASED ON THE TRANSTHEORETICAL MODEL

Prochaska (1999) identified five phases for planning interventions based on the TTM:

1. Recruitment
2. Retention
3. Progress
4. Process
5. Outcomes

In the *recruitment phase*, measures are taken to persuade a large number of people to join the program. In this phase professionals must proactively reach out to the target population. With regard to the stage of change people are in for any given behavior to be changed, DiClemente and Prochaska (1998) suggest a thumb rule of 40, 40, 20. That is, 40% of the target population are in the precontemplation stage, 40% in the contemplation stage, and 20% in the preparation stage.

> *The strong principle of progress holds that to progress from precontemplation to effective action, the pros of changing must increase 1 standard deviation.*
>
> *The weak principle of progress holds that to progress from contemplation to effective action, the cons of changing must decrease ½ standard deviation.*
>
> —James O. Prochaska
> (2000, p. 117)

In the *retention phase*, efforts must be taken to retain people who join the program. This can be done by matching the processes of change with the stage of change a person is in today. In the *progress phase*, efforts must be taken to help people progress during and after the intervention. In the *process phase*, efforts must be made to help participants move from one stage to another, and processes of change must be applied. The pros for changing must be underscored in precontemplation. The cons must be decreased during contemplation to progress to action. Processes of change must be matched with the stage. In the *outcomes phase*, the end results are measured.

APPLICATIONS OF THE TRANSTHEORETICAL MODEL

Some examples of behavioral research in which the TTM has been used are studying gender differences in intimate partner violence (Babcock, Canady, Senior, & Eckhardt, 2005; Burke, Mahoney, Gielen, McDonnell, & O'Campo, 2009), modeling to remedy alcohol abuse among patients with mental illness (Zhang, Harmon, Werkner, & McCormick, 2006), studying patients' participation in medical decision making (Arora, Ayanian, & Guadagnoli, 2005), predicting physician behavior to recommend colonoscopy (Honda & Gorin, 2006), predictive modeling for bicycle helmet use (Weiss, Okun, & Quay, 2004), predictive modeling for chlamydia and gonorrhea (Chacko et al., 2006), predictive modeling for physical activity (Dishman et al., 2009; Rhodes & Plotnikoff, 2006), predictive modeling in ethnically diverse women at risk for HIV (Gazabon, Morokoff, Harlow, Ward, & Quina, 2006), evaluating a processes of change scale for alcohol misuse (Freyer et al., 2006), profiling youth who do not use drugs (J. L. Johnson et al., 2006), developing a scale for mammography on processes of change (Pruitt et al., 2010), and developing a scale for osteoporosis prevention behaviors in older adults (Popa, 2005). **Table 4.3** summarizes these applications.

Some examples in which the transtheoretical model has been used for primary prevention are for increasing acceptance of contraceptives in men (Ha, Jayasuriya, & Owen, 2005); changing sun protection behaviors (Falk & Anderson, 2008; Kristjansson, Ullen, & Helgason, 2004); HIV, STD, and pregnancy prevention in adolescents (Hacker, Brown, Cabral, & Dodds, 2005); increasing fruit and vegetable consumption (Henry, Reimer, Smith, & Reicks, 2006); overweight and obesity reduction in primary care (Logue et al., 2005); promoting physical activity (Fahrenwald, Atwood, Walker, Johnson, & Berg, 2004; Fahrenwald & Shangreaux, 2006; Fahrenwald, & Sharma, 2002);

TABLE 4.3   Applications of the Transtheoretical Model in Behavioral Research
Gender differences in intimate partner violence
Modeling to remedy alcohol abuse among patients with mental illness
Patients' participation in medical decision making
Predicting physician behavior to recommend colonoscopy
Predictive modeling for bicycle helmet use
Predictive modeling for chlamydia and gonorrhea
Predictive modeling for physical activity
Predictive modeling in ethnically diverse women at risk for HIV
Processes of change scale for alcohol misuse
Profiling youth who do not use drugs
Scale for mammography on processes of change
Scale for osteoporosis prevention behaviors in older adults

training lay health advisors (Kobetz, Vatalaro, Moore, & Earp, 2005); tobacco cessation counseling by dental hygienists (Monson & Engeswick, 2005); promoting use of a food thermometer when cooking meat (Takeuchi, Edlefsen, McCurdy, & Hillers, 2006); and promoting use of hearing protection devices by workers (Raymond & Lusk, 2006). **Table 4.4** summarizes these applications.

Some examples in which the TTM has been used for secondary and tertiary prevention are adherence to activity recommendations in chronic low back pain (Basler, Bertalanffy, Quint, Wilke, & Wolf, 2007), adherence to antiretroviral therapy in AIDS (Highstein, Willey, & Mundy, 2006), adherence to lipid-lowering drugs (S. S. Johnson et al., 2006), adherence to medication for treatment of multiple sclerosis (Berger, Liang, & Hudmon, 2005), cardiac rehabilitation intervention (Beckie, 2006; Paradis, Cossette, Frasure-Smith, Heppell, & Guertin, 2010), cervical cancer screening (Tung, 2010; Tung, Nguyen, & Tran, 2008), colorectal cancer screening (Zimmerman, Tabbarah, Trauth, Nowalk, & Ricci, 2006), adherence to continuous positive airway pressure treatment in sleep apnea (Stepnowsky, Marler, Palau, & Annette Brooks, 2006), dietary fat modification in breast cancer survivors (Politi, Rabin, & Pinto, 2006), hypercholesterolemia education classes (Kotani, Saiga, Sakane, & Kurozawa, 2005), mammography participation (Hur, Kim, & Park, 2005; Lin & Wang 2009), a physical activity program for prostate cancer patients (Taylor et al., 2006), sexually transmitted diseases (STD) screening (Chacko et al., 2010), smoking cessation (Aveyard et al., 2006; Roig et al., 2010; Schumann, John, Rumpf, Hapke, &

TABLE 4.4   Applications of the Transtheoretical Model in Primary Prevention
Acceptance of contraceptives in men
Changing sun protection behaviors
HIV, STD, and pregnancy prevention in adolescents
Increasing fruit and vegetable consumption
Overweight and obesity reduction in primary care
Physical activity promotion
Tobacco cessation counseling by dental hygienists
Training lay health advisors
Use of food thermometer when cooking meat
Use of hearing protection devices by workers

TABLE 4.5   Applications of the Transtheoretical Model in Secondary and Tertiary Prevention

Adherence to activity recommendations in chronic low back pain

Adherence to antiretroviral therapy in AIDS

Adherence to lipid-lowering drugs

Adherence to medication for treatment of multiple sclerosis

Cardiac rehabilitation intervention

Cervical cancer screening

Colorectal cancer screening

Continuous positive airway pressure (CPAP) treatment adherence in sleep apnea

Dietary fat modification in breast cancer survivors

Hypercholesterolemia education classes

Mammography participation

Physical activity program for prostate cancer patients

Sexually transmitted diseases (STD) screening

Smoking cessation

Web-based physical activity promotion in persons with disabilities

Meyer, 2006), and Web-based physical activity promotion in persons with disabilities (Kosma, Cardinal, & McCubbin, 2005). **Table 4.5** summarizes these applications.

LIMITATIONS OF THE TRANSTHEORETICAL MODEL

Despite the great popularity enjoyed by the transtheoretical model, there have been several criticisms of this model. Some critics have even argued that the model should be completely abandoned (West, 2005). Many critics (Bandura, 1997; Davidson, 1992; Littell & Girvin, 2002; Sutton, 1996; West, 2005) have argued that the stages in the model are arbitrary and that classifying a population into different stages has little utility. They see change as a continuous process that cannot be categorized. Whitelaw, Baldwin, Bunton, and Flynn (2000) noted that classifying people in stages has several problems. First, people can move through the stages of the model in minutes.

Second, the validity of self-reported behavior with regard to stage is questionable. Third, a significant number of people cannot be assigned to recognized stages. Herzog (2005, p. 1040) noted "that there has never been a peer-reviewed account of the developmental research that led to the creation of the stages of change algorithm." Littell and Girvin (2002) noted that there is little empirical evidence regarding sequential transition between the stages and that no single study has documented movement through the entire spectrum of stages. Etter (2005) pointed out that classifying people in stages such as precontemplation means lumping different categories together, and people who have never thought of changing their behavior may be grouped with people who have relapsed after making successful behavior change.

In rejoinder, Prochaska (2006) has clarified that stage of change is a discrete variable that some people mistakenly consider a theory, which leads to confusion. Migneault, Adams, and Read (2005) also noted that most applications of the TTM in the area of substance abuse have focused on the construct of stages of change and very few have focused on other constructs such as processes, decisional balance, and self-efficacy. More constructs of the model need to be used.

Another limitation of the TTM that has been pointed out in the literature is its lack of predictive potential (West, 2005). Migneault, Adams, and Read (2005) noted that application of the TTM to substance abuse behaviors has yielded mixed results and that the model is descriptive rather than predictive. There is definitive need to make the model robust in its predictive potential.

Another limitation of the model is that theories aim for parsimony, or use of few constructs to predict the phenomenon, and the TTM is not parsimonious (West, 2006). Salient constructs that account for the majority of the variance need to be identified to make TTM parsimonious so that it can be of more practical utility.

Although there are definite limitations to this model, just like all other models and theories, there is no need to completely abandon its use as some of its critics have suggested. What is needed is better measurement of the constructs of the model, particularly the processes of change; better and more rigorous reification of its constructs; and further refinement of the model.

APPLICATION EXERCISE

In this chapter you have been given examples of applications of the transtheoretical model in behavioral research, in primary prevention, and in secondary and tertiary prevention. Choose an area of application that you like and locate the full text article of the example in that area. Critically examine how the model has been used in that application.

One such example is the development of a physical activity intervention, "Moms on the Move," for mothers in the Women, Infants, and Children (WIC) program (Fahrenwald, Atwood, Walker, Johnson, & Berg, 2004; Fahrenwald, & Sharma, 2002). The intervention was designed for women in the contemplation and preparation stages of physical activity behavior change. The constructs used in the intervention were decisional balance, self-efficacy for physical activity, three behavioral processes (self-liberation, helping relationships, and counterconditioning), and an experiential process (environmental reevaluation). The primary delivery mode was provider-delivered counseling supplemented with an interactive brochure and four biweekly provider-delivered telephone contacts. Using an experimental design the authors were able to demonstrate statistically significant changes in the transtheoretical model constructs and physical activity behavior.

Read these two articles and prepare a 250 word critique.

SKILL-BUILDING ACTIVITY

Let us see how we can apply the transtheoretical model to the issue of smoking cessation. Let us assume that most of the group of smokers are in the precontemplation stage of change. The TTM is an extensive model and is difficult to fully operationalize. Thus, we will choose a few constructs that would be important to move the participants from precontemplation to action: decisional balance, consciousness raising, dramatic relief, self-liberation, and self-efficacy. The scheme is depicted diagrammatically in **Figure 4.2**.

To modify the construct of decisional balance, the educational process of discussion can be used. In the discussion, the pros of abstaining from smoking must be underscored and alternatives to smoking should be highlighted. The cons or costs of quitting must be reduced through the discussion. Discussion can be used to modify the construct of consciousness raising for quitting smoking and exploring alternatives to smoking. In the discussion, specific techniques of confrontation about the unhealthy behavior and feedback regarding healthy behaviors need to be used. The construct of dramatic relief can be modified through a role play in which a smoker goes through various kinds of problems because of the habit of smoking. The construct of self-liberation can be modified through use of the method of contracting, in which each participant creates a contract about quitting smoking and agrees to adhere to it. Finally, to modify the construct of self-efficacy, small steps to use for quitting smoking could be outlined and relaxation as an alternative for coping with stress could be demonstrated. Role models can be used to emphasize the message.

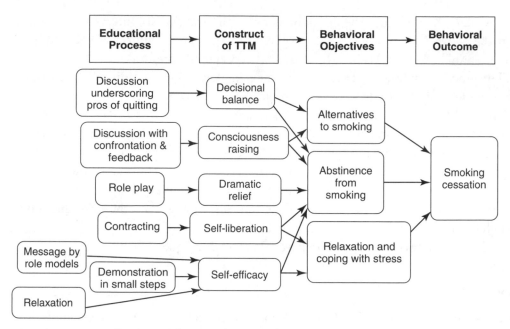

FIGURE 4.2   Application of the transtheoretical model for a smoking cessation program.

Using this approach, you can apply the TTM to a health behavior issue of your choice for any given target population. **Table 4.6** provides a set of questions to assist you in choosing an educational method that corresponds to various constructs of the TTM.

SUMMARY

The transtheoretical model (TTM) or stages of change (SOC) model, which originated from the field of psychotherapy, is at present the most popular model in research and practice related to health education. The TTM is a model of behavior change that posits that people move through five stages of change, from precontemplation (not thinking about change) to contemplation (thinking about change over the next 6 months) to preparation (thinking about change in the next month) to action (having made meaningful change but not completed 6 months) and finally to maintenance (acquisition of the healthy behavior for 6 or more months).

TABLE 4.6   Choosing the Educational Method for Planning a Health Education Program Using the Transtheoretical Model

1. What is the best approach to determine the stage of change?
   - Self-report survey
   - Group discussion
   - Individual interview
   - Other
2. What is the best educational method to facilitate decisional balance?
   - Lecture
   - Discussion
   - Brainstorming
   - Role play
   - Simulation
   - Other
3. What is the best educational method to facilitate self-efficacy?
   - Demonstration
   - Role play
   - Video with a credible role model
   - Stress reduction techniques
     - Progressive muscle relaxation
     - Visual imagery
     - Autogenic training
     - Yoga
     - Other
   - Other
4. What is the best educational method to facilitate overcoming temptations?
   - Demonstration
   - Role play
   - Psychodrama
   - Stress reduction techniques
     - Progressive muscle relaxation
     - Visual imagery
     - Autogenic training
     - Yoga
     - Other
   - Other
5. What is the best educational method to facilitate consciousness raising?
   - Discussion with confrontation
   - Discussion with feedback
   - Discussion with interpretations
   - Lecture
   - Other

(Continued)

TABLE 4.6   *(Continued)*

6. What is the best educational method to facilitate dramatic relief?
   - Psychodrama
   - Role play
   - Opportunity to grieve
   - Personal testimonies
   - Other

7. What is the best educational method to facilitate self-reevaluation?
   - Discussion about values
   - Use of healthy role models
   - Imagery
   - Other

8. What is the best educational method to facilitate environmental reevaluation?
   - Discussion with empathy
   - Screening documentaries
   - Lecture
   - Other

9. What is the best educational method to facilitate self-liberation?
   - Contracting
   - Making resolutions
   - Giving public testimony
   - Brainstorming
   - Other

10. What is the best educational method to facilitate helping relationships?
    - Alliance with health educator
    - Buddy system
    - Self-help group
    - Other

11. What is the best educational method to facilitate counterconditioning?
    - Stress reduction techniques
      - Progressive muscle relaxation
      - Visual imagery
      - Autogenic training
      - Yoga
      - Other
    - Assertion
    - Positive self-statements
    - Other

12. What is the best educational method to facilitate reinforcement management?
    - Contracting
    - Discussion
    - Group recognition
    - Other

TABLE 4.6 *(Continued)*

13. What is the best health promotion method to facilitate stimulus control?
    - Environmental engineering
    - Avoidance of stimuli
    - Self-help groups
    - Other
14. What is the best health promotion method to facilitate social liberation?
    - Advocacy
    - Empowerment training
    - Changing policies
    - Other

Source: Data from Montano, D. E., & Kaspryzk, D. (2002). *The theory of reasoned action and the theory of planned behavior*. In K. Glanz, B. Rimer, & F. M. Lewis (Eds.), *Health behavior and health education: Theory, research and practice* (3rd ed., p. 68). San Francisco: Jossey Bass.

The TTM identifies 10 processes of change and the constructs of decisional balance, self-efficacy, and overcoming temptations, which aid the behavior change. Decisional balance is the construct of TTM that addresses the relative importance placed by an individual on the advantages (pros) of behavior change as opposed to the disadvantages (cons). Self-efficacy is the confidence that a person has in his or her ability to pursue a given behavior. Temptation refers to the urge to engage in unhealthy behavior when confronted with a difficult situation.

The processes of change are categorized as either experiential or behavioral in nature. Experiential processes include consciousness raising, dramatic relief, environmental reevaluation, social liberation, and self reevaluation. Behavioral processes include stimulus control, counterconditioning, helping relationships, reinforcement management, and self-liberation. The TTM has been widely used in behavioral research, primary prevention, and secondary prevention. Some critics have raised objections to the robustness of TTM, but it continues to be a popular model.

IMPORTANT TERMS

action stage
consciousness raising
contemplation stage
contingency management
counterconditioning

decisional balance
dramatic relief
environmental reevaluation
helping relationships
levels of change

maintenance stage
precontemplation stage
preparation stage
reinforcement management
self-efficacy
self-liberation
self-reevaluation

social liberation
stages of change
stimulus control
temptation
termination
transtheoretical model (TTM)

REVIEW QUESTIONS

1. Describe the historical genesis of the transtheoretical model.
2. Discuss the five stages of behavior change in the TTM.
3. List and define the 10 key processes of change in the TTM.
4. How can stimulus control be modified?
5. Differentiate between self-liberation and social liberation.
6. Describe the five phases for planning interventions based on the TTM.
7. Discuss the limitations of the TTM.
8. Apply TTM for promoting leisure time physical activity in a group of African American women.

WEBSITES TO EXPLORE

Applying TTM to Exercise Adherence

http://www.findarticles.com/p/articles/mi_m0CTG/is_1_19/ai_n6072012

This website presents a research study describing the application of TTM to exercise adherence. The article was published by Guillot and colleagues in the *American Journal of Health Studies* in 2004. *Read this article and discuss its strengths and weaknesses.*

Applying TTM to Financial Behavior

http://www.rce.rutgers.edu/money2000/pdfs/acci01m2k-proceedings.pdf

This website presents an interesting application of TTM to financial behavior in a consumer education program. *Read the article and identify which processes were used more by the participants who met their financial goals when compared to those who did not.*

Boston University: Webcast by Dr. James Prochaska

http://www.bu.edu/cpr/webcast/change/index.html

This website sponsored by the Center for Psychiatric Rehabilitation at Boston University includes a 2001 webcast featuring Dr. James Prochaska who discusses the

TTM. You will have to complete a free registration in order to see the webcast. The title of his talk is "Helping Populations Progress through Stages of Change." *Visit this website and view the webcast. Summarize your reaction to the presentation.*

Cancer Prevention Research Center (CPRC): Transtheoretical Model

http://www.uri.edu/research/cprc/transtheoretical.htm

The originator of the TTM, Dr. James Prochaska, is the director of this center. The website provides a summary of the TTM with a link to retrieve a detailed version of the model. The other links pertain to stages of change, processes of change, decisional balance, self-efficacy, about the CPRC, and several measures related to TTM. *Visit the link with the measures and review one instrument in an area of your choice. Discuss its strengths and weaknesses.*

The State University of New York at Buffalo: Webcast

http://nursing.buffalo.edu/Research/TranstheoreticalModel.aspx

This website from the School of Nursing at The State University of New York, Buffalo presents a series of videoclips from 2003 in which Dr. James Prochaska speaks about the TTM and its applications. *Visit this website, download the clips, and write your reaction to the presentation.*

University of Maryland: HABITS—Health and Addictive Behaviors: Investigating Transtheoretical Solutions

http://www.umbc.edu/psyc/habits/

This website was developed by Dr. Carlo DiClemente and his team at the University of Maryland. It summarizes the publications, assessment tools, presentation of team members, and many other things. *Visit this website and review some of the assessment tools. Discuss the strengths and weaknesses of any one tool of your choice.*

REFERENCES

Adler, A. (1929). *Problems of neurosis.* London: Kegan Paul.

Arora, N. K., Ayanian, J. Z., & Guadagnoli, E. (2005). Examining the relationship of patients' attitudes and beliefs with their self-reported level of participation in medical decision-making. *Medical Care, 43*(9), 865–872.

Aveyard, P., Lawrence, T., Cheng, K. K., Griffin, C., Croghan, E., & Johnson, C. (2006). A randomized controlled trial of smoking cessation for pregnant women to test the effect of a transtheoretical model-based intervention on movement in stage and interaction with baseline stage. *British Journal of Health Psychology, 11*(Pt. 2), 263–278.

Babcock, J. C., Canady, B. E., Senior, A., & Eckhardt, C. I. (2005). Applying the transtheoretical model to female and male perpetrators of intimate partner violence: Gender differences in stages and processes of change. *Violence and Victims, 20*(2), 235–250.

Bandura, A. (1986). *The social foundations of thought and action: A social cognitive theory.* Upper Saddle River, NJ: Prentice-Hall.

Bandura, A. (1997). *Self-efficacy: The exercise of control.* New York: W. H. Freeman.

Basler, H. D., Bertalanffy, H., Quint, S., Wilke, A., & Wolf, U. (2007). TTM-based counselling in physiotherapy does not contribute to an increase of adherence to activity recommendations in older adults with chronic low back pain—a randomised controlled trial. *European Journal of Pain, 11*(1), 31–37.

Beckie, T. M. (2006). A behavior change intervention for women in cardiac rehabilitation. *Journal of Cardiovascular Nursing 21*(2), 146–153.

Berger, B. A., Liang, H., & Hudmon, K. S. (2005). Evaluation of software-based telephone counseling to enhance medication persistency among patients with multiple sclerosis. *Journal of the American Pharmacists Association, 45*(4), 466–472.

Berne, E. (1966). *Principles of group treatment.* New York: Oxford University Press.

Binswanger, L. (1958). The existential analysis school of thought. In R. May, E. Angel, & H. Ellenberger (Eds.), *Existence.* New York: Basic Books.

Burke, J. G., Mahoney, P., Gielen, A., McDonnell, K. A., & O'Campo, P. (2009). Defining appropriate stages of change for intimate partner violence survivors. *Violence & Victims, 24*(1), 36–51.

Chacko, M. R., Wiemann, C. M., Kozinetz, C. A., Diclemente, R. J., Smith, P. B., Velasquez, M. M., et al. (2006). New sexual partners and readiness to seek screening for chlamydia and gonorrhoea: Predictors among minority young women. *Sexually Transmitted Infections, 82*(1), 75–79.

Chacko, M. R., Wiemann, C. M., Kozinetz, C. A., von Sternberg, K., Velasquez, M. M., Smith, P. B., et al. (2010). Efficacy of a motivational behavioral intervention to promote chlamydia and gonorrhea screening in young women: A randomized controlled trial. *The Journal of Adolescent Health, 46*(2), 152–161.

Davidson, R. (1992). Prochaska and DiClemente's model of change: A case study? *British Journal of Addiction, 87,* 821–822.

DiClemente, C. C., & Prochaska, J. O. (1998). Toward a comprehensive, transtheoretical model of change. Stages of change and addictive behaviors. In W. R. Miller & N. Heather (Eds.), *Treating addictive behaviors* (2nd ed., pp. 3–24). New York: Plenum Press.

Dishman, R. K., Thom, N. J., Rooks, C. R., Motl, R. W., Horwath, C., & Nigg, C. R. (2009). Failure of post-action stages of the transtheoretical model to predict change in regular physical activity: A multiethnic cohort study. *Annals of Behavioral Medicine, 37*(3), 280–293.

Ellis, A. (1973). *Humanistic psychotherapy: The rational emotive approach.* New York: McGraw-Hill.

Etter, J. (2005). Theoretical tools for the industrial era in smoking cessation counseling: A comment on West (2005). *Addiction, 100,* 1041–1042.

Fahrenwald, N. L., Atwood, J. R., Walker, S. N., Johnson, D. R., & Berg, K. (2004). A randomized pilot test of "Moms on the Move": A physical activity intervention for WIC mothers. *Annals of Behavioral Medicine, 27*(2), 82–90.

Fahrenwald, N. L., & Shangreaux, P. (2006). Physical activity behavior of American Indian mothers. *Orthopaedic Nursing, 25*(1), 22–29.

Fahrenwald, N. L., & Sharma, M. (2002). Development and expert evaluation of "Moms on the Move": A physical activity intervention for WIC mothers. *Public Health Nursing, 19*(6), 423–439.

Falk, M., & Anderson, C. (2008). Prevention of skin cancer in primary healthcare: An evaluation of three different prevention effort levels and the applicability of a phototest. *The European Journal of General Practice, 14*(2), 68–75.

Freud, S. (1959). The question of lay analysis. In J. Strachey (Ed.), *The standard edition of the complete psychological works of Sigmund Freud*. London: Hogarth Press.

Freud, S. (1960). *The ego and the id*. New York: Norton. (Original work published 1923)

Freyer, J., Bott, K., Riedel, J., Wedler, B., Meyer, C., Rumpf, H. J., et al. (2006). Psychometric properties of the "Processes of Change" scale for alcohol misuse and its short form (POC-20). *Addictive Behaviors, 31*, 821–832.

Gazabon, S. A., Morokoff, P. J., Harlow, L. L., Ward, R. M., & Quina, K. (2006). Applying the transtheoretical model to ethnically diverse women at risk for HIV. *Health Education and Behavior*, Epub PMID: 16740521.

Ha, B. T., Jayasuriya, R., & Owen, N. (2005). Predictors of men's acceptance of modern contraceptive practice: Study in rural Vietnam. *Health Education and Behavior, 32*(6), 738–750.

Hacker, K., Brown, E., Cabral, H., & Dodds, D. (2005). Applying a transtheoretical behavioral change model to HIV/STD and pregnancy prevention in adolescent clinics. *Journal of Adolescent Health, 37*(3 Suppl.), S80–S93.

Henry, H., Reimer, K., Smith, C., & Reicks, M. (2006). Associations of decisional balance, processes of change, and self-efficacy with stages of change for increased fruit and vegetable intake among low-income, African-American mothers. *Journal of American Dietetic Association, 106*(6), 841–849.

Herzog, T. A. (2005). When popularity outstrips the evidence: Comments on West (2005). *Addiction, 100*, 1040–1041.

Highstein, G. R., Willey, C., & Mundy, L. M. (2006). Development of stage of readiness and decisional balance instruments: Tools to enhance clinical decision-making for adherence to antiretroviral therapy. *AIDS and Behavior, 10*(5), 563–573.

Honda, K., & Gorin, S. S. (2006). A model of stage of change to recommend colonoscopy among urban primary care physicians. *Health Psychology, 25*(1), 65–73.

Hur, H. K., Kim, G. Y., & Park, S. M. (2005). Predictors of mammography participation among rural Korean women age 40 and over. *Taehan Kanho Hakhoe Chi, 35*, 1443–1450.

Janis, I. L., & Mann, L. (1977). *Decision making: A psychological analysis of conflict, choice, and commitment*. New York: Free Press.

Johnson, J. L., Evers, K. E., Paiva, A. L., Van Marter, D. F., Prochaska, J. O., Prochaska, J. M., et al. (2006). Prevention profiles: Understanding youth who do not use substances. *Addictive Behaviors, 31*(9),1593–1606.

Johnson, S. S., Driskell, M. M., Johnson, J. L., Dyment, S. J., Prochaska, J. O., Prochaska, J. M., et al. (2006). Transtheoretical model intervention for adherence to lipid-lowering drugs. *Disease Management, 9*(2), 102–114.

Kobetz, E., Vatalaro, K., Moore, A., & Earp, J. A. (2005). Taking the transtheoretical model into the field: A curriculum for lay health advisors. *Health Promotion Practice, 6*(3), 329–337.

Kosma, M., Cardinal, B. J., & McCubbin, J. A. (2005). A pilot study of a Web-based physical activity motivational program for adults with physical disabilities. *Disability and Rehabilitation, 27*, 1435–1442.

Kotani, K., Saiga, K., Sakane, N., & Kurozawa, Y. (2005). The effects of interval length between sessions in a hypercholesterolemia education class. *Acta Medica Okayama, 59*(6), 271–277.

Kristjansson, S., Ullen, H., & Helgason, A. R. (2004). The importance of assessing the readiness to change sun-protection behaviours: A population-based study. *European Journal of Cancer, 40,* 2773–2780.

Lin, Z. C., & Wang, S. F. (2009). A tailored Web-based intervention to promote women's perceptions of and intentions for mammography. *The Journal of Nursing Research, 17*(4), 249–260.

Littell, J. H., & Girvin, H. (2002). Stages of change. A critique. *Behavior Modification, 26,* 223–273.

Logue, E., Sutton, K., Jarjoura, D., Smucker, W., Baughman, K., & Capers, C. (2005). Transtheoretical model-chronic disease care for obesity in primary care: A randomized trial. *Obesity Research, 13,* 917–927.

McConnaughy, E. A., DiClemente, C. C., Prochaska, J. O., & Velicer, W. F. (1989). Stages of change in psychotherapy: A follow-up report. *Psychotherapy, 4,* 494–503.

Migneault, J. P., Adams, T. B., & Read, J. P. (2005). Application of the transtheoretical model to substance abuse: Historical development and future directions. *Drug and Alcohol Review, 24,* 437–448.

Migneault, J. P., Velicer, W. F., Prochaska, J. O., & Stevenson, J. F. (1999). Decisional balance for immoderate drinking in college students. *Substance Use and Misuse, 34,* 1325–1346.

Miller, W. R., & Tonigan, J. S. (1996). Assessing drinkers' motivations for change: The Stages of Readiness and Treatment Eagerness Scale (SOCRATES). *Psychology of Addictive Behaviors, 10,* 81–89.

Monson, A. L., & Engeswick, L. M. (2005). Promotion of tobacco cessation through dental hygiene education: A pilot study. *Journal of Dental Education, 69,* 901–911.

Olsen, P. (1976). *Emotional flooding.* New York: Human Sciences Press.

Paradis, V., Cossette, S., Frasure-Smith, N., Heppell, S., & Guertin, M. C. (2010). The efficacy of a motivational nursing intervention based on the stages of change on self-care in heart failure patients. *Journal of Cardiovascular Nursing, 25*(2), 130–141.

Perls, F. (1969). *Gestalt therapy verbatim.* Lafayette, CA: Real People Press.

Politi, M. C., Rabin, C., & Pinto, B. (2006). Biologically based complementary and alternative medicine use among breast cancer survivors: Relationship to dietary fat consumption and exercise. *Support Care Cancer, 14*(10), 1064–1069.

Popa, M. A. (2005). Stages of change for osteoporosis preventive behaviors: A construct validation study. *Journal of Aging and Health, 17,* 336–350.

Prochaska, J. O. (1979). *Systems of psychotherapy: A transtheoretical analysis.* Homewood, IL: Dorsey Press.

Prochaska, J. O. (1995). An eclectic and integrative approach: Transtheoretical therapy. In A. S. Gurman & S. B. Messer (Eds.), *Essential psychotherapies: Theory and practice* (pp. 403–440). New York: Guilford Press.

Prochaska, J. O. (1999). How do people change, and how can we change to help many more people? In M. A. Hubble, B. L. Duncan, & S. D. Miller (Eds.), *The heart and soul of change: What works in therapy* (pp. 227–255). Washington, DC: American Psychological Association.

Prochaska, J. O. (2000). Change at differing stages. In C. R. Snyder & R. E. Ingram (Eds.), *Handbook of psychological change: Psychotherapy processes and practices for the 21st century* (pp. 109–127). New York: Wiley.

Prochaska, J. O. (2006). Moving beyond the transtheoretical model. *Addiction, 101*, 768–774.

Prochaska, J. O., & DiClemente, C. C. (1983). Stages and processes of self change in smoking: Toward an integrative model of change. *Journal of Consulting and Clinical Psychology, 5*, 390–395.

Prochaska, J. O., DiClemente, C. C., & Norcross, J. C. (1992). In search of how people change: Applications to addictive behaviors. *American Psychologist, 47*, 1102–1114.

Prochaska, J. O., Redding, C. A., & Evers, K. E. (2008). The transtheoretical model and stages of change. In K. Glanz, B. K. Rimer, & K. Viswanath (Eds.), *Health behavior and health education:. Theory, research, and practice* (4th ed., pp. 97–121). San Francisco: Jossey-Bass.

Pruitt, S. L., McQueen, A., Tiro, J. A., Rakowski, W., Diclemente, C. C., & Vernon, S. W. (2010). Construct validity of a mammography processes of change scale and invariance by stage of change. *Journal of Health Psychology, 15*(1), 64–74.

Raymond, D. M., 3rd, & Lusk, S. L. (2006). Staging workers' use of hearing protection devices: Application of the transtheoretical model. *AAOHN Journal, 54*(4),165–172.

Rhodes, R. E., & Plotnikoff, R. C. (2006). Understanding action control: Predicting physical activity intention-behavior profiles across 6 months in a Canadian sample. *Health Psychology, 25*(3), 292–299.

Rogers, C. (1951). *Client centered therapy*. Boston: Houghton Mifflin.

Rogers, C. R. (1961). *On becoming a person*. Boston: Houghton Mifflin.

Roig, L., Perez, S., Prieto, G., Martin, C., Advani, M., Armengol, A., et al. (2010). Cluster randomized trial in smoking cessation with intensive advice in diabetic patients in primary care. ITADI Study. *BMC Public Health, 10*, 58.

Rollnick, S., Heather N., Gold, R., & Hall, W. (1992). Development of a short readiness to change questionnaire for use in brief opportunistic interventions among excessive drinkers. *British Journal of Addiction, 87*, 743–754.

Schumann, A., John, U., Rumpf, H. J., Hapke, U., & Meyer, C. (2006). Changes in the "stages of change" as outcome measures of a smoking cessation intervention: A randomized controlled trial. *Preventive Medicine, 43*(2), 101–106.

Skinner, B. F. (1953). *Science and human behavior*. New York: Macmillan.

Stepnowsky, C. J., Marler, M. R., Palau, J., & Annette Brooks, J. (2006). Social-cognitive correlates of CPAP adherence in experienced users. *Sleep Medicine, 7*(1), 350–356.

Sutton, S. (1996). Can stages of change provide guidance in the treatment of addictions? A critical examination of Prochaska and DiClemente's model. In G. Edwards & C. Dare (Eds.), *Psychotherapy, psychological treatments and the addictions* (pp. 189–205). Cambridge, UK: Cambridge University Press.

Takeuchi, M. T., Edlefsen, M., McCurdy, S. M., & Hillers, V. N. (2006). Development and validation of stages-of-change questions to assess consumers' readiness to use a food thermometer when cooking small cuts of meat. *Journal of American Dietetic Association, 106*(2), 262–266.

Taylor, C. L., Demoor, C., Smith, M. A., Dunn, A. L., Basen-Engquist, K., Nielsen, I., et al. (2006). Active for life after cancer: A randomized trial examining a lifestyle physical activity program for prostate cancer patients. *Psycho-oncology, 15*(10), 847–862.

Tung, W. C. (2010). Benefits and barriers of pap smear screening: Differences in perceptions of Vietnamese American women by stage. *Journal of Community Health Nursing, 27*(1), 12–22.

Tung, W. C., Nguyen, D. H., & Tran, D. N. (2008). Applying the transtheoretical model to cervical cancer screening in Vietnamese-American women. *International Nursing Review, 55*(1), 73–80.

Weiss, J., Okun, M., & Quay, N. (2004). Predicting bicycle helmet stage-of-change among middle school, high school, and college cyclists from demographic, cognitive, and motivational variables. *Journal of Pediatrics, 145*, 360–364.

West, R. (2005). Time for a change: Putting the transtheoretical (stages of change) model to rest [Editorial]. *Addiction, 100*, 1036–1039.

West, R. (2006). The transtheoretical model of behavior change and the scientific method. *Addiction, 101*, 774–778.

Whitelaw, S., Baldwin, S., Bunton, R., & Flynn, D. (2000). The status of evidence and outcomes in stages of change research. *Health Education Research, 15*, 707–718.

Wolpe, J. (1973). *The practice of behavior therapy* (2nd ed.). New York: Pergamon Press.

Zhang, A. Y., Harmon, J. A., Werkner, J., & McCormick, R. A. (2006). The long-term relationships between the motivation for change and alcohol use severity among patients with severe and persistent mental illness. *Journal of Addictive Diseases, 25*(1), 121–128.

Zimmerman, R. K., Tabbarah, M., Trauth, J., Nowalk, M. P., & Ricci, E. M. (2006). Predictors of lower endoscopy use among patients at three inner-city neighborhood health centers. *Journal of Urban Health, 83*(2), 221–230.

CHAPTER 5

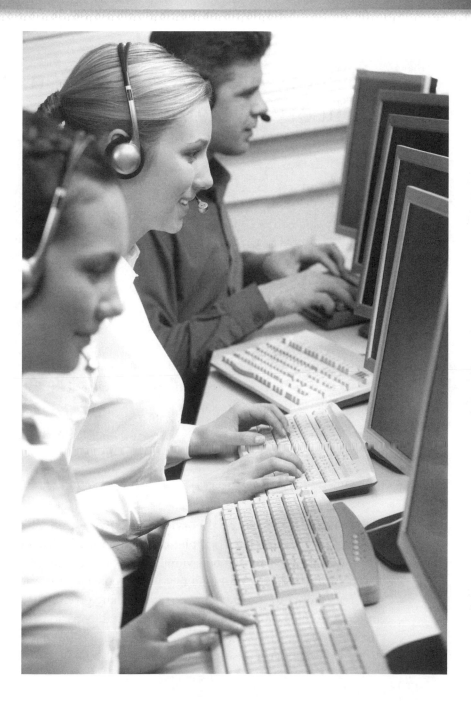

Theory of Reasoned Action and Theory of Planned Behavior

KEY CONCEPTS

- attitude toward the behavior
- behavior
- behavioral beliefs
- behavioral intention
- control beliefs
- motivation to comply
- normative beliefs

- outcome evaluations
- perceived behavioral control
- perceived power
- subjective norm
- theory of planned behavior
- theory of reasoned action

AFTER READING THIS CHAPTER YOU SHOULD BE ABLE TO

- Describe the historical genesis of the theory of reasoned action (TRA) and the theory of planned behavior (TPB)
- List the constructs of the TRA and TPB
- Summarize the applications of the TRA and TPB in health education and health promotion
- Identify educational methods and match these to modify each construct from the TRA and TPB
- Apply the TRA and TPB in changing a health behavior of your choice

This chapter discusses the **theory of reasoned action (TRA)** and its newer, more evolved version, the **theory of planned behavior (TPB)**. The salient feature of both theories is their claim that behavioral intention is the most important determinant of behavior. Both theories contend that people consider the implications of their actions before deciding to engage in or refrain from any given behavior. Freudian theory and others view behavior as being controlled by unconscious motives or desires. These two theories emphasize the role of thought in decision making about engaging in behaviors. The TRA states that a person's intention is determined by two antecedents, one comprising personal factors and the other social influence. However, it is not assumed that these beliefs and attitudes are necessarily reasonable or correct, which is why it is not called the theory of *reasonable* action. The TPB adds a third predictor, that of control over the behavior. These theories also provide strong guidance with regard to construct measurement, which is invaluable for both practitioners and researchers.

> *Theory of Reasoned Action is designed to explain virtually any human behavior, whether we want to understand why a person bought a new car, voted against a school bond issue, was absent from work, or engaged in premarital sexual intercourse.*
>
> —Ajzen and Fishbein
> (1980, p. 4)

This chapter begins with a description of the historical genesis of these theories. Next we describe the various constructs that make up the theories. Then we discuss the applications of the TRA and TPB in health education and health promotion. Finally, we discuss the limitations of the TRA and TPB and presents a skill-building application.

HISTORICAL PERSPECTIVE

In the mid- to late-1960s, Martin Fishbein (1965, 1967), a social psychologist at the University of Illinois at Urbana, examined the relationship between beliefs and attitudes. He defined *attitudes* as learned predispositions to respond to an object or class of objects in a favorable or unfavorable way. He defined *beliefs* as hypotheses concerning the nature of objects. He differentiated between beliefs and attitudes and also talked about the distinction between "belief in" an object and "belief about" an object. "Belief in" an object refers to the existence of an object, whereas "belief about" an object deals with the nature of that object. He also differentiated between attitudes toward objects and attitudes toward behaviors. For example, a health educator working with women seeking a Pap test may look at attitudes regarding cervical cancer (object) or at attitudes regarding getting a Pap test (behavior). Emphasis on the latter aspect, attitude toward behavior, served as the origin of the present-day TRA.

In the 1970s, Fishbein teamed up with Icek Ajzen of the University of Massachusetts at Amherst to write *Belief, Attitude, Intention and Behavior: An Introduction to Theory and Research* (Fishbein & Ajzen, 1975), which formed the basis of the TRA. The theory linked beliefs to attitudes, which in turn were linked to intentions, which led to behaviors. In coming up with this theory, they reviewed several then-existing theories, such as learning theories (Hull, 1943; Spence, 1956), value expectancy theories (Atkinson, 1957; Rotter, 1954; Tolman, 1955), consistency theories such as the balance theory (Heider, 1946), the congruity principle (Osgood & Tannenbaum, 1955), Festinger's (1957) theory of cognitive dissonance, and attribution theories (Bem, 1965; Kelley, 1971).

Learning theories describe when a given response is associated with a given stimulus. Value expectancy theories postulate that a behavior depends on the value placed by an individual on an outcome (value) and the individual's estimate of the likelihood that a given action will result in that outcome (expectancy). Consistency theories deal with the effects of inconsistencies among beliefs, attitudes, intentions, and behaviors. Attribution theories purport to explain how people make causal explanations and how they answer questions beginning with "why."

In 1980, Ajzen and Fishbein published a second book, *Understanding Attitudes and Predicting Social Behavior*, which simplified the TRA and made it more accessible for use in a variety of fields. The theory was popular among researchers and practitioners throughout the early 1980s. Sheppard, Hartwick, and Warshaw (1988) performed a meta-analysis and found that the TRA had strong predictive utility. Still, some researchers, including Professor Ajzen, felt that the theory was deficient in explaining behavior, especially the behavior of people who have little power or feel they have little power over their behaviors. As a result, he added the construct of perceived behavioral control to the TRA (Ajzen, 1991). His new thinking was based on Rotter's (1966) locus of control theory, Atkinson's (1964) theory of achievement motivation, and Bandura's (1986) social cognitive theory. The addition of this construct resulted in the theory of planned behavior (TPB).

> *The centrality of the attitude concept remains unchallenged and, if anything, its importance has increased.*
>
> —Fishbein and Ajzen
> (1975, p. v)

In 2004, Francis and colleagues developed a manual for health service researchers to construct questionnaires based on the TPB. Today both theories are among the popular theories in health education and health promotion, and researchers and practitioners continue to use them in various applications.

CONSTRUCTS OF THE THEORY OF REASONED ACTION AND THEORY OF PLANNED BEHAVIOR

Figure 5.1 represents the TRA and TPB diagrammatically. The first construct is **behavior**. Usually this is a single action performed by an individual that is observable. In health education and health promotion, we are interested in many such behaviors, such as condom use, eating five servings of vegetables and fruits, and so on. Ajzen and Fishbein (1980) also talk about behavioral categories that involve sets of actions rather than a single action, which are not easily observable. In health education and health promotion, we are interested in many such behaviors, such as being physically active

FIGURE 5.1   The upper portion including proximal constructs of attitude toward behavior and subjective norm constitute the theory of reasoned action; all three proximal constructs together constitute the theory of planned behavior

every day, healthy eating, and so on. The behavior should be defined in terms of its target, action, context, and time (TACT). For example, let us consider the behavior of helping sedentary African American women practice 30 minutes of aerobic dancing at a local church. Here the target is the African American women, the action is aerobic dancing, the context is the sedentary nature of the women, and the time is 30 minutes. In TRA and TPB, defining and measuring the behavior accurately is very important. Often the behavior is measured by self-reports.

The second construct in the TRA and TPB is **behavioral intention**. This is the thought to perform the behavior, which is an immediate determinant of the given behavior. This construct is the hallmark of this model, which was the first to posit that intention is a proximal measure of behavior. The intention also has the components of TACT. It is usually measured on a 7-point bipolar scale that includes the categories of extremely probable (+3), quite probable (+2), slightly probable (+1), neither proba-ble nor improbable (0), slightly improbable (–1), quite improbable (–2), and extremely improbable (–3). There should be a high degree of correspondence between intention and behavior. Intentions change over time, so the intention must be measured as close to the occurrence of the behavior as possible. The advantage of measuring behavioral intention is that if actual behavior cannot be easily measured in an intervention, then the behavioral intention serves as a useful indicator.

The third construct in the TRA and TPB is **attitude toward the behavior**, which refers to the overall feeling of like or dislike toward any given behavior. The more favorable a person's attitude is toward a behavior, the more likely it is that he or she will intend to perform the behavior; conversely, the more unfavorable a person's attitude is toward the behavior, the more likely it is that he or she will intend not to perform the behavior. Attitude is measured on a 7-point semantic differential scale ranging from favorable to unfavorable or from good to bad. The attitude toward a behavior is shaped by the fourth and fifth constructs of the TRA and TPB, namely, behavioral beliefs and outcome evaluations.

The fourth construct of the TRA and TPB, which is a determinant of attitude to-ward behavior, is **behavioral beliefs**. Behavioral beliefs are beliefs that performing a given behavior will lead to certain outcomes. The fifth construct is **outcome evalua-tions**, or the value a person places on each outcome resulting from performance of the behavior. Together the behavioral beliefs and outcome evaluations determine the attitude toward the behavior. Behavioral beliefs are measured on a 7-point unipolar scale such as extremely unlikely (1) to extremely likely (7). Outcome evaluations are measured on a 7-point bipolar scale such as extremely good (+3), quite good (+2), slightly good (+1), neither good nor bad (0), slightly bad (–1), quite bad (–2), and ex-tremely bad (–3).

A multiplicative score between the behavioral beliefs and the outcome evaluations is derived to assess attitudes toward a behavior. For example, let us look at the behav-ior of exercising. A person may think of exercising and say that it makes him or her sweaty and thus rate exercise as extremely unlikely (1) to occur and as quite bad (–2). Such a person would have an attitude score of –2, or a negative attitude toward exer-cise. Another person might think of exercising and say it gives him or her a feeling of high energy and thus rate it as extremely likely (7) to occur and as quite good (+2). Such a person would have an attitude score of +14, or a positive attitude toward exer-cise. Behavioral beliefs can be modified by brainstorming all possible outcomes in an educational session. To modify outcome evaluations, a discussion on positive outcomes needs to be undertaken.

The sixth construct in TRA and TPB is **subjective norm**, which refers to a person's belief that most of the significant others in his or her life think the person should or should not perform the behavior. For example, a person might think, "If I exercise, my spouse will be proud of me." This is the second predictor of behavioral intention. In forming a subjective norm, people consider the normative expectations of others in their environment. It is usually measured on a 7-point unipolar scale with a range of strongly agree (7) to strongly disagree (1). The subjective norm is shaped by two constructs—normative beliefs and motivation to comply—which form the seventh and eighth constructs of the TRA and TPB.

The seventh construct of the TRA and TPB is **normative beliefs**, which refer to how a person thinks others who are significant in his or her life would like him or her to behave. For example, a person might think that his or her spouse, parents, and friends believe exercise is good and approve of people who exercise. Normative beliefs are measured on a 7-point bipolar scale with a range of strongly agree (+3), moderately agree (+2), slightly agree (+1), neither agree nor disagree (0), slightly disagree (−1), moderately disagree (−2), and strongly disagree (−3). In educational settings normative beliefs can be influenced by using a role play or psychodrama that helps the person become cognizant of how others may think about him or her. Discussion or arranging a panel discussion can help the person think more critically about the perception of significant others in his or her life.

The eighth construct of TRA and TPB is **motivation to comply**, which refers to the degree to which a person wants to act in accordance with the perceived wishes of those significant in his or her life. For example, a person might think that what his or her spouse, parents, and friends think about that person's plans for exercise matters a lot. Motivation to comply is usually measured on a 7-point unipolar scale with a range of extremely likely (7) to extremely unlikely (1). To influence motivation to comply, educational techniques such as role play, psychodrama, or discussion can be used, whereby people may become cognizant of their motivations to comply. With these eight constructs the TRA is complete. **Table 5.1** summarizes these constructs and describes how to modify each one.

In subsequent research, Ajzen added the following three constructs to create the TPB. The ninth construct in TPB is **perceived behavioral control**, which refers to how much a person feels he or she is in command of enacting the given behavior. It is dependent on the constructs of control belief and perceived power (Montano & Kasprzyk, 2002). Perceived behavioral control is measured on a 7-point unipolar scale with a range of strongly agree (7) to strongly disagree (1). Perceived behavioral

	TABLE 5.1	Key Constructs of the Theory of Reasoned Action	
	Construct	**Definition**	**How to Modify?**
	Behavior	Single, observable action performed by an individual, or a category of actions with a specific target, action, context, and time (TACT)	By influencing a behavioral intention, which is dependent on attitude toward the behavior and subjective norms
	Behavioral intention	The thought to perform the behavior, which is an immediate determinant of the given behavior	By influencing attitude toward the behavior and subjective norms
	Attitude toward the behavior	Overall feeling of like or dislike toward any given behavior	By influencing behavioral beliefs and outcome evaluations
✓	Behavioral beliefs	Beliefs that performing a given behavior leads to certain outcomes	Brainstorming all possible outcomes
✓	Outcome evaluations	Value a person places on each outcome resulting from performance of the behavior	Discussion about positive outcomes
✗	Subjective norm	One's belief that most of the significant others in one's life think one should or should not perform the behavior	By influencing normative beliefs and motivation to comply
✓	Normative beliefs	How a person thinks that other people who are significant in his or her life would like him or her to behave	• Role play • Psychodrama • Panel discussion • Discussion
⌣	Motivation to comply	Degree to which a person wants to act in accordance with the perceived wishes of those significant in his or her life	• Role play • Psychodrama • Discussion

control is a proxy measure of actual behavioral control and is hypothesized to be directly linked in predicting or explaining the behavior.

The tenth construct in TPB is **control beliefs**, which are beliefs about internal and external factors that may inhibit or facilitate the performance of the behavior. For example, a person may believe that he or she can exercise at any time, whereas another person may believe that he or she can exercise only during the times when the gym is open. These are measured on a 7-point scale with unipolar adjectives ranging from unlikely (1) to likely (7). To modify control beliefs, one can use discussion about factors that facilitate behavior, provide incentives, and reduce inhibiting factors.

The eleventh, and final, construct in TPB is **perceived power**, which refers to a person's perception of how easy or difficult it is to perform the behavior in each condition identified in that person's control beliefs. For example, a control belief may be that a person is able to exercise only during the times when the gym is open. Perceived power would explore how easy or how difficult it would be for the person to exercise when the gym is open. It is usually measured on a 7-point scale with bipolar adjectives ranging from extremely difficult (–3), moderately difficult (+2), slightly difficult (+1), neither difficult nor easy (0), slightly easy (+1), and moderately easy (+2), to extremely easy (+3). To modify perceived power, educational methods such as having role models model the desired behavior, removing barriers, and breaking down the behavior into small steps could be used. **Table 5.2** summarizes these additional constructs and how to modify them.

TABLE 5.2	Additional Constructs of the Theory of Planned Behavior	
Construct	**Definition**	**How to Modify?**
Perceived behavioral control	How much a person feels he or she is in command of enacting the given behavior	By influencing control beliefs and perceived power
Control beliefs	Beliefs about internal and external factors that may inhibit or facilitate the performance of the behavior	• Discussion about factors that facilitate behavior • Incentives • Reduction of inhibiting factors
Perceived power	Perception about how easy or difficult it is to perform the behavior in each condition identified in the control beliefs	• Having role models model the behavior • Removing barriers • Breaking down the behavior into small steps

APPLICATIONS OF THE THEORY OF REASONED ACTION AND THEORY OF PLANNED BEHAVIOR

It is possible to distinguish between beliefs, attitude, intentions, and behaviors, obtain valid and reliable measures for these, and to show that these are systematically related.

—Fishbein and Ajzen
(1975, p. 16)

Some examples in which the TRA has been used in health education and health promotion are for acceptance of the diagnosis of depression (Van Voorhees et al., 2005), attitudes about genetically modified foods (Silk, Weiner, & Parrott, 2005), colorectal cancer screening (Zimmerman, Tabbarah, Trauth, Nowalk, & Ricci, 2006), condom use (Fife-Schaw, & Abraham, 2009; Vanlandingham, Suprasert, Grandjean, & Sittitrai, 1995), a developmental care training program for neonatal nurses (Milette, Richard, & Martel, 2005), exercise/physical activity (Downs, Graham, Yang, Bargainnier, & Vasil, 2006; Wang, Worsley, & Cunningham, 2009), an HIV prevention program in adolescent mothers (Koniak-Griffin & Stein, 2006), mammography behavior and intention (Ham, 2006), modeling alcohol use (Zamboanga, Schwartz, Ham, Jarvis, & Olthuis, 2009), osteoporosis prevention (Tussing & Chapman-Novakofski, 2005), patient compliance during orthodontic treatment (Bos, Hoogstraten, & Prahl-Andersen, 2005), physician intention to prescribe emergency contraception (Sable, Schwartz, Kelly, Lisbon, & Hall, 2006), predicting mothers' infant feeding intentions (Manstead, Proffitt, & Smart, 1983), predicting pneumococcal vaccination (Zimmerman et al., 2005), predicting problem gambling (Moore & Ohtsuka, 1997), promoting healthy diet (Peng, 2009), promoting milk with 1% or less fat (Booth-Butterfield & Reger, 2004), prostate cancer genetic screening (Doukas, Localio, & Li, 2004), school-based intervention for HIV/AIDS prevention (Kinsler, Sneed, Morisky, & Ang, 2004), substance abuse behavior in pregnant adolescents (Morrison, Spencer, & Gillmore, 1998), sunscreen use behavior (Abroms, Jorgensen, Southwell, Geller, & Emmons, 2003), teaching testicular self-examination by nurse practitioners (Kleier, 2004), and violence prevention (Meyer, Roberto, Boster, & Roberto, 2004). **Table 5.3** summarizes these applications.

Some examples in which the TPB has been used in health education and health promotion are for condom use (Boer & Mashamba, 2005), controlling preschoolers' sugar snacking (Astrom & Kiwanuka, 2006), exercise/physical activity behavior (Hagger et al., 2009; Marsh, Papaioannou, & Theodorakis, 2006; Rhodes, Warburton, & Bredin, 2009), hand washing in healthcare workers (Whitby, McLaws, & Ross, 2006), healthy eating behaviors (Fila & Smith, 2006), hoist usage for moving a dependent patient among health care workers (Rickett, Orbell, & Sheeran, 2006), hypoglycemic medication among type 2 diabetics (Farmer, Kinmonth, & Sutton, 2006), mammography (O'Neill et al., 2008; Tolma, Reininger, Evans, & Ureda, 2006), mental health problems among prison inmates (Skogstad, Deane, & Spicer, 2006), multivitamin use among women (Pawlak, Connell, Brown, Meyer, & Yadrick, 2005), organ donation (Park, Smith, & Yun, 2009), predicting alcohol use (Park, Klein, Smith, & Martell, 2009; Quinlan, Jaccard, & Blanton, 2006), predicting binge drinking behavior (Norman & Conner, 2006), predicting fruit consumption (Brug, de Vet, de Nooijer, & Verplanken, 2006; de Bruijn, Brug, & Van Lenthe, 2009), predicting smoking among

TABLE 5.3 Applications of the Theory of Reasoned Action in Health Education and Health Promotion
Acceptance of a diagnosis of depression
Attitudes about genetically modified foods
Colorectal cancer screening
Condom use
Developmental care training program for neonatal nurses
Exercise/physical activity behavior
HIV prevention program in adolescent mothers
Mammography behavior and intention
Modeling alcohol use
Osteoporosis prevention
Patient compliance during orthodontic treatment
Physician intention to prescribe emergency contraception
Predicting mothers' infant feeding intentions
Predicting pneumococcal vaccination
Predicting problem gambling
Promoting healthy diet
Promoting milk with 1% or less fat
Prostate cancer genetic screening
School-based intervention for HIV/AIDS prevention
Substance abuse behavior in pregnant adolescents
Sunscreen use behavior
Teaching testicular self-examination by nurse practitioners
Violence prevention

We have long been convinced to demonstrate the utility of a theory in applied settings as well as in laboratory settings. This has led us to investigate such diverse problems as voting behavior, family planning, consumer behavior, occupational choice, and weight reduction.

—Ajzen and Fishbein
(1980, p. 97)

adolescents (van den Eijnden, Spijkerman, & Engels, 2006; Van De Ven, Engels, Otten, & Van Den Eijnden, 2007), school-based intervention to promote physical activity (Angelopoulos, Milionis, Grammatikaki, Moschonis, & Manios, 2009; Tsorbatzoudis, 2005), self-management of rheumatoid arthritis (Strating, van Schuur, & Suurmeijer, 2006), sexual and reproductive health in early adolescence (Aaro et al., 2006), small business owners' health and safety intentions (Brosseau & Li, 2005), smoking cessation (Bledsoe, 2005; Kim, 2008), use of assistive devices by home nurses (Roelands, Van Oost, Depoorter, Buysse, & Stevens, 2006), and vaccination against influenza (Gallagher & Povey, 2006). **Table 5.4** summarizes these applications.

LIMITATIONS OF THE THEORY OF REASONED ACTION AND THEORY OF PLANNED BEHAVIOR

Both TRA and TPB predict behavioral intention and behavior but do not necessarily explain behavior change, which is the primary concern in health education and health promotion programs. Hence, they do not provide detailed and specific guidance for behavior modification. Another limitation of the TRA and TPB is that they do not consider personality-related factors, cultural factors, and demographic variables, which also shape behavior. In his later work, Fishbein (2008) suggested adding an integrative model (IM) of behavioral prediction to the theory of reasoned action to account for environmental and other factors that moderate the intention–behavior relationship. Also, the theory of planned behavior assumes that perceived behavioral control predicts actual behavioral control, which may not always happen. Finally, these theories focus only on rational thoughts and do not account for irrational thoughts or fears, which health educators often encounter.

Jane Ogden (2003) noted that the TRA and TPB are pragmatic theories, but she criticized their conceptual bases and discussed several limitations of these theories. First, based on a literature review, Ogden observed that some studies of TPB reported no role for subjective norms, others showed no predictive role for perceived behavioral control, and some showed no role for attitudes. She contended that these theories may not be predictive or account for low variance, but often investigators rationalize this by arguing that the variables were not adequately operationalized rather than questioning the predictive potential of these theories. Ogden questioned the

TABLE 5.4	Applications of the Theory of Planned Behavior in Health Education and Health Promotion

Condom use

Controlling preschoolers' sugar snacking

Exercise/physical activity behavior

Hand washing in health care workers

Healthy eating behaviors

Hoist usage for moving a dependent patient among healthcare workers

Hypoglycemic medication among type 2 diabetics

Mammography

Mental health problems among prison inmates

Multivitamin use among women

Organ donation

Predicting alcohol use

Predicting binge drinking behavior

Predicting fruit consumption

Predicting smoking among adolescents

School-based intervention to promote physical activity

Self-management of rheumatoid arthritis

Sexual and reproductive health in early adolescence

Small business owners' health and safety intentions

Smoking cessation

Use of assistive devices by home nurses

Vaccination against influenza

testability of these theories. Ajzen and Fishbein (2004), in a rejoinder, clarified that the relative importance of attitudes, subjective norms, and perceptions of behavioral control for the prediction of intentions is expected to vary from behavior to behavior and from population to population. They argued that of the three theoretical antecedents, sometimes only one or two may be necessary in a given situation.

Ogden (2003) also talked about two types of truth in the philosophy of science: synthetic truth, which can be known through exploration and testing, and analytic truth, which is known by definition. She contended that the TRA and TPB focus on analytic truth, whereby the conclusions are not supported by observation. She also noted that behavior is mostly measured by self-reports rather than objective measures. In their rejoinder, Ajzen and Fishbein (2004) presented evidence from structural equation modeling that supported the path mentioned in the theories. They also defended self-reports because it is virtually impossible to obtain objective measurement of some behaviors (such as condom use) and extremely expensive and time consuming for others (such as exercise).

Finally, Ogden (2003) noted that answering questions about an individual's cognition in the operationalization of these theories may change and create an individual's thinking rather than tap into how that person thought to begin with. Ajzen and Fishbein (2004) noted that this concern is universal to all behavioral science research.

APPLICATION EXERCISE

In this chapter we have presented several examples of applications of TRA and TPB in health education and health promotion. Choose one application in which you are interested and locate the full text article for that application. Review and critique that example.

One example is the study by O'Neill and colleagues (2008) that examined behavioral intentions for adherence to mammography using TPB. In addition to the constructs of TPB, they included previous barriers, previous mammography maintenance, and age as potential predictors. A cross-sectional survey design was utilized and administered to 2062 currently adherent women who were due for their mammograms in 3 to 4 months. All TPB variables significantly predicted ($p < 0.05$) behavioral intention except subjective norms.

Locate the full text article of this study and in a critique of 250 words comment on how TPB was used.

SKILL-BUILDING ACTIVITY

Let us see how we can apply the TPB to the behavior of condom use. (Application of the TRA is a subset of the application of the TPB.) This application is depicted in **Figure 5.2**.

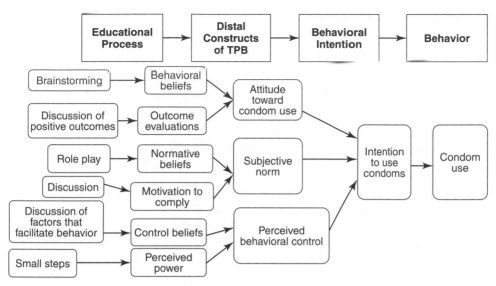

FIGURE 5.2 How the theory of planned behavior can be used for promoting condom use behavior.

Let us first define the target as college students; the action, which is condom use; the context, which is while having sex; and the time, which is every time an individual had sex. According to the TPB, the behavioral intention precedes the behavior. The proximal predictive constructs of intention include attitude toward condom use, subjective norm, and perceived behavioral control. To influence the construct of attitude toward condom use, the constructs of behavioral beliefs and outcome evaluations need to be modified. To modify behavioral beliefs, a brainstorming session can be organized in which the participants share their perceived outcomes about condom use. Instead of brainstorming, elicitation interviews with 15 to 20 members of the target audience could be organized. To modify outcome evaluations, a discussion on the positive outcomes of condom use, such as prevention of diseases and prevention of pregnancy, can be organized that would help all participants develop their outlook about positive effects.

To modify subjective norms, we would need to modify normative beliefs and motivation to comply. Normative beliefs can be modified by use of a role play that depicts the most significant others in a family situation approving of the behavior of condom use. The participants would then perhaps be able to apply that observation to their own lives and make a deduction that significant others in their lives would also approve of the behavior. To modify motivation to comply, a discussion can be organized that would try to sway the participants' belief that parents, friends, teachers, and all significant others consider using condoms important and that each person must use condoms.

To modify perceived behavioral control, the constructs of control beliefs and perceived power must be modified. To modify control beliefs, we can organize a discussion about factors that facilitate condom use behavior, such as keeping condoms readily accessible, having a prior discussion with one's partner, and so on. To modify perceived power, the condom use can be demonstrated in small steps, and role models can demonstrate the behavior of condom use. Using this approach, you can apply the TRA or TPB to any health behavior for a target group of your choice. **Table 5.5** provides a set of questions to assist you in choosing an educational method that corresponds to different constructs.

SUMMARY

In the late 1960s and early 1970s, Martin Fishbein and Icek Ajzen propounded the theory of reasoned action (TRA). The theory claims that behavioral intention precedes behavior and is determined by attitude toward the behavior and subjective norm. Attitude toward the behavior is the individual's overall like or dislike of any given behavior and is determined by behavioral beliefs (beliefs that performing a given behavior lead to certain outcomes) and outcome evaluations (the value a person places on each outcome resulting from performance of a given behavior). Subjective norm is one's belief that most of the significant others in one's life think one should or should not perform the behavior and is determined by normative beliefs (a person's beliefs about how other people who are significant in his or her life would like him or her to behave) and motivation to comply (degree to which a person wants to act in accordance with the perceived wishes of those significant in his or her life).

In the late 1980s and early 1990s, Ajzen added the construct of perceived behavioral control (how much a person feels that he or she is in command of enacting the given behavior) and created the theory of planned behavior (TPB). The construct of perceived behavioral control is dependent on control beliefs (beliefs about internal and external factors that may inhibit or facilitate the performance of the behavior) and perceived power (perception about how easy or difficult it is to perform the behavior in each condition identified in the control beliefs).

TABLE 5.5   Choosing the Educational Method for Health Education Program Planning Using the TRA and TPB

1. How will you define the behavior and behavioral intention?
   - Action: _____
   - Target: _____
   - Context: _____
   - Time: _____
2. What is the best educational method to facilitate behavioral beliefs?
   - Brainstorming
   - Discussion
   - Elicitation interviews
   - Other
3. What is the best educational method to facilitate outcome evaluations?
   - Discussion on positive outcomes
   - Lecture
   - Video with a credible role model
   - Other
4. What is the best educational method to facilitate normative beliefs?
   - Discussion
   - Role play
   - Psychodrama
   - Panel discussion
   - Simulation
   - Other
5. What is the best educational method to facilitate motivation to comply?
   - Discussion
   - Role play
   - Psychodrama
   - Simulation
   - Other
6. What is the best educational method to facilitate control beliefs?
   - Discussion about factors that facilitate behavior
   - Incentives
   - Reduction of inhibiting factors
   - Other
7. What is the best educational method to facilitate perceived power?
   - Demonstration of behavior in small steps
   - Having a role model model the behavior
   - Removing barriers
   - Other

Both the TRA and TPB have been used widely in health education and health promotion and continue to be applied. Lack of focus on behavior change, not considering all predictors, gap between perceived behavioral control and actual behavioral control, exclusive focus on rational thoughts, variations in predictive constructs, reliance on self-reports, and influences from measuring questionnaires are some identified limitations of the TRA and TPB.

IMPORTANT TERMS

attitude toward the behavior	outcome evaluations
behavior	perceived behavioral control
behavioral beliefs	perceived power
behavioral intention	subjective norm
control beliefs	theory of planned behavior (TPB)
motivation to comply	theory of reasoned action (TRA)
normative beliefs	

REVIEW QUESTIONS

1. Discuss the historical genesis of the theory of reasoned action (TRA) and the theory of planned behavior (TPB).
2. List and define the constructs of the TRA.
3. List and define the constructs of the TPB.
4. Differentiate between subjective norms and normative beliefs.
5. Discuss the limitations of the TRA and TPB.
6. Apply TPB to the promotion of condom use in college students.

WEBSITES TO EXPLORE

Applying TRA to Condom Use Among Sexual Workers

http://www.findarticles.com/p/articles/mi_qa3852/is_199801/ai_n8796585

This article by Sneed and Morisky was published in 1998 in the journal *Social Behavior and Personality*. The article examines the relationship between constructs from the TRA on condom use in a sample of Filipina sex workers. *Read this article and see how TRA has been used. Comment on its strengths and weaknesses.*

Professor Icek Aizen (Ajzen)

http://www.people.umass.edu/aizen/ *faq . html*

The website of Professor Icek Ajzen contains his contact information, professional background, teaching interests, research interests, a list of publications, and information on the theory of planned behavior. The link to theory of planned behavior provides a depiction of the model, bibliography of the model, tips on constructing a questionnaire based on TPB, tips on designing an intervention based on TPB, a research manual on TPB developed by researchers at University of New Castle, and frequently asked questions. *Read the frequently asked questions. Summarize what new things you learned.*

Resource Center for Adolescent Pregnancy Prevention (RECAPP)

522

http://www.etr.org/recapp/index.cfm?fuseaction=pages.TheoriesDetail&PageID=517

The RECAPP website summarizes the TRA, discusses its key concepts, explains how the TRA was developed, includes two research study summaries, discusses how TRA can be applied, discusses challenges, and lists resources. *Review one of the research study summaries and comment on its strengths and weaknesses.*

TRA to Explain Physician Intention to Prescribe Emergency Contraception

http://www.findarticles.com/p/articles/mi_m0NNR/is_1_38/ai_n16119587

This article by Sable and colleagues, published in March 2006 in the journal *Perspectives on Sexual and Reproductive Health,* uses TRA to explain physician intention to prescribe emergency contraception. *Read this article and discuss how well TRA has been applied.*

University of Twente: TPB & TRA

http://www.tcw.utwente.nl/theorieenoverzicht/Theory%20clusters/Health%20Communication/theory_planned_behavior.doc/

This website at the University of Twente in the Netherlands summarizes the TRA and TPB. Included in the presentation are history, core assumptions and statements, favorite methods, scope and application, and references. *Review this website and locate an account of an application of this theory. Discuss its strengths and weaknesses.*

REFERENCES

Aaro, L. E., Flisher, A. J., Kaaya, S., Onya, H., Fuglesang, M., Klepp, K. I., et al. (2006). Promoting sexual and reproductive health in early adolescence in South Africa and Tanzania: Development of a theory- and evidence-based intervention programme. *Scandinavian Journal of Public Health*, *34*(2), 150–158.

Abroms, L., Jorgensen, C. M., Southwell, B. G., Geller, A. C., & Emmons, K. M. (2003). Gender differences in young adults' beliefs about sunscreen use. *Health Education and Behavior*, *30*(1), 29–43.

Ajzen, I. (1991). The theory of planned behavior. *Organizational Behavior and Human Decision Process*, *50*, 179–211.

Ajzen, I., & Fishbein, M. (1980). *Understanding attitudes and predicting social behavior*. Englewood Cliffs, NJ: Prentice-Hall.

Ajzen, I., & Fishbein, M. (2004). Questions raised by a reasoned action approach: Comment on Ogden (2003). *Health Psychology*, *23*, 431–434.

Angelopoulos, P. D., Milionis, H. J., Grammatikaki, E., Moschonis, G., & Manios, Y. (2009). Changes in BMI and blood pressure after a school based intervention: The CHILDREN study. *European Journal of Public Health*, *19*(3), 319–325.

Astrom, A. N., & Kiwanuka, S. N. (2006). Examining intention to control preschool children's sugar snacking: A study of carers in Uganda. *International Journal of Paediatric Dentistry*, *16*(1), 10–18.

Atkinson, J. W. (1957). Motivational determinants of risk taking behavior. *Psychological Review*, *64*, 359–372.

Atkinson, J. W. (1964). *An introduction to motivation*. Princeton, NJ: Van Nostrand.

Bandura, A. (1986). *Social foundations of thought and action: A social cognitive theory*. Englewood Cliffs, NJ: Prentice-Hall.

Bem, D. J. (1965). An experimental analysis of self persuasion. *Journal of Experimental Social Psychology*, *1*, 199–218.

Bledsoe, L. K. (2005). Smoking cessation: An application of theory of planned behavior to understanding progress through stages of change. *Addictive Behaviors*, *31*(7), 1271–1276.

Boer, H., & Mashamba, M. T. (2005). Psychosocial correlates of HIV protection motivation among black adolescents in Venda, South Africa. *AIDS Education and Prevention*, *17*(6), 590–602.

Booth-Butterfield, S., & Reger, B. (2004). The message changes belief and the rest is theory: The "1% or less" milk campaign and reasoned action. *Preventive Medicine*, *39*(3), 581–588.

Bos, A., Hoogstraten, J., & Prahl-Andersen, B. (2005). The theory of reasoned action and patient compliance during orthodontic treatment. *Community Dentistry and Oral Epidemiology*, *33*(6), 419–426.

Brosseau, L. M., & Li, S. Y. (2005). Small business owners' health and safety intentions: A cross-sectional survey. *Environmental Health*, *4*, 23.

Brug, J., de Vet, E., de Nooijer, J., & Verplanken, B. (2006). Predicting fruit consumption: Cognitions, intention, and habits. *Journal of Nutrition Education and Behavior*, *38*(2), 73–81.

de Bruijn, G. J., Brug, J., & Van Lenthe, F. J. (2009). Neuroticism, conscientiousness and fruit consumption: Exploring mediator and moderator effects in the theory of planned behaviour. *Psychology & Health*, *24*(9), 1051–1069.

Doukas, D. J., Localio, A. R., & Li, Y. (2004). Attitudes and beliefs concerning prostate cancer genetic screening. *Clinical Genetics*, *66*(5), 445–451.

Downs, D. S., Graham, G. M., Yang, S., Bargainnier, S., & Vasil, J. (2006). Youth exercise intention and past exercise behavior: Examining the moderating influences of sex and meeting exercise recommendations. *Research Quarterly for Exercise and Sport*, 77(1), 91–99.

Farmer, A., Kinmonth, A. L., & Sutton, S. (2006). Measuring beliefs about taking hypoglycaemic medication among people with type 2 diabetes. *Diabetic Medicine*, 23(3), 265–270.

Festinger, L. (1957). *A theory of cognitive dissonance*. Evanston, IL: Row, Peterson.

Fife-Schaw, C., & Abraham, C. (2009). How much behaviour change should we expect from health promotion campaigns targeting cognitions? An approach to pre-intervention assessment. *Psychology & Health*, 24(7), 763–776.

Fila, S., & Smith, C. (2006). Applying the theory of planned behavior to healthy eating behaviors in urban Native American youth. *International Journal of Behavioral Nutrition and Physical Activity*, 3(1), 11.

Fishbein, M. (1965). A consideration of beliefs, attitudes, and their relationship. In I. D. Steiner & M. Fishbein (Eds.), *Current studies in social psychology* (pp. 107–120). New York: Holt Rinehart and Winston.

Fishbein, M. (1967). Attitude and the prediction of behavior. In M. Fishbein (Ed.), *Readings in attitude theory and measurement* (pp. 477–492). New York: Wiley.

Fishbein, M. (1980). A theory of reasoned action: Some applications and implications. *Nebraska Symposium on Motivation*, 27, 65–116.

Fishbein, M. (2008). A reasoned action approach to health promotion. *Medical Decision Making*, 28(6), 834–844.

Fishbein, M., & Ajzen, I. (1975). *Belief, attitude, intention and behavior: An introduction to theory and research*. Reading, MA: Addison-Wesley.

Francis, J. J., Eccles, M. P., Johnston, M., Walker, A., Grimshaw, J., Foy, R., et al. (2004). *Constructing questionnaires based on the theory of planned behaviour*. Newcastle upon Tyne, UK: Centre for Health Services Research, University of Newcastle.

Gallagher, S., & Povey, R. (2006). Determinants of older adults' intentions to vaccinate against influenza: A theoretical application. *Journal of Public Health*, 28(2), 139–144.

Ham, O. K. (2006). Factors affecting mammography behavior and intention among Korean women. *Oncology Nursing Forum*, 33(1), 113–119.

Hagger, M., Chatzisarantis, N. L., Hein, V., Soos, I., Karsai, I., Lintunen, T., et al. (2009). Teacher, peer and parent autonomy support in physical education and leisure-time physical activity: A trans-contextual model of motivation in four nations. *Psychology & Health*, 24(6), 689–711.

Heider, F. (1946). Attitudes and cognitive organization. *Journal of Psychology*, 21, 107–112.

Hull, C. L. (1943). *The principles of behavior*. New York: Appleton-Century-Crofts.

Kelley, H. H. (1971). *Attribution in social interaction*. New York: General Learning Press.

Kim, S. S. (2008). Predictors of short-term smoking cessation among Korean American men. *Public Health Nursing*, 25(6), 516–525.

Kinsler, J., Sneed, C. D., Morisky, D. E., & Ang, A. (2004). Evaluation of a school-based intervention for HIV/AIDS prevention among Belizean adolescents. *Health Education Research*, 19(6), 730–738.

Kleier, J. A. (2004). Nurse practitioners' behavior regarding teaching testicular self-examination. *Journal of the American Academy of Nurse Practitioners*, 16(5), 206–208, 210, 212.

Koniak-Griffin, D., & Stein, J. A. (2006). Predictors of sexual risk behaviors among adolescent mothers in a human immunodeficiency virus prevention program. *Journal of Adolescent Health*, *38*(3), 297.e1–11.

Manstead, A. S., Proffitt, C., & Smart, J. L. (1983). Predicting and understanding mothers' infant-feeding intentions and behavior: Testing the theory of reasoned action. *Journal of Personality and Social Psychology*, *44*(4), 657–671.

Marsh, H. W., Papaioannou, A., & Theodorakis, Y. (2006). Causal ordering of physical self-concept and exercise behavior: Reciprocal effects model and the influence of physical education teachers. *Health Psychology*, *25*(3), 316–328.

Meyer, G., Roberto, A. J., Boster, F. J., & Roberto, H. L. (2004). Assessing the Get Real About Violence curriculum: Process and outcome evaluation results and implications. *Health Communication*, *16*(4), 451–474.

Milette, I. H., Richard, L., & Martel, M. J. (2005). Evaluation of a developmental care training programme for neonatal nurses. *Journal of Child Health Care*, *9*(2), 94–109.

Montano, D. E., & Kasprzyk, D. (2002). The theory of reasoned action and the theory of planned behavior. In K. Glanz, B. Rimer, & F. M. Lewis (Eds.), *Health behavior and health education: Theory, research and practice* (3rd ed., pp. 67–98). San Francisco: Jossey-Bass.

Moore, S. M., & Ohtsuka, K. (1997). Gambling activities of young Australians: Developing a model of behaviour. *Journal of Gambling Studies*, *13*(3), 207–236.

Morrison, D. M., Spencer, M. S., & Gillmore, M. R. (1998). Beliefs about substance use among pregnant and parenting adolescents. *Journal of Research on Adolescence*, *8*(1), 69–95.

Norman, P., & Conner, M. (2006). The theory of planned behaviour and binge drinking: Assessing the moderating role of past behaviour within the theory of planned behaviour. *British Journal of Health Psychology*, *11*(Pt. 1), 55–70.

Ogden, J. (2003). Some problems with social cognition models: A pragmatic and conceptual analysis. *Health Psychology*, *22*, 424–428.

O'Neill, S. C., Bowling, J. M., Brewer, N. T., Lipkus, I. M., Skinner, C. S., Strigo, T. S., et al. (2008). Intentions to maintain adherence to mammography. *Journal of Women's Health*, *17*(7), 1133–1141.

Osgood, C. E., & Tannenbaum, P. H. (1955). The principle of congruity in the prediction of attitude change. *Psychological Review*, *62*, 42–55.

Park, H. S., Klein, K. A., Smith, S., & Martell, D. (2009). Separating subjective norms, university descriptive and injunctive norms, and U. S. descriptive and injunctive norms for drinking behavior intentions. *Health Communication*, 24(8), 746–751.

Park, H. S., Smith, S. W., & Yun, D. (2009). Ethnic differences in intention to enroll in a state organ donor registry and intention to talk with family about organ donation. *Health Communication*, *24*(7), 647–659.

Pawlak, R., Connell, C., Brown, D., Meyer, M. K., & Yadrick, K. (2005). Predictors of multivitamin supplement use among African-American female students: A prospective study utilizing the theory of planned behavior. *Ethnicity and Disease*, *15*(4), 540–547.

Peng, W. (2009). Design and evaluation of a computer game to promote a healthy diet for young adults. *Health Communication*, *24*(2), 115–127.

Quinlan, S. L., Jaccard, J., & Blanton, H. (2006). A decision theoretic and prototype conceptualization of possible selves: Implications for the prediction of risk behavior. *Journal of Personality*, *74*(2), 599–630.

Rhodes, R. E., Warburton, D. E., & Bredin, S. S. (2009). Predicting the effect of interactive video bikes on exercise adherence: An efficacy trial. *Psychology, Health & Medicine, 14*(6), 631–640.

Rickett, B., Orbell, S., & Sheeran, P. (2006). Social-cognitive determinants of hoist usage among health care workers. *Journal of Occupational Health Psychology, 11*(2), 182–196.

Roelands, M., Van Oost, P., Depoorter, A. M., Buysse, A., & Stevens, V. (2006). Introduction of assistive devices: Home nurses' practices and beliefs. *Journal of Advanced Nursing, 54*(2), 180–188.

Rotter, J. B. (1954). *Social learning and clinical psychology.* New York: Prentice-Hall.

Rotter, J. B. (1966). Generalized expectancies for internal versus external control of reinforcement. *Psychological Monographs, 80*(1, No. 609).

Sable, M. R., Schwartz, L. R., Kelly, P. J., Lisbon, E., & Hall, M. A. (2006). Using the theory of reasoned action to explain physician intention to prescribe emergency contraception. *Perspectives on Sexual and Reproductive Health, 38*(1), 20–27.

Sheppard, B. H., Hartwick, J., & Warshaw, P. R. (1988). The theory of reasoned action: A meta-analysis of past research with recommendations for modifications and future research. *Journal of Consumer Research, 15*, 325–343.

Silk, K. J., Weiner, J., & Parrott, R. L. (2005). Gene cuisine or Frankenfood? The theory of reasoned action as an audience segmentation strategy for messages about genetically modified foods. *Journal of Health Communication, 10*, 751–767.

Skogstad, P., Deane, F. P., & Spicer, J. (2006). Social-cognitive determinants of help-seeking for mental health problems among prison inmates. *Criminal Behavior and Mental Health, 16*(1), 43–59.

Spence, K. W. (1956). *Behavior theory and conditioning.* New Haven, CT: Yale University Press.

Strating, M. M., van Schuur, W. H., & Suurmeijer, T. P. (2006). Contribution of partner support in self-management of rheumatoid arthritis patients. An application of the theory of planned behavior. *Journal of Behavioral Medicine, 29*(1), 51–60.

Tolma, E. L., Reininger, B. M., Evans, A., & Ureda, J. (2006). Examining the theory of planned behavior and the construct of self-efficacy to predict mammography intention. *Health Education and Behavior, 33*(2), 233–251.

Tolman, E. C. (1955). Principles of performance. *Psychological Review, 62*, 315–326.

Tsorbatzoudis, H. (2005). Evaluation of a school-based intervention programme to promote physical activity: An application of the theory of planned behavior. *Perceptual and Motor Skills, 101*(3), 787–802.

Tussing, L., & Chapman-Novakofski, K. (2005). Osteoporosis prevention education: Behavior theories and calcium intake. *Journal of American Dietetic Association, 105*, 92–97.

van den Eijnden, R. J., Spijkerman, R., & Engels, R. C. (2006). Relative contribution of smoker prototypes in predicting smoking among adolescents: A comparison with factors from the theory of planned behavior. *European Addiction Research, 12*(3), 113–120.

Van De Ven, M. O., Engels, R. C., Otten, R., & Van Den Eijnden, R. J. (2007). A longitudinal test of the theory of planned behavior predicting smoking onset among asthmatic and non-asthmatic adolescents. *Journal of Behavioral Medicine, 30*(5), 435–445.

Vanlandingham, M. J., Suprasert, S., Grandjean, N., & Sittitrai, W. (1995). Two views of risky sexual practices among northern Thai males: The health belief model and the theory of reasoned action. *Journal of Health and Social Behavior, 36*, 195–212.

Van Voorhees, B. W., Fogel, J., Houston, T. K., Cooper, L. A., Wang, N. Y., & Ford, D. E. (2005). Beliefs and attitudes associated with the intention to not accept the diagnosis of depression among young adults. *Annals of Family Medicine, 3*(1), 38–46.

Wang, W. C., Worsley, A., & Cunningham, E. G. (2009). Social ideological influences on food con-
    sumption, physical activity and BMI. *Appetite, 53*(3), 288–296.

Whitby, M., McLaws, M. L., & Ross, M. W. (2006). Why healthcare workers don't wash their
    hands: A behavioral explanation. *Infection Control and Hospital Epidemiology, 27*(5), 484–492.

Zamboanga, B. L., Schwartz, S. J., Ham, L. S., Jarvis, L. H., & Olthuis, J. V. (2009). Do alcohol
    expectancy outcomes and valuations mediate peer influences and lifetime alcohol use among
    early adolescents? *Journal of Genetic Psychology, 170*(4), 359–376.

Zimmerman, R. K., Tabbarah, M., Nowalk, M. P., Raymund, M., Jewell, I. K., Block, B., et al.
    (2005). Predictors of pneumococcal polysaccharide vaccination among patients at three inner-
    city neighborhood health centers. *American Journal of Geriatric Pharmacotherapy, 3*(3), 149–159.

Zimmerman, R. K., Tabbarah, M., Trauth, J., Nowalk, M. P., & Ricci, E. M. (2006). Predictors of
    lower endoscopy use among patients at three inner-city neighborhood health centers. *Journal of
    Urban Health, 83*(2), 221–230.

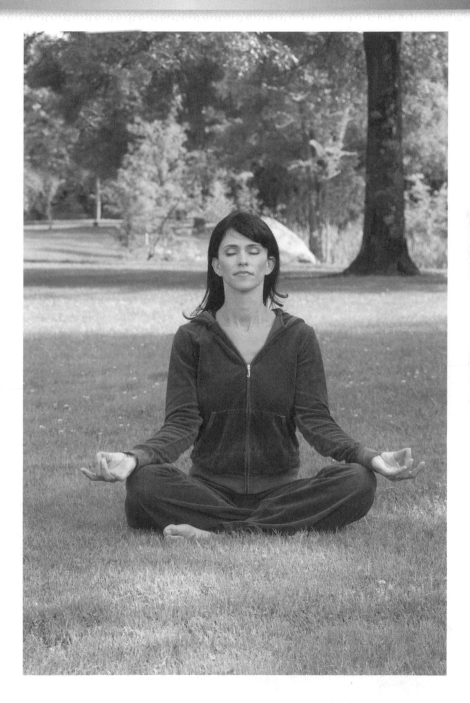

CHAPTER 6

Theories of Stress and Coping

KEY CONCEPTS

- challenge
- chronic strains
- chronic stressors
- commitment
- community-wide strains
- comprehensibility
- control
- coping
- daily hassles
- emotion-focused coping
- event-based models
- general adaptation syndrome
- hardiness
- life events or life change events
- manageability
- meaningfulness

- nonevents
- optimism
- persistent life difficulties
- problem-focused coping
- recent life events
- remote life events
- response-based models
- role strains
- sense of coherence
- social support
- stress
- stressors
- transactional model
- type A personality
- type B personality

AFTER READING THIS CHAPTER YOU SHOULD BE ABLE TO

- Describe the historical genesis of theories of stress and coping
- List the constructs of the expanded transactional model, the theory of hardiness, and the theory of sense of coherence
- Summarize the applications of theories of stress and coping in health education and health promotion
- Identify educational methods and match these to modify each construct from theories of stress and coping
- Apply the theories of stress and coping in reducing stress

This chapter discusses theories of stress and coping. Stress is an integral part of any behavior change. People experience some amount of stress when changing any given behavior.

If this stress is very high, new behavior cannot be acquired. Stress can be produced by a variety of external and internal events other than acquiring a new behavior. Often this stress is harmful and causes negative sequelae. Various theories, models, and constructs have been developed to explain the stress process. Some of these theories and models focus on the effects of stress, some on the causes of stress, others on personality characteristics, and some on coping responses. This chapter integrates the understanding of stress across these various models and theories. In health education and health promotion, we are interested in understanding the stress process as well as in finding ways to reduce negative stress, so the emphasis is on modifying those constructs that can be altered.

The chapter begins by describing the historical aspects of the genesis of these theories. Next we describe the various constructs that make up these theories and discuss the applications of theories of stress and coping in health education and health promotion. We then discuss the limitations of the theories of stress and coping and present a skill-building application.

> *It is not the stressor but your perception of the stress that is important.*
>
> —Romas and Sharma (2007, p. 1)

HISTORICAL PERSPECTIVE

The concept of **stress** was unknown in physiology and psychology prior to 1932. The term had been used mainly in physical sciences to denote cracks in the structure of buildings that were caused by pressure. Walter Cannon (1932), a physiologist, first defined stress as a "fight or flight" syndrome. He stated that when an organism is presented with a stressful stimulus, it responds by either fighting with it or running away from it. This was the origin of **response-based models** of stress.

The response-based concept was further elaborated by the work of Swedish physiologist Hans Selye (1936, 1974a, 1974b, 1982), who described the **general adaptation syndrome**. While trying to isolate a new sex hormone in rats, Selye observed that exposing rats to events such as cold, heat, injury, infection, loss of blood, pain, and other noxious stimuli resulted in their adrenal glands secreting corticoid hormones (a steroid) and their bodies going through three stages that he called the general adaptation syndrome (**Figure 6.1**). He labeled the first stage the *alarm reaction*, in which a living organism's homeostasis, or balance, is disrupted by the noxious stimuli. In this phase the endocrine glands (ductless glands that pour their secretions directly into the blood), especially the adrenal glands, begin secreting hormones (corticosteroids) that help to supply more energy to the body. This is accompanied by a

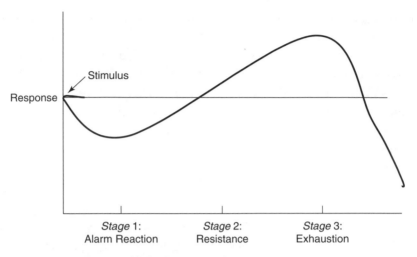

FIGURE 6.1   Stages of general adaptation syndrome.

shrinkage of lymphatic structures, a decrease in blood volume, and development of ulcers in the stomach. The second stage is *resistance*, in which the body tries to resist the noxious stimuli. In this stage the adaptation energy continues to be depleted. The third and final stage of the general adaptation syndrome is *exhaustion*. Exhaustion causes permanent damage to the system; if the noxious agent is not removed, the organism's energy becomes depleted, and death may follow.

The response-based modeling of stress that originated from the work of physiologists and discussed hormonal and physiological responses remained the major model of stress until the 1960s, when event-based models and the concept of coping began to be understood in psychology. Thomas Holmes and Richard Rahe (1967) developed the Social Readjustment Rating Scale, which listed 43 life events, each with a predetermined weight, and asked a person to identify events he or she had experienced in the past year. They empirically found that the higher a person's score was on the scale, the greater the chances of that individual developing sickness in the subsequent year. The **event-based models** changed the paradigm from the effect (response) to the cause (stressor).

Alongside the event-based models, the concept of **coping** also developed, which led to establishment of the transactional model of coping. The term *coping* can be traced back to the concept of **defense mechanisms** described in the psychoanalytical model by the famous Austrian neurologist Sigmund Freud (1923). In the 1920s, Freud described the mechanisms of defense that a person's mind uses to protect itself. These included methods such as introjection, isolation, projection reversal, reaction formation, regression, repression, sublimation, turning against the self, and undoing. According to Freud, defense mechanisms were the devices that the mind used to alter the individual's perception of situations that disturbed the internal milieu or mental balance. He applied this concept in identifying sources of anxiety using a free association technique on patients.

In the 1930s one of Freud's associates, Austrian-born physician Alfred Adler, differed from Freud and argued that defense mechanisms were protective against external threats or challenges (Sharma, 2003). Sigmund Freud's daughter and renowned psychologist, Anna Freud (1937), included both these viewpoints and underscored the role of defense mechanisms as being protective against both internal and external threats. She also extended the repertoire of defense mechanisms to include denial, intellectualization, ego restriction, and identifying with the aggressor. Therefore, it appears that the concept of defense mechanisms is very similar to that of coping, which it preceded. However, in the 1970s, psychologist Norma Haan (1977) distinguished defense mechanisms from coping. She explained that coping is purposeful and involves choices, whereas defense mechanisms are rigid and set. Coping, according to Haan, is focused on the present, whereas defense mechanisms are premised on the past and distort the present.

Using the concept of coping, Richard Lazarus (1966, 1984), a professor of psychology at the University of California–Berkley, developed the transactional model. According to this model, all stressful experiences, including chronic illnesses, are perceived as person–environment transactions. In these transactions, the person undertakes a four-stage assessment known as *appraisal* (Lazarus & Folkman, 1984). When confronted with any stressor, the first stage is the *primary appraisal* of the event. In this stage, the person internally determines the severity of the stressor and whether he or she is in trouble. If the stressor is perceived to be severe or threatening, has caused harm or loss in the past, or has affected someone known to the person, then the stage of secondary appraisal occurs. If, on the other hand, the stressor is judged to be irrelevant or poses minimal threat, then stress does not develop any further, and no further coping occurs. The *secondary appraisal* determines how much control the person has over the stressor. Based on this understanding, the individual ascertains what means of control are available to him or her. This is the stage known as *coping*. According to the transactional model, there are two broad categories of coping: problem-focused coping and emotion-focused coping. Finally, the fourth stage is *reappraisal*, during which the person determines whether the effects of the stressor have been effectively negated.

In the 1970s Suzanne Kobasa (1979a, 1979b) conducted an eight-year study of executives undergoing the major stress of losing their jobs or being reassigned and found that individuals who displayed a certain set of personality characteristics remained healthier and happier during the crisis. She labeled such personality traits **hardiness**. Friedman and Rosenman (1974) classified people into type A and type B personalities. The **type A personality** was characterized by hurrying, exercising control over people and things, a sense of urgency, and a challenging nature. The **type B personality** was more laid back and had a more relaxed disposition. It was found that people with type B personalities had less stress than those with type A personalities. In the late 1970s and 1980s, a medical sociologist, Aaron Antonovsky (1979, 1987), proposed the theory of **sense of coherence**, which postulated that people who possess a higher sense of coherence tend to cope with life better. In the 1980s another construct that moderates the influence of stressors was discovered, namely, social support. Scheier and Carver (1985) also suggested the construct of optimism as having a beneficial effect on coping.

> *The nature and severity of the stress disorder could depend on at least three factors: (1) the formal characteristics of the environmental demands, (2) the quality of the emotional response generated by the demands, or in particular individuals facing these demands, and (3) the process of coping mobilized by the stressful commerce.*
>
> —Lazarus (1974, p. 327)

CONSTRUCTS OF THEORIES OF STRESS AND COPING

A model incorporating theories of stress and coping is depicted in **Figure 6.2**. The primary construct of theories of stress and coping is that of **stressors**, which are demands from the internal or external environment that an individual perceives as being harmful or threatening (Lazarus & Folkman, 1984). These are divided into three general classes: discrete, major life events; ongoing, everyday chronic stressors; and the absence of major happenings, or nonevents (Romas & Sharma, 2010).

Life events, or **life change events**, are discrete, observable, and objectively reportable events that require some social or psychological adjustment, or both, on the part of the individual (Wheaton, 1994). Examples of such events are the death of a family member, starting a new job, and buying a new home. If these happened in the recent past (within the last year), they are called **recent life events**; if they occurred

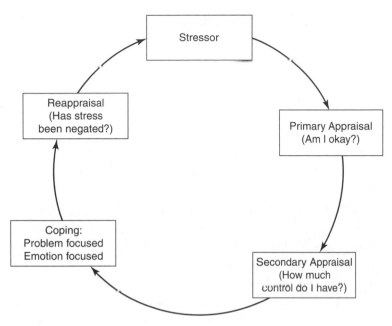

FIGURE 6.2 Model of stress and coping.

further in the past (such as childhood events) and are bothersome as memories, they are called **remote life events**.

McLean and Link (1994) classified **chronic stressors** into five types:

1. **Persistent life difficulties**: Life events lasting longer than six months, such as long term disability.
2. **Role strains**: Strain from either performing a specific role (such as parenting, working, or being in a relationship) or performing a multiplicity of roles at the same time.
3. **Chronic strains**: Responses of one social group to another, such as overt or covert, intentional or unintentional discriminatory behavior due to race, ethnicity, and so on.
4. **Daily hassles**: Everyday problems, such as getting stuck in traffic.
5. **Community-wide strains**: Stressors that operate at an ecological level, such as residing in a high-crime neighborhood.

Nonevents are of three kinds: (1) when desired or anticipated events do not occur (e.g., wanting to graduate but not having enough credits), (2) when desired events do not occur even though their occurrence is normative for people of a certain group (e.g., a person does not get married when most people of his or her age are married), and (3) not having anything to do (e.g., being bored).

Most of the time stressors cannot be modified and have to be endured. However, a person's perception of the stressors can be changed. Some stressors can be changed by modifying the environment. For example, if one is stressed about taking a class from a certain instructor and that class is also offered by another instructor, signing up for the class with the second instructor can alleviate the stress.

The second construct of the theories of stress and coping is that of **primary appraisal**, in which the person determines the severity of the stressor and makes an assessment regarding whether he or she is in trouble. To modify this construct in an educational program, participants could be asked to keep a stress diary, participate in a brainstorming session to identify the stressors affecting them at any given time, or participate in a discussion of the stressors and their severity.

In **secondary appraisal**, the person determines how much control he or she has over the stressor. If control is high, no stress develops; if control is low, stress develops. To modify secondary appraisal in an educational program, stress diaries, brainstorming, or discussion can be helpful.

The construct of **problem-focused coping** is based on a person's capability to think and to alter the environmental event or situation. Examples of this strategy at the thought process level include utilization of problem-solving skills, interpersonal conflict resolution, advice seeking, time management, goal setting, and gathering more information about what is causing the stress. Problem solving requires thinking through various alternatives, evaluating the pros and cons of different solutions, and then implementing a solution that seems most advantageous to reduce the stress. Examples of this strategy at the behavioral or action level include activities such as joining a smoking cessation program, compliance with a prescribed medical treatment, adherence to a diabetic diet plan, and scheduling and prioritizing tasks for managing time.

In the construct of **emotion-focused coping**, the focus is on altering the way one thinks or feels about a situation or an event. Examples of this strategy at the thought process level include denying the existence of the stressful situation, freely expressing emotions, avoiding the stressful situation, making social comparisons, and looking at the bright side of things. Examples of this strategy at the behavioral or action level include seeking social support to negate the influence of the stressful situation; use of exercise, relaxation, or meditation; joining support groups; and practicing religious rituals. Negative examples include escaping through the use of alcohol and drugs.

The final construct of the theories of stress and coping is **reappraisal**, which is the feedback loop by which the person determines whether the effects of the stressor have been effectively negated. To modify this construct, techniques such as stress diaries, brainstorming, or discussion can again be helpful. **Table 6.1** summarizes the constructs.

TABLE 6.1 Key Constructs of Theories of Stress and Coping		
Construct	**Definition**	**How to Modify?**
Stressors	Demands from the internal or external environment that one perceives as being harmful or threatening. These are of three kinds: life events, chronic stressors, and nonevents.	Most stressors cannot be modified and must be endured. What can be modified is the person's perception of the stressors. Some stressors can be modified by environmental engineering.
Primary appraisal	Person determines the severity of the stressor and makes an assessment regarding whether he or she is in trouble.	Stress diary Brainstorming Discussion
Secondary appraisal	Person determines how much control he or she has over the stressor.	Stress diary Brainstorming Discussion
Problem-focused coping	Method of dealing with a given stressor that focuses on the ability to think about and alter the environmental event or situation.	Problem-solving skills Interpersonal conflict resolution Advice seeking Time management Goal setting Discussion to gather more information about what is causing the stress
Emotion-focused coping	Method of dealing with a stressor in which the focus is on altering the way one thinks or feels about a situation or an event.	Exercise Relaxation Meditation Joining support groups
Reappraisal	Feedback loop in which the person determines whether the effects of the stressor have been effectively negated.	Stress diary Brainstorming Discussion

As we have seen, the theory of hardiness also originated in the 1970s. Hardiness has three constructs (Taylor & Aspinwall, 1996): control, commitment, and challenge (**Table 6.2**). **Control** refers to a person's belief that he or she causes the events of his or her life and can influence the environment. The greater a person's belief in his or her control, the better that person is able to endure the adverse effects of stress. Control can be modified in an educational program by conducting a discussion on this topic or by having participants role-play situations in which they experience control and relate it to their lives.

> *The mechanism whereby stressful life events produce illness is presumably physiological. Whatever this physiological response is, the personality characteristics of hardiness may cut into it, decreasing the likelihood of breakdown into illness.*
>
> —Kobasa (1985, p. 187)

Commitment refers to a person's tendency to become involved in whatever he or she encounters or to a feeling of deep involvement in the activities of life. The higher a person's commitment, the higher that person's ability to cope with stress. To modify commitment in an educational program, the educator can facilitate a discussion on the topic, or the effects of commitment can be portrayed in a role play.

Challenge refers to a person's willingness to undertake change, confront new activities, and obtain opportunities for growth. The greater a sense of challenge a person has, the easier he or she is able to cope with stress. To modify the construct of challenge, one can use goal setting, whereby participants set incrementally challenging goals for themselves.

Another theory that originated in the 1970s was that of the sense of coherence (Antonovsky, 1979, 1987). The three constructs of the sense of coherence are comprehensibility, manageability, and meaningfulness (**Table 6.3**). **Comprehensibility** refers to the extent to which the individual perceives that the stressors he or she confronts make cognitive sense, which implies that there is some set structure, consistency,

TABLE 6.2	Key Constructs of the Theory of Hardiness	
Construct	**Definition**	**How to Modify?**
Control	Belief that one causes the events of one's life and can influence the environment.	Discussion Role-play
Commitment	Tendency to involve oneself in whatever one encounters, or a feeling of deep involvement in the activities of life.	Discussion Role-play
Challenge	Willingness to undertake change, confront new activities, and obtain opportunities for growth.	Goal setting

TABLE 6.3	Key Constructs for the Theory of Sense of Coherence	
Construct	**Definition**	**How to Modify?**
Comprehensibility	The extent to which one perceives that the stressors that confront one make cognitive sense, implying that there is some set structure, consistency, order, clarity, and predictability.	Clarify the stressors and interpret them such that they have clarity and predictability.
Manageability	The extent to which one feels that the resources under one's control are adequate to meet the demands posed by the stressors.	Brainstorming to identify all resources Support group to increase resources
Meaningfulness	The extent to which one feels that life makes sense emotionally and that at least some of the stressors in life are worth investing energy in and are worthy of commitment and engagement.	Discussion about perspective toward stressors

order, clarity, and predictability. To modify comprehensibility in an educational program, a discussion session that clarifies the stressors and interprets them can provide clarity and predictability.

Manageability refers to the extent to which a person feels that the resources under his or her control are adequate to meet the demands posed by the stressors. To modify this construct in educational sessions, the educator can facilitate a brainstorming session in which all the potential resources can be enlisted. A support group that is able to provide additional resources can be built into the educational program.

Meaningfulness refers to the extent to which the person feels that life makes sense emotionally and that at least some of the stressors in life are worth investing energy in and are worthy of commitment and engagement. It entails looking at challenges in life as something welcome rather than burdensome. It can be modified in an educational session by organizing a discussion about changing one's perspective regarding stressors.

Another construct that has been found to moderate the negative effects of stressors is **social support**, which is the help obtained through social relationships and interpersonal exchanges (Heaney & Israel, 2008). House (1981) classified social support into four types: (1) emotional support, which entails providing understanding, love, caring, and reliance; (2) informational support, which entails providing information, guidance, and counsel; (3) instrumental support, which entails providing concrete assistance and support; and (4) appraisal support, which entails providing evaluative assistance.

Social support can be naturally occurring, in the form of parents, spouse, other family members, and friends, or it can be created artificially by the health educator. Social support buffers the effects of stressors and shields a person from negative consequences.

A final construct that has been linked to resistance to stress is **optimism** (Scheier & Carver, 1985), which is the tendency to expect the best possible outcome or to think about the most hopeful aspects of any situation. Several studies have linked optimism to better coping and health. Optimism acts through several pathways to ensure better health. First, optimism affects a person's efforts to avoid illness by increasing attention to information about potential health threats. Second, optimism directly improves coping. Third, optimism acts through its influence on the maintenance of positive mood. Martin Seligman has talked about the modifiability of this construct in his books *Learned Optimism* (1990) and *What You Can Change and What You Can't* (1994). To modify the construct of optimism in an educational program, the educator can facilitate a lecture or discussion on its value.

APPLICATIONS OF THE THEORIES OF STRESS AND COPING

Theories of stress and coping have been used in a variety of health education and promotion applications, including for cardiac rehabilitation following myocardial infarction (Macinnes, 2005), coping following traumatic brain injury (Anson & Ponsford, 2006; Strom & Kosciulek, 2007), coping in breast cancer survivors (Lebel, Rosberger, Edgar, & Devins, 2008; Wonghongkul, Dechaprom, Phumivichuvate, & Losawatkul, 2006), coping in the elderly (Poderico, Ruggiero, Iachini, & Iavarone, 2006), coping with arthritis (Rosenzweig et al., 2010; Tak, 2006), coping in head and neck cancer patients (Vidhubala, Latha, Ravikannan, Mani, & Karthikesh, 2006), coping in newly incarcerated adolescents (Brown & Ireland, 2006), coping in old-age psychosis (Berry, Barrowclough, Byrne, & Purandare, 2006), coping in siblings with sickle cell disease (Gold, Treadwell, Weissman, & Vichinsky, 2008), coping in survivors of domestic violence (Lewis et al., 2006; Watlington & Murphy, 2006), coping with diabetes mellitus (Samuel-Hodge, Watkins, Rowell, & Hooten, 2008; Thoolen, Ridder, Bensing, Gorter, & Rutten, 2009), coping with exacerbation of psoriasis and eczema (Wahl, Mork, Hanestad, & Helland, 2006), prevention of atherosclerosis (Jedryka-Goral et al., 2006), prevention of recurrent depression (Bockting et al., 2006), quality of life assessment for stroke caregivers (Van Puymbroeck & Rittman, 2005), smoking cessation (Friis, Forouzesh, Chhim, Monga, & Sze, 2006), and a worksite stress management program (Shimazu, Umanodan, & Schaufeli, 2006). **Table 6.4** summarizes these applications.

The theory of hardiness has been used in a variety of health education and promotion applications, including for adaptation in families of young children with chronic

TABLE 6.4 Applications of Theories of Stress and Coping in Health Education and Health Promotion

Cardiac rehabilitation following myocardial infarction

Coping following traumatic brain injury

Coping in breast cancer survivors

Coping with elderly health conditions

Coping with arthritis

Coping in head and neck cancer patients

Coping in newly incarcerated adolescents

Coping in old-age psychosis

Coping in siblings with sickle cell disease

Coping in survivors of domestic violence

Coping with diabetes mellitus

Coping with exacerbation of psoriasis and eczema

Prevention of atherosclerosis

Prevention of recurrent depression

Quality of life assessment for stroke caregivers

Smoking cessation

Worksite stress management program

asthma (Svavarsdottir, Rayens, & McCubbin, 2005), family-level intervention for parents of children with cancer (Svavarsdottir & Sigurdardottir, 2005, 2006), military cadets participating in survival training (Eid & Morgan, 2006), modeling coping in spousal caregivers of persons with dementia (DiBartolo & Soeken, 2003), modeling for mental health among mothers of adult children with intellectual disability (Ben-Zur, Duvdevany, & Lury, 2005), modeling health in women with physical and sexual abuse (Heckman & Clay, 2005), modeling psychological status and physical function in osteoarthritis patients (Kee, 2003), modeling well-being in older women (Smith, Young, & Lee, 2004), modeling work stress and job satisfaction (Lambert, Lambert, Petrini, Li, & Zhang, 2007; McCalister, Dolbier, Webster, Mallon, & Steinhardt, 2006), organizational and psychological adjustment in managers (Ghorbani & Watson, 2005), psychological distress in police officers (Andrew et al., 2008), qualitative study of adults aging with HIV (Vance & Woodley, 2005), qualitative study of hardiness in intensive care unit nurses (Hurst & Koplin-Baucum, 2005; Whitmer, Hurst, & Prins, 2009), qualitative study of women with paraplegia (Kinder, 2005), and workplace stress reduction (Lambert, Lambert, & Yamase, 2003). **Table 6.5** summarizes these applications.

The theory of sense of coherence has been used in a variety of health education and promotion applications, including for an addiction recovery program (Chen, 2006), associations with quality of life among women with systemic lupus erythematosus (Abu-Shakra et al., 2006), coping in the next of kin of cancer patients who are in palliative home care (Milberg & Strang, 2003), coping with serious accidental injury (Hepp, Moergeli, Buchi, Wittmann, & Schnyder, 2005), couple therapy aimed at reducing marital distress and psychiatric symptoms (Lundblad & Hansson, 2005), determinants of mental health (Malinauskiene, Leisyte, & Malinauskas, 2009), an educational program after breast cancer surgery (Koinberg, Langius-Eklof, Holmberg, & Fridlund, 2006),

TABLE 6.5   Applications of the Theory of Hardiness in Health Education and Health Promotion
Adaptation in families of young children with chronic asthma
Family-level intervention for parents of children with cancer
Military cadets participating in survival training
Modeling coping in spousal caregivers of persons with dementia
Modeling for mental health among mothers of adult children with intellectual disability
Modeling health in women with physical and sexual abuse
Modeling psychological status and physical function in osteoarthritis patients
Modeling well-being in older women
Modeling work stress and job satisfaction
Organizational and psychological adjustment in managers
Psychological distress in police officers
Qualitative study of adults aging with HIV
Qualitative study of hardiness in intensive care unit nurses
Qualitative study of women with paraplegia
Workplace stress reduction

modeling sick leave absence in parents of children with Down syndrome (Hedov, Wikblad, & Anneren, 2006), pain management in spinal cord injury patients (Norrbrink Budh, Kowalski, & Lundeberg, 2006), predicting depression in mass-evacuated adults from Kosovo (Roth & Ekblad, 2006), predicting oral and general health behaviors (Savolainen et al., 2009), predicting quality of life among spouses of stroke patients (Larson et al., 2005), quality of life in older people (Borglin, Jakobsson, Edberg, & Hallberg, 2006; Volanen et al., 2010), relationship with stress in parents of children with developmental disabilities (Oelofsen & Richardson, 2006), and relationship with tobacco use (Glanz, Maskarinec, & Carlin, 2005). **Table 6.6** summarizes these applications.

> *Each person must find a way to relieve his pent-up energy without creating conflicts with his fellow men. Such an approach not only insures peace of mind but also earns goodwill, respect, and even love of our neighbors, the highest degree of security and the noblest status symbol to which the human being can aspire.*
>
> —Selye (1985, p. 28)

TABLE 6.6   Applications of the Theory of Sense of Coherence in Health Education and Health Promotion

Addiction recovery program

Associations with quality of life among women with systemic lupus erythematosus

Coping in the next of kin of cancer patients who are in palliative home care

Coping with serious accidental injury

Couple therapy aimed at reducing marital distress and psychiatric symptoms

Determinants of mental health

Educational program after breast cancer surgery

Modeling sick leave absence in parents of children with Down syndrome

Pain management in spinal cord injury patients

Predicting depression in mass-evacuated adults from Kosovo

Predicting oral and general health behaviors

Predicting quality of life among spouses of stroke patients

Quality of life in older people

Relationship with stress in parents of children with developmental disabilities

Relationship with tobacco use

LIMITATIONS OF THE THEORIES OF STRESS AND COPING

We have seen that there are three major kinds of theories of stress and coping. The strength of response-based models is that they explicate the physiological relationships involved in stress, but some of the limitations of this model are the nonspecificity of stimuli, the lack of accounting for individual variations, the lack of accounting for differences in stressors, and lack of attention to cognitive processing of stressors. Event-based models are strong in terms of clarifying stressors, introducing the notion of coping, and explaining the differences in stressors, but have the limitations of not covering physiological mechanisms and not distinguishing between cause and effect (e.g., disease is an event that produces stress as well as being an outcome of stress).

The strengths of the transactional model of stress are that it explains coping in steps; underscores the importance of thinking, perception, and determination of controllability; emphasizes the role of chronic stressors or daily hassles as being more important than once-in-a-while life events; takes into account the interaction between individual and environment; and has a feedback mechanism or "closed loop" system in the form of reappraisal. The chief limitations of this model are that coping is not measured objectively, does not cover personality characteristics, and does not cover physiological mechanisms. **Table 6.7** summarizes the strengths and weaknesses of the three major models of stress and coping.

APPLICATION EXERCISE

In this chapter we have presented several applications of theories of stress and coping, hardiness, and sense of coherence in health education and health promotion. Locate the full text of an article of any application that interests you and read and critique that article. One such article is from Japan in which Tomotsune and colleagues (2009) examined the association between sense of coherence and coping profile in Tsukuba Research Park City workers. They used the Sense of Coherence Scale and the Brief Scale for Coping Profile (BSCP) and mailed these surveys to 20,742 employees at educational and research institutions in Tsukuba Research Park City, Japan. They had a response rate of 57.9% with 12,009 returned surveys. It was found that workers with higher sense of coherence scores utilized problem-focused coping, whereas workers with lower sense of coherence scores used emotion-focused coping.

Read and critique this article in 250 words.

TABLE 6.7   Comparison of Response-Based, Event-Based, and Transactional Models of Stress and Coping

Model	Strengths	Weaknesses
Response-based models	Explicates the physiological mechanisms	Nonspecificity of stimuli/stressors Does not account for individual variations Multiplicity of stressors not addressed No attention to the cognitive processing of the stressor(s)
Event-based models	Clarifies stressors Introduces the notion of coping (or dealing with environmental events) Explains multiplicity of stressors	Does not cover physiological mechanisms Does not distinguish between cause and effect (e.g., disease is an event that produces stress as well as being considered an outcome of stress)
Transactional model	Explains coping in steps Underscores the importance of thinking, perception, and determination of controllability Emphasizes the role of chronic stressors or daily hassles as being more important than once-in-a-while life events Takes into account the communication process or interaction between individual and environment, including other people Existence of a feedback mechanism, or "closed loop" system, in this model (reappraisal)	Lack of objective measurement of coping Does not consider personality characteristics Does not cover physiological mechanisms

SKILL-BUILDING ACTIVITY

Let us see how we can apply the transactional model of stress and coping for developing healthy coping behavior in a group of college students. **Figure 6.3** depicts each of the constructs of the transactional model of coping and links these with the educational processes and behavioral objectives in this example.

The health education intervention would start with the primary appraisal, or stressor identification. This can be done by keeping a stress diary. Secondary appraisal can be modified through a brainstorming session. Problem-focused coping can be used to help students build problem-solving skills. A demonstration of how to apply the steps of problem solving to help participants think through many solutions and identify the pros and cons of each solution before choosing one solution will be used as an educational method. Emotion-focused coping would involve teaching the behavioral skill of relaxation to the students using the technique of progressive muscle relaxation. The final construct, reappraisal, can be facilitated through a discussion in which participants think about how successful they have been in identifying stressors, using problem-solving skills, and learning relaxation. Using this approach, you can plan a coping intervention either as a stand-alone program such as the one discussed here or as one part of a larger behavior change program. **Table 6.8** provides a set of questions to help you define this program.

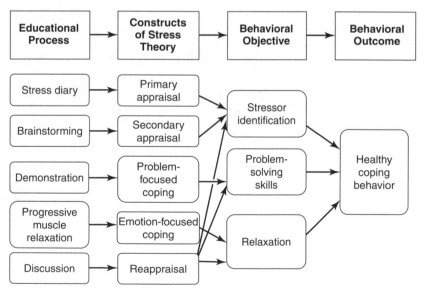

FIGURE 6.3 How the transactional model can be used to develop healthy coping.

TABLE 6.8   **Choosing the Educational Methods for Health Education Program Planning Using Theories of Stress and Coping**

1. What is the best method to facilitate primary appraisal?
   - Stress diary
   - Brainstorming
   - Discussion
   - Other
2. What is the best educational method to facilitate secondary appraisal?
   - Stress diary
   - Brainstorming
   - Discussion
   - Other
3. What is the best educational method to facilitate problem-focused coping?
   - Demonstration of problem-solving skills
   - Interpersonal conflict resolution
   - Advice seeking
   - Time management
   - Goal setting
   - Discussion
   - Other
4. What is the best educational method to facilitate emotion-focused coping?
   - Exercise
   - Relaxation
   - Meditation
   - Support groups
   - Other
5. What is the best educational method to facilitate reappraisal?
   - Stress diary
   - Brainstorming
   - Discussion
   - Other
6. What is the best educational method to facilitate control (theory of hardiness)?
   - Discussion
   - Role-play
   - Simulation
   - Other
7. What is the best educational method to facilitate commitment (theory of hardiness)?
   - Discussion
   - Role-play
   - Simulation
   - Other

(continued)

TABLE 6.8   Choosing the Educational Methods for Health Education Program Planning Using Theories of Stress and Coping (*Continued*)

8. What is the best educational method to facilitate challenge (theory of hardiness)?
   - Discussion
   - Goal setting
   - Other
9. What is the best educational method to facilitate comprehensibility (sense of coherence)?
   - Discussion clarifying the stressors
   - Lecture
   - Other
10. What is the best educational method to facilitate manageability (sense of coherence)?
    - Brainstorming
    - Support groups
    - Other
11. What is the best educational method to facilitate meaningfulness (sense of coherence)?
    - Lecture
    - Discussion
    - Other
12. What is the best educational method to facilitate optimism?
    - Lecture
    - Discussion
    - Other

SUMMARY

In physiology and psychology, the concept of stress originated in the 1930s with the response-based models based on the work of Walter Cannon and Hans Selye. These models looked at myriad physiological effects of stress on the body. This conceptualization was followed by the event-based models, which looked at the role of life events or discrete stressors in the causation of stress. Between the 1960s and 1980s, Richard Lazarus proposed the transactional model of stress, in which a person interacts with the environment while going through four stages: primary appraisal, secondary appraisal, coping, and reappraisal.

In addition to these models, several sets of personality characteristics were identified as predictors of healthier coping. One such personality trait, identified by Suzanne Kobasa, is hardiness, which comprises three factors: commitment, control, and challenge. Similarly, Friedman and Rosenman classified personality into types A and B and found that type B personalities had less stress compared with type A. Aaron Antonovsky proposed a theory of the sense of coherence, which suggested that people who possess a higher sense of coherence tend to cope better in life. A sense of coherence comprises comprehensibility, manageability, and meaningfulness. Another construct is social support, which entails the help obtained through social relationships and interpersonal exchanges and is protective against negative effects arising from stressors. Finally, the construct of optimism (a personality disposition that refers to the tendency to expect the best possible outcome) has been found to have a beneficial effect on coping.

IMPORTANT TERMS

challenge

chronic strains

chronic stressors

commitment

community-wide strains

comprehensibility

control

coping

daily hassles

defense mechanisms

emotion-focused coping

event-based models

general adaptation syndrome

hardiness

life events (life change events)

manageability

meaningfulness

nonevents

optimism

persistent life difficulties

primary appraisal

problem-focused coping

reappraisal

recent life events

remote life events

response-based models

role strains

secondary appraisal

sense of coherence

social support

stress

stressors

transactional model

type A personality

type B personality

REVIEW QUESTIONS

1. Differentiate between response-based and event-based models.
2. Describe the transactional model.
3. Discuss the general adaptation syndrome.
4. Define stressors. Provide a classification of stressors.
5. Describe the constructs of hardiness.
6. Describe the constructs of the sense of coherence.
7. Differentiate between problem-focused and emotion-focused coping.
8. Apply the transactional model of stress and coping for developing healthy coping behavior in a group of college students.

WEBSITES TO EXPLORE

American Institute of Stress

http://www.stress.org/

This website provides information about the American Institute of Stress, a not-for-profit organization established in 1978 to serve as a clearinghouse for information on stress-related issues. *Use this website to explore the contributions of some of the well-known personalities in the stress field.*

Sense of Coherence and Food Selection

http://www.nutritionj.com/content/4/1/9

This website provides a link to an article published in *Nutrition Journal* by Lindmark and colleagues in 2005. The purpose of this study was to evaluate associations between dietary intake and sense of coherence (SOC) in adults. *Read this article and comment on the association between SOC and dietary intake.*

Sense of Coherence Scale

http://jech.bmjjournals.com/cgi/content/abstract/59/6/460

This website provides the abstract and link to an article published in the *Journal of Epidemiology and Community Health* in 2005 by Monica Eriksson and Bengt Lindstrom that systematically reviews and analyzes the psychometric properties of Antonovsky's Sense of Coherence (SOC) Scale. *Read and comment on the various types of reliability and validity of the SOC scale reported in the article.*

Stress and Disease: Contributions of Hans Selye

http://home.cc.umanitoba.ca/~berczii/page2.htm

This website at the University of Manitoba summarizes the contributions of Hans Selye. It also provides links to the Canadian Institute of Stress, several books, and sites related to neuroimmunobiology. *Review this website and summarize the contributions of Hans Selye to the stress field.*

Stress Free Net

http://www.stressfree.com/

Review the graphic model of stress provided as a link on this website. *Check the featured item and write a brief summary of what was on the featured item.*

Transactional Model of Stress and Coping: University of Twente

http://www.tcw.utwente.nl/theorieenoverzicht/Theory%20clusters/Health%20Communication/transactional_model_of_stress_and_coping.doc/

This website at University of Twente, Netherlands, summarizes the transactional model of stress and coping. Its history, assumptions, conceptual model, favorite methods, scope and application, and examples are presented. *Review the website and determine which constructs were discussed in the chapter and which were new.*

REFERENCES

Abu-Shakra, M., Keren, A., Livshitz, I., Delbar, V., Bolotin, A., Sukenik, S., et al. (2006). Sense of coherence and its impact on quality of life of patients with systemic lupus erythematosus. *Lupus, 15*(1), 32–37.

Andrew, M. E., McCanlies, E. C., Burchfiel, C. M., Charles, L. E., Hartley, T. A., Fekedulegn, D., et al. (2008). Hardiness and psychological distress in a cohort of police officers. *International Journal of Emergency Mental Health, 10*(2), 137–147.

Anson, K., & Ponsford, J. (2006). Coping and emotional adjustment following traumatic brain injury. *Journal of Head Trauma Rehabilitation, 21*(3), 248–259.

Antonovsky, A. (1979). *Health, stress, and coping.* San Francisco: Jossey-Bass.

Antonovsky, A. (1987). *Unraveling the mystery of health: How people manage stress and stay well.* San Francisco: Jossey-Bass.

Ben-Zur, H., Duvdevany, I., & Lury, L. (2005). Associations of social support and hardiness with mental health among mothers of adult children with intellectual disability. *Journal of Intellectual Disability Research, 49*(Pt. 1), 54–62.

Berry, K., Barrowclough, C., Byrne, J., & Purandare, N. (2006). Coping strategies and social support in old age psychosis. *Social Psychiatry and Psychiatric Epidemiology, 41*(4), 280–284.

Bockting, C. L., Spinhoven, P., Koeter, M. W., Wouters, L. F., Visser, I., & Schene, A. H. (2006). Differential predictors of response to preventive cognitive therapy in recurrent depression: A 2-year prospective study. *Psychotherapy and Psychosomatics, 75*(4), 229–236.

Borglin, G., Jakobsson, U., Edberg, A. K., & Hallberg, I. R. (2006). Older people in Sweden with various degrees of present quality of life: Their health, social support, everyday activities and sense of coherence. *Health and Social Care in the Community, 14*(2), 136–146.

Brown, S. L., & Ireland, C. A. (2006). Coping style and distress in newly incarcerated male adolescents. *Journal of Adolescent Health, 38*(6), 656–661.

Cannon, W. B. (1932). *The wisdom of the body.* New York: Norton.

Chen, G. (2006). Social support, spiritual program, and addiction recovery. *International Journal of Offender Therapy and Comparative Criminology, 50*(3), 306–323.

DiBartolo, M. C., & Soeken, K. L. (2003). Appraisal, coping, hardiness, and self-perceived health in community-dwelling spouse caregivers of persons with dementia. *Research in Nursing and Health, 26*(6), 445–458.

Eid, J., & Morgan, C. A., III. (2006). Dissociation, hardiness, and performance in military cadets participating in survival training. *Military Medicine, 171*(5), 436–442.

Freud, A. (1937). *The ego and mechanism of defense*. London: Hogarth Press.

Freud, S. (1923). *The ego and the id*. New York: Norton.

Friedman, M., & Rosenman, R. H. (1974). *Type A behavior and your heart*. New York: Fawcett Crest.

Friis, R. H., Forouzesh, M., Chhim, H. S., Monga, S., & Sze, D. (2006). Sociocultural determinants of tobacco use among Cambodian Americans. *Health Education Research, 21*(3), 355–365.

Ghorbani, N., & Watson, P. J. (2005). Hardiness scales in Iranian managers: Evidence of incremental validity in relationships with the five factor model and with organizational and psychological adjustment. *Psychological Reports, 96*(3 Pt. 1), 775–781.

Glanz, K., Maskarinec, G., & Carlin, L. (2005). Ethnicity, sense of coherence, and tobacco use among adolescents. *Annals of Behavioral Medicine, 29*(3), 192–199.

Gold, J. I., Treadwell, M., Weissman, L., & Vichinsky, E. (2008). An expanded transactional stress and coping model for siblings of children with sickle cell disease: Family functioning and sibling coping, self-efficacy and perceived social support. *Child: Care, Health, & Development, 34*(4), 491–502.

Haan, N. (1977). *Coping and defending: Processes of self-environment organization*. New York: Academic Press.

Heaney, C. A., & Israel, B. A. (2008). Social networks and social support. In K. Glanz, B. K. Rimer, & K. Viswanath (Eds.), *Health behavior and health education: Theory, research and practice* (4th ed., pp. 189–210). San Francisco: Jossey-Bass.

Heckman, C. J., & Clay, D. L. (2005). Hardiness, history of abuse and women's health. *Journal of Health Psychology, 10*(6), 767–777.

Hedov, G., Wikblad, K., & Anneren, G. (2006). Sickness absence in Swedish parents of children with Down's syndrome: Relation to self-perceived health, stress and sense of coherence. *Journal of Intellectual Disability Research, 50*(7), 546–552.

Hepp, U., Moergeli, H., Buchi, S., Wittmann, L., & Schnyder, U. (2005). Coping with serious accidental injury: A one-year follow-up study. *Psychotherapy and Psychosomatics, 74*(6), 379–386.

Holmes, T. H., & Rahe, R. H. (1967). The Social Readjustment Rating Scale. *Journal of Psychosomatic Research, 11*, 213–218.

House, J. S. (1981). *Work stress and social support*. Reading, MA: Addison-Wesley.

Hurst, S., & Koplin-Baucum, S. (2005). A pilot qualitative study relating to hardiness in ICU nurses: Hardiness in ICU nurses. *Dimensions of Critical Care Nursing, 24*(2), 97–100.

Jedryka-Goral, A., Pasierski, T., Zabek, J., Widerszal-Bazyl, M., Radkiewicz, P., Szulczyk, G. A., et al. (2006). Risk factors for atherosclerosis in healthy employees—a multidisciplinary approach. *European Journal of Internal Medicine, 17*(4), 247–253.

Kee, C. C. (2003). Older adults with osteoarthritis. Psychological status and physical function. *Journal of Gerontological Nursing, 29*(12), 26–34.

Kinder, R. A. (2005). Psychological hardiness in women with paraplegia. *Rehabilitation Nursing, 30*(2), 68–72.

Kobasa, S. C. (1979a). Personality and resistance to illness. *American Journal of Community Psychology, 7*, 413–423.

Kobasa, S. C. (1979b). Stressful life events, personality, and health: An inquiry into hardiness. *Journal of Personality and Social Psychology, 37*, 1–11.

Kobasa, S. C. (1985). Stressful life events, personality, and health: An inquiry into hardiness. In A. Monat & R. S. Lazarus (Eds.), *Stress and coping: An anthology* (pp. 174–188). New York: Columbia University Press.

Koinberg, I., Langius-Eklof, A., Holmberg, L., & Fridlund, B. (2006). The usefulness of a multidisciplinary educational program after breast cancer surgery: A prospective and comparative study. *European Journal of Oncology Nursing, 10*(4), 273–282.

Lambert, V. A., Lambert, C. E,, Petrini, M., Li, X. M., & Zhang, Y. J. (2007). Workplace and personal factors associated with physical and mental health in hospital nurses in China. *Nursing and Health Sciences, 9*(2), 120–126.

Lambert, V. A., Lambert, C. E., & Yamase, H. (2003). Psychological hardiness, workplace stress and related stress reduction strategies. *Nursing and Health Sciences, 5*(2), 181–184.

Larson, J., Franzen-Dahlin, A., Billing, E., Arbin, M., Murray, V., & Wredling, R. (2005). Predictors of quality of life among spouses of stroke patients during the first year after the stroke event. *Scandinavian Journal of Caring Science, 19*(4), 439–445.

Lazarus, R. S. (1966). *Psychological stress and the coping process.* New York: McGraw-Hill.

Lazarus, R. S. (1974). Psychological stress and coping in adaptation and illness. *International Journal of Psychiatry in Medicine, 5,* 321–333.

Lazarus, R. S. (1984). Puzzles in the study of daily hassles. *Journal of Behavioral Medicine, 7,* 375–389.

Lazarus, R. S., & Folkman, S. (1984). *Stress, appraisal, and coping.* New York: Springer.

Lebel, S., Rosberger, Z., Edgar, L., & Devins, G. M. (2008). Predicting stress-related problems in long-term breast cancer survivors. *Journal of Psychosomatic Research, 65*(6), 513–523.

Lewis, C. S., Griffing, S., Chu, M., Jospitre, T., Sage, R. E., Madry, L., & Primm, B. J. (2006). Coping and violence exposure as predictors of psychological functioning in domestic violence survivors. *Violence Against Women, 12*(4), 340–354.

Lundblad, A. M., & Hansson, K. (2005). Outcomes in couple therapy: Reduced psychiatric symptoms and improved sense of coherence. *Nordic Journal of Psychiatry, 59*(5), 374–380.

Macinnes, J. D. (2005). The illness perceptions of women following acute myocardial infarction: Implications for behaviour change and attendance at cardiac rehabilitation. *Women and Health, 42*(4), 105–121.

Malinauskienc, V., Leisyte, P., & Malinauskas, R. (2009). Psychosocial job characteristics, social support, and sense of coherence as determinants of mental health among nurses. *Medicina, 45*(11), 910–917.

McCalister, K. T., Dolbier, C. L., Webster, J. A., Mallon, M, W, & Steinhardt, M. A. (2006). Hardiness and support at work as predictors of work stress and job satisfaction. *American Journal of Health Promotion, 20*(3), 183–191.

McLean, D. E., & Link, B. G. (1994). Unraveling complexity: Strategies to refine concepts, measures, and research designs in the study of life events and mental health. In W. R. Avison & I. H. Gotlib (Eds.), *Stress and mental health: Contemporary issues and prospects for the future* (pp. 15–42). New York: Plenum Press.

Milberg, A., & Strang, P. (2003). Meaningfulness in palliative home care: An interview study of dying cancer patients' next of kin. *Palliative and Supportive Care, 1*(2), 171–180.

Norrbrink Budh, C., Kowalski, J., & Lundeberg, T. (2006). A comprehensive pain management programme comprising educational, cognitive and behavioural interventions for neuropathic pain following spinal cord injury. *Journal of Rehabilitation Medicine, 38*(3), 172–180.

Oelofsen, N., & Richardson, P. (2006). Sense of coherence and parenting stress in mothers and fathers of preschool children with developmental disability. *Journal of Intellectual and Developmental Disability, 31*(1), 1–12.

Poderico, C., Ruggiero, G., Iachini, T., & Iavarone, A. (2006). Coping strategies and cognitive functioning in elderly people from a rural community in Italy. *Psychological Reports*, *98*(1), 159–168.

Romas, J. A., & Sharma, M. (2010). *Practical stress management. A comprehensive workbook for managing change and promoting health* (5th ed.). San Francisco: Benjamin Cummings.

Roth, G., & Ekblad, S. (2006). A longitudinal perspective on depression and sense of coherence in a sample of mass-evacuated adults from Kosovo. *Journal of Nervous and Mental Disease*, *194*(5), 378–381.

Rosenzweig, S., Greeson, J. M., Reibel, D. K., Green, J. S., Jasser, S. A., & Beasley, D. (2010). Mindfulness-based stress reduction for chronic pain conditions: Variation in treatment outcomes and role of home meditation practice. *Journal of Psychosomatic Research*, *68*(1), 29–36.

Samuel-Hodge, C. D., Watkins, D. C., Rowell, K. L., & Hooten, E. G. (2008). Coping styles, well-being, and self-care behaviors among African Americans with type 2 diabetes. *The Diabetes Educator*, *34*(3), 501–510.

Savolainen, J., Suominen-Taipale, A., Uutela, A., Aromaa, A., Härkänen, T., & Knuuttila, M. (2009). Sense of coherence associates with oral and general health behaviours. *Community Dental Health*, *26*(4), 197–203.

Scheier, M. F., & Carver, C. S. (1985). Optimism, coping, and health: Assessment and implications of generalized outcome expectancies. *Health Psychology*, *4*, 219–247.

Seligman, M.E.P. (1990). *Learned optimism*. New York: Pocket Books.

Seligman, M.E.P. (1994). *What you can change and what you can't: The complete guide to self improvement*. New York: Alfred A. Knopf.

Selye, H. (1936). A syndrome produced by diverse nocuous agents. *Nature*, *138*, 32.

Selye, H. (1974a). *Stress without distress*. Philadelphia: Lippincott.

Selye, H. (1974b). *The stress of life*. New York: McGraw-Hill.

Selye, H. (1982). History and present status of stress concept. In L. Goldberger & S. Breznitz (Eds.), *Handbook of stress: Theoretical and clinical aspects* (pp. 7–17). New York: Free Press.

Selye, H. (1985). History and present status of the stress concept. In A. Monat & R. S. Lazarus (Eds.), *Stress and coping: An anthology* (pp. 17–29). New York: Columbia University Press.

Sharma, M. (2003). Coping: Strategies. In N. A. Pitrowski (Ed.), *Magill's encyclopedia of social science: Psychology* (pp. 442–446). Pasadena, CA: Salem Press.

Shimazu, A., Umanodan, R., & Schaufeli, W. B. (2006). Effects of a brief worksite stress management program on coping skills, psychological distress and physical complaints: A controlled trial. *International Archives of Occupational and Environmental Health*, *80*(1), 60–69.

Smith, N., Young, A., & Lee, C. (2004). Optimism, health-related hardiness and well-being among older Australian women. *Journal of Health Psychology*, *9*(6), 741–752.

Strom, T. Q., & Kosciulek, J. (2007). Stress, appraisal and coping following mild traumatic brain injury. *Brain Injury*, *21*(11), 1137–1145.

Svavarsdottir, E. K., Rayens, M. K., & McCubbin, M. (2005). Predictors of adaptation in Icelandic and American families of young children with chronic asthma. *Family and Community Health*, *28*(4), 338–350.

Svavarsdottir, E. K., & Sigurdardottir, A. O. (2005). The feasibility of offering a family level intervention to parents of children with cancer. *Scandinavian Journal of Caring Sciences*, *19*(4), 368–372.

Svavarsdottir, E. K., & Sigurdardottir, A. O. (2006). Developing a family-level intervention for families of children with cancer. *Oncology Nursing Forum*, *33*(5), 983–990.

Tak, S. H. (2006). An insider perspective of daily stress and coping in elders with arthritis. *Orthopaedic Nursing*, *25*(2), 127–132.

Taylor, S. E., & Aspinwall, L. G. (1996). Mediating and moderating processes in psychosocial stress. Appraisal, coping, resistance, and vulnerability. In H. B Kaplan (Ed.), *Psychosocial stress: Perspectives on structure, theory, life course and methods* (pp. 71–110). San Diego: Academic Press.

Thoolen, B. J., Ridder, D., Bensing, J., Gorter, K., & Rutten, G. (2009). Beyond good intentions: The role of proactive coping in achieving sustained behavioural change in the context of diabetes management. *Psychology & Health*, *24*(3), 237–254.

Tomotsune, Y., Sasahara, S., Umeda, T., Hayashi, M., Usami, K., Yoshino, S., et al. (2009). The association of sense of coherence and coping profile with stress among Research Park City workers in Japan. *Industrial Health*, *47*(6), 664–672.

Vance, D. E., & Woodley, R. A. (2005). Strengths and distress in adults who are aging with HIV: A pilot study. *Psychological Reports*, *96*(2), 383–386.

Van Puymbroeck, M., & Rittman, M. R. (2005). Quality-of-life predictors for caregivers at 1 and 6 months poststroke: Results of path analyses. *Journal of Rehabilitation Research and Development*, *42*(6), 747–760.

Vidhubala, E., Latha, Ravikannan, R., Mani, C. S., & Karthikesh, M. (2006). Coping preferences of head and neck cancer patients—Indian context. *Indian Journal of Cancer*, *43*(1), 6–11.

Volanen, S. M., Suominen, S., Lahelma, E., Koskenvuo, K., Koskenvuo, M., & Silventoinen, K. (2010). Sense of coherence and intentions to retire early among Finnish women and men. *BMC Public Health*, *10*, 22.

Wahl, A. K., Mork, C., Hanestad, B. R., & Helland, S. (2006). Coping with exacerbation in psoriasis and eczema prior to admission in a dermatological ward. *European Journal of Dermatology*, *16*(3), 271–275.

Watlington, C. G., & Murphy, C. M. (2006). The roles of religion and spirituality among African American survivors of domestic violence. *Journal of Clinical Psychology*, *62*(7), 837–857.

Wheaton, B. (1994). Sampling the stress universe. In W. R. Avison & I. H. Gotlib (Eds.), *Stress and mental health: Contemporary issues and prospects for the future* (pp. 15–42). New York: Plenum Press.

Whitmer, M., Hurst, S., & Prins, M. (2009). Intergenerational views of hardiness in critical care nurses. *Dimensions of Critical Care Nursing*, *28*(5), 214–220.

Wonghongkul, T., Dechaprom, N., Phumivichuvate, L., & Losawatkul, S. (2006). Uncertainty appraisal coping and quality of life in breast cancer survivors. *Cancer Nursing*, *29*(3), 250–257.

CHAPTER 7

Social Cognitive Theory

KEY CONCEPTS

- emotional coping
- environment
- forethought capability
- goal setting or self-control
- knowledge
- outcome expectations
- outcome expectancies
- reciprocal determinism
- self-efficacy

- self-efficacy in overcoming impediments
- self-reflective capability
- self-regulatory capability
- situational perception
- social cognitive theory
- social learning theory
- symbolizing capability
- vicarious capability

AFTER READING THIS CHAPTER YOU SHOULD BE ABLE TO

- Identify the five basic human capabilities according to social cognitive theory
- List the constructs of social cognitive theory
- Summarize the applications of social cognitive theory in health education and health promotion
- Identify educational methods and match these to modify each construct from social cognitive theory
- Apply social cognitive theory for changing a health behavior of your choice

This chapter discusses **social cognitive theory (SCT)**, which was earlier known as social learning theory (SLT). The word *social* refers to the social origins of thought and action. *Cognitive* refers to the influential causal contributions of thought processes to human motivation, affect, and action. The word *theory* alludes to the fact that this model has been empirically tested can explain, describe, predict, or control behavior.

Social cognitive theory posits that human behavior can be explained as a triadic reciprocal causation. One angle of the tripod consists of the behavior. The second angle consists of environmental factors, and the third angle consists of personal factors such as cognitions, affect, and biological events. The unique interaction among these three dimensions results in behavior change. Hence, all three dimensions—personal factors, behavioral factors, and environmental factors—must be targeted in designing health education and health promotion interventions. This is known as reciprocal determinism. Over the past three decades many research studies, articles, and books by Albert Bandura and other research workers have substantiated the application of this theory in predicting, explaining, and changing behavior in a variety of settings. Some examples are clinical psychology for the treatment of phobias, counseling for parenting, career development, educational programs, and health education and health promotion.

This chapter begins with a description of the historical aspects of the genesis of social cognitive theory. Next we describe the underpinnings of SCT and the various constructs that make up this theory and discuss the applications of SCT in health education and health promotion. Finally, we discuss the limitations of SCT and provide a skill-building application.

> *A theory that denies that thoughts can regulate actions does not lend itself readily to the explanation of complex human behavior.*
>
> —Bandura (1986)

HISTORICAL PERSPECTIVE

Historically, social cognitive theory superseded several earlier theories developed to explain behavior. In the early part of the 20th century, the psychodynamic theory developed by Sigmund Freud (1923/1960) proposed that behavior was shaped by a dynamic interplay of subconscious and unconscious needs, drives, impulses, and instincts. However, this theory lacked predictive value, was difficult to test, and entailed no social dimension, thereby offering limited utility. Another early behavior theory was Gordon Allport's (1937) trait theory, which emphasized determination of behavior through broad, enduring dispositions. Weak empirical support and inconsistency of behavior across situations and over time did not provide much credence to this line of thought.

Learning theories were also popular in psychology, such as those by Dollard and Miller (1950), Rotter (1954), and Skinner (1953). A major limitation of these theories was that they were tested either on animal models or on human subjects in one-person situations and therefore did not consider the social aspects of learning.

In 1963 Albert Bandura at Stanford University, in collaboration with Richard Walters of the University of Waterloo, Ontario, proposed **social learning theory** (Bandura & Walters, 1963), which described the existence of three important influences on learning. The first is the role of *imitation*. Imitation provides three possible effects that contribute to learning: (1) a modeling effect, whereby the person directly copies the behavior; (2) an inhibitory or disinhibitory effect, whereby there is an increase or decrease in the behavior as a result of the observation; and (3) an eliciting effect, whereby imitation serves as a cue for releasing similar responses in the observer.

The second important influence in learning, according to Bandura and Walters (1963), is that of *reinforcement patterns*. Positive reinforcement, in the form of verbal approval or material rewards, tends to reinforce the occurrence of the behavior. Negative reinforcement, in the form of verbal or physical punishment by an authority figure, inhibits aggression as long as the punitive agent is present; however, children who receive a great deal of negative reinforcement display aggression toward objects other than the punitive agent.

The third important influence in learning is that of *self-control*. There are three forms of self-controlling behavior: (1) resistance to deviation, (2) regulation of self-administered rewarding resources, and (3) postponement of immediate reinforcements in lieu of some more valued reward in the future. Self-control is acquired and maintained by direct reinforcement that takes the form of disciplinary interventions, both negative and positive.

In 1969 Bandura wrote the *Principles of Behavior Modification*, which explained how social learning theory could be applied to a variety of behaviors. This approach was used in designing the Stanford three-community study, which began in 1972 in three northern California communities (Farquhar, 1978; Farquhar et al., 1977). The intervention targeted three risk factors: smoking, high serum cholesterol, and high blood pressure. The primary objectives of the intervention were to compare a mass media campaign alone in one community; a mass media campaign with high-risk screening and face-to-face instruction for high-risk individuals in the second community; and no health education with regard to knowledge and behavior related to cardiovascular disease, and measurement of various physiological indicators in the third community. The health education approach of this project had three distinct features: (1) mass media materials focused on teaching specific behavioral skills and affecting attitudes and motivation, (2) traditional behavior and self-control training, and (3) assessment of the knowledge deficits and media consumption patterns of intended audiences before the intervention. The study was able to demonstrate that mass media campaigns can increase knowledge and change habits, and that the approach is cost effective.

By 1977 Bandura had refined his approach, which he presented in his book *Social Learning Theory*. This refined approach formed the basis of the Stanford five-city project, which began in 1978 (Farquhar et al., 1985; Young, Haskell, Jatulis, & Fortmann, 1993).

This intervention was implemented in northern California for six years in two treatment cities and two control cities, and in one city for surveillance only. The use of social learning theory in these two trials popularized this theory in health education and health promotion. In the 1980s, it was used in the Minnesota Heart Health Program (Luepker et al., 1994) and the Pawtucket Heart Health Program (Carleton, Lasater, Assaf, Feldman, & McKinlay, 1995), among other applications.

In 1986, Bandura renamed the theory social cognitive theory in his book *Social Foundations of Thought and Action*. Social cognitive theory continues to be popular today. In 1995, Bandura published *Self-Efficacy in Changing Societies*, which underscored the role of self-efficacy in behavior change. This construct accounts for the largest proportion of variance in work with this theory. In his recent works (1997, 2001a, 2001b, 2002, 2004, 2005), Bandura has emphasized an agentic perspective; that is, the role of the person as an agent shaping and controlling his or her own life. In 2002, he was awarded the Healthtrac Award. He delivered a lecture at the convention of the Society for Public Health Education that focused mainly on the theory's applications in health education and promotion (Bandura, 2004).

> *Self-efficacy is the belief in one's capabilities to organize and execute the sources of action required to manage prospective situations.*
>
> —Bandura (1986)

UNDERPINNINGS OF SOCIAL COGNITIVE THEORY

One of the distinctive features of SCT is the importance it places on the potential of human beings. According to this theory, five basic human capabilities describe human beings. These are depicted in **Figure 7.1**. The first such capability is the **symbolizing capability**, which refers to the use of symbols in attributing meaning to experiences. It is an important tool for understanding, creating, and managing one's environment. Most environmental events are interpreted cognitively rather than directly. By using symbols, people give structure, meaning, and continuity to their experiences. The symbolizing capability also helps in communicating with others at any distance in time and space.

The **vicarious capability** refers to the ability to learn from observing other people's behavior and the consequences they face. This ability is important because it enables people to generate and regulate behavior without tedious trial and error. Some complex skills can be mastered only through modeling. Modeling is not simply a process of response mimicry but entails creativity and innovativeness as well.

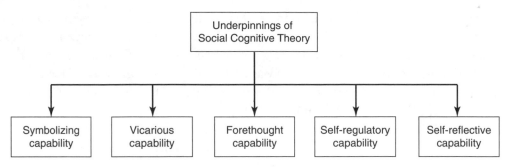

FIGURE 7.1   Underpinnings of social cognitive theory.

Forethought capability refers to the fact that most behavior is purposive and regulated by prior thoughts. People motivate themselves and plan their actions using their forethought capability. Although future events do not have actual existence, they can be imagined and can serve as motivators in the present. Usually the course of action that is likely to bring positive rewards is easily adopted, whereas the course that is likely to produce negative outcomes is not adopted.

Self-regulatory capability refers to setting internal standards and self-evaluative reactions for one's behavior. Self-satisfaction is gained from meeting desirable standards, and dissatisfaction results from below-standard performance. People are proactive and constantly set challenging goals for themselves, which also plays an important role in self-regulation.

The final capability is **self-reflective capability**, which is the analysis of experiences and examination of one's own thought processes. People are not just agents of action but also self-examine and critique their own actions. They generate ideas, act on them based on an anticipated outcome, and then in retrospect judge the accuracy and value of the outcomes, finally modifying their thinking as needed. According to Bandura (2001a), verification of one's thought processes happens in four ways: (1) enactive verification, in which one looks at the closeness between one's thoughts and the results of one's action; (2) vicarious verification, in which one looks at other people's actions and compares that with one's thinking; (3) persuasive verification, in which one evaluates one's beliefs against what others believe; and (4) logical verification, in which one compares one's thinking against knowledge that is known.

> *People are not only agents of action but self-examiners of their own functioning.*
>
> —Bandura (2001a, p. 10)

CONSTRUCTS OF SOCIAL COGNITIVE THEORY

The constructs of Bandura's theory have been described in the literature in several ways. This chapter uses the depiction elaborated by Bandura in his presentation regarding the application of SCT in health promotion (Bandura, 2004). The constructs, their definitions, and ways to modify each construct are summarized in **Table 7.1** and depicted in **Figure 7.2**.

TABLE 7.1	Key Constructs of Social Cognitive Theory	
Construct	**Definition**	**How to Modify?**
Knowledge	Learning facts and gaining insights related to an action, idea, object, person, or situation	Lecture Informational talk Providing fact sheets
Outcome expectations	Anticipation of the probable outcomes that would ensue as a result of engaging in the behavior under discussion	Discussion of benefits Brainstorming Role play
Outcome expectancies	Value a person places on the probable outcomes that result from performing a behavior	Discussion of values Brainstorming Role play
Situational perception	How one perceives and interprets the environment around oneself	Rectify misperceptions
Environment	Physical or social circumstances or conditions that surround a person	Provide opportunities to overcome personal and situational impediments Provide access to the health system Build social support around the person
Self-efficacy	Confidence in one's ability to pursue a behavior	Practice in small steps (e.g., breaking down the complex behavior of physical activity into doable small steps) Have a role model demonstrate (e.g., a video of a well-known movie star with whom the

(continued)

TABLE 7.1 Key Constructs of Social Cognitive Theory (*Continued*)		
Construct	**Definition**	**How to Modify?**
		target audience can associate performing the same behaviors) Use persuasion and reinforcement (e.g., tell participants that they have what it takes to perform the behavior, and attribute past failures to external reasons) Reduce stress associated with implementing a new behavior (e.g., have women take a relaxing shower before doing a breast self-examination)
Self-efficacy in overcoming impediments	Confidence that a person has in overcoming barriers while performing a given behavior	Practice overcoming barriers in small steps Have a role model demonstrate overcoming barriers Use persuasion and reinforcement in overcoming barriers Reduce stress while overcoming barriers
Goal setting or self-control	Setting goals and developing plans to accomplish chosen behaviors	Provide opportunities for setting goals Self-monitoring Provide personal rewards to reinforce accomplishment of goals
Emotional coping	Techniques employed by the person to control the emotional and physiological states associated with acquisition of a new behavior	Progressive muscle relaxation Yoga/meditation Autogenic training Visual imagery Other stress management techniques

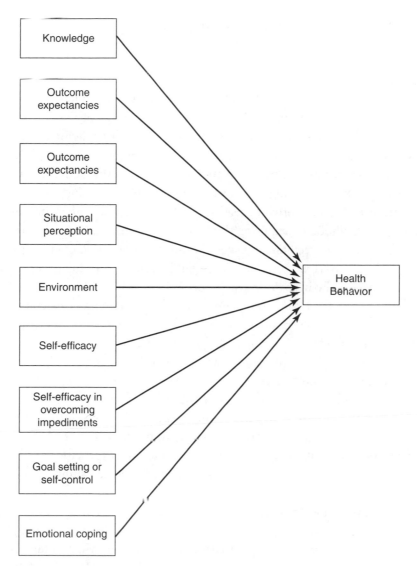

FIGURE 7.2 Constructs of social cognitive theory.

The first construct of SCT is *knowledge*, which is learning facts and gaining insights related to an action, idea, object, person, or situation. Knowledge is an essential
component for any behavior change. It is a necessary precondition for change, but often
is not sufficient for making the behavior change. In the context of health education
and health promotion, knowledge of the risks and benefits of different health practices is required for behavior change interventions. To modify knowledge, the health

educator can provide information in the form of a lecture, a demonstration, or fact sheets on the topic.

The second construct of SCT is **outcome expectations**, which is the anticipation of the probable outcomes that would ensue as a result of engaging in the behavior under discussion. Bandura (2004) identifies three types of outcomes: (1) physical outcomes, which include positive and negative consequences of the behavior; (2) the outcome of social approval or disapproval of engaging or disengaging in the behavior; and (3) positive and negative self-evaluations. For example, some possible outcome expectations for a person being motivated to be physically active may be losing weight, looking attractive, being able to make more friends, having less chance of acquiring heart disease, and improving his or her self-image. The higher the expectations, the greater the likelihood of acquiring the behavior. To modify outcome expectations, the health educator can facilitate a discussion on the possible outcomes from engaging in the desired behavior. Other methods could be brainstorming or a role play that depicts the effects of the behavior on a person.

The construct of SCT that goes hand-in-hand with outcome expectations is **outcome expectancies**, which refers to the value a person places on the probable outcomes that result from performing a behavior. The higher the expectancies, the greater the chance that the individual will perform the behavior. For example, in motivating students, possible outcomes of getting an A grade could be to graduate early, to have more friends, to learn more about the subject, and so on. If students value these outcomes, they are likely to work harder to get an A in the course. Students who do not value these associated outcomes are likely to put in less effort. Likert scales are often used to measure outcome expectations and outcome expectancies. The expectations are multiplied with corresponding expectancies and then summed to arrive at a score of expectations (outcome expectations plus outcome expectancies). To modify expectancies, a discussion or brainstorming on values associated with outcomes can be organized. Expectancies also can be influenced by a psychodrama or a role play.

The fourth construct of SCT is **situational perception**, which refers to how one perceives and interprets the environment (Baranowski, Perry, & Parcel, 2002). Any misperceptions hinder the behavior change. Thus efforts must be made to remove misperceptions and to promote social norms that are healthy. For example, in a teen pregnancy program, a large number of teens may believe it is normative for most teens to be sexually active, but the statistical evidence does not support this belief. Providing correct information and explaining it would rectify the situational perception. To modify situational perception, misperceptions can be modified in either a discussion or a lecture.

The fifth construct of SCT, **environment**, refers to the physical or social circumstances or conditions that surround a person. Whereas situational perception involves a person's interpretation of his or her surroundings, environment consists of the actual conditions. Some effective means of modifying this construct are creating opportunities to overcome personal and situational impediments, providing access to the health system, and building social support around the person. Example applications of this construct are creating facilities for physical activity in the community (physical environment) and creating learning experiences for eliciting and maintaining social support from friends to maintain exercise behavior (social environment).

The sixth construct of SCT is **self-efficacy**, which is the confidence a person has in his or her ability to pursue a behavior. Self-efficacy is behavior specific and is in the present. It is not about the past or future. Self-efficacy plays a central role in behavior change. Bandura (2004) notes that unless people believe that they can produce the desired changes by their own efforts, there will be very little incentive to put in that effort. Four strategies can be used in building self-efficacy:

1. *Break down the complex behavior into practical and doable small steps.* For example, instead of simply telling people to read food labels, the educator may teach participants how to find the title and then how to find information on serving size, total calories, calories from fat, the constitution of different food groups, and so on, using small steps.
2. *Use a demonstration from credible role models.* For example, in facilitating an educational program about obesity prevention, having a movie star who has successfully gone through the process of losing weight share his or her story would help in enhancing the self-efficacy of the participants.
3. *Use persuasion and reassurance.* If a person has failed in the past to make a behavior change, those failures can be attributed to external reasons. If the person has succeeded in related fields, those successes can be compared with the behavior the person is trying to change. For example, in a quitting alcohol program, the health educator could ask participants to identify one instance when they were successful in changing a negative behavior or in acquiring a positive behavior and then could state that they can do the same thing with the alcohol behavior.
4. *Reduce stress.* Any behavior change is associated with some amount of stress, which hinders the change process. Reducing stress is an effective means of building self-efficacy. For example, if children find giving up watching television to be stressful, they can be instructed in how to relax either by listening to music or by practicing progressive muscle relaxation.

The seventh construct is **self-efficacy in overcoming impediments**, which refers to the confidence that a person has in overcoming barriers while performing a given behavior. This construct is related to self-efficacy in that it is situation specific, pertains to the present, and represents a level of confidence. Sometimes considered as a subset of self-efficacy, it is better to think of it as a separate construct. For example, to become more physically active, one must overcome several barriers, such as being tired, feeling depressed, feeling anxious, encountering bad weather, and having other interesting things to do. To modify the construct of self-efficacy in overcoming impediments, helpful techniques include practicing to overcome each barrier in small steps, having role models demonstrate success, using persuasion, and reducing stress.

The eighth construct is **goal setting** or **self-control**, which refers to setting goals and developing plans to accomplish chosen behaviors. When one sets goals and develops concrete plans, behavior change becomes easier. Goals are proximal and distal. Proximal goals are immediate accomplishments, whereas distal goals set the course of making change. To modify the construct of goal setting or self-control, educators need to provide opportunities for setting goals, show individuals how to monitor their progress, and provide personal rewards to reinforce the attainment of goals.

Social cognitive theory acknowledges the influential role of evolved factors in human adaptation and change, but it rejects one-sided evolutionism in which evolved biology shapes behavior but the selection pressures of social and technological innovations on biological evolutions get ignored.

—Bandura (2001a, p. 20)

The final construct in SCT is **emotional coping**, which refers to the techniques employed by the person to control the emotional and physiological states associated with acquisition of a new behavior. This construct is often reified in association with self-efficacy. To modify emotional coping, stress management techniques such as progressive muscle relaxation, yoga, autogenic training, and visual imagery are useful. For example, a program that teaches aerobics to a group of sedentary employees at a worksite may also need to utilize stress management techniques that reduce the anxiety associated with learning a new skill.

APPLICATIONS OF SOCIAL COGNITIVE THEORY

Some examples of behavior research in which SCT has been used include assessing medication adherence (Diiorio et al., 2009; Kalichman et al., 2005), defining correlates of physical activity in fibromyalgia patients (Oliver & Cronan, 2005), defining predictors of exercise participation (Kaewthummanukul, Brown, Weaver, & Thomas, 2006), identifying perceptions of whole-grain foods and the factors influencing their intake by children (Burgess-Champoux, Marquart, Vickers, & Reicks, 2006), modeling adolescents' sexual behavior on exposure to sexual content on television (Martino, Collins, Kanouse, Elliott, & Berry, 2005), modeling father-son communication about sex (Diiorio, McCarty, & Denzmore, 2006), predicting bullying and victimization (Mouttapa, Valente,

Gallaher, Rohrbach, & Unger, 2004), predicting condom use among university students (Mashegoane, Moalusi, Peltzer, & Ngoepe, 2004), predicting fruit and vegetable intake in children (Bere & Klepp, 2005), predicting heavy drinking in college students (Gilles, Turk, & Fresco, 2006), predicting obesity prevention behaviors (Sharma, Mehan, & Surabhi, 2008–2009; Sharma, Wagner, & Wilkerson, 2005–2006), predicting physical activity behavior (Rhodes & Plotnikoff, 2005; Tavares, Plotnikoff, & Loucaides, 2009), predicting physician behavior to recommend colonoscopy (Honda & Gorin, 2006), predicting reproductive health behavioral intention in adolescent women with diabetes (Wang, Charron-Prochownik, Sereika, Siminerio, & Kim, 2006), predicting sexually risky behaviors among adolescent mothers (Koniak-Griffin & Stein, 2006), and profiling community-based rehabilitation volunteers (Sharma & Deepak, 2003). **Table 7.2** summarizes these applications.

TABLE 7.2 Applications of Social Cognitive Theory in Behavioral Research
Assessing medication adherence
Defining correlates of physical activity in fibromyalgia patients
Defining predictors of exercise participation
Identifying perceptions of whole-grain foods and the factors influencing their intake by children
Modeling adolescents' sexual behavior on exposure to sexual content on television
Modeling father-son communication about sex
Predicting bullying and victimization
Predicting condom use among university students
Predicting fruit and vegetable intake in children
Predicting heavy drinking in college students
Predicting obesity prevention behaviors
Predicting physical activity behavior
Predicting physician behavior to recommend colonoscopy
Predicting reproductive health behavioral intention in adolescent women with diabetes
Predicting sexually risky behaviors among adolescent mothers
Profiling community-based rehabilitation volunteers

Some examples in which SCT has been used for primary prevention include an active ergonomics training program in computer users (Greene, DeJoy, & Olejnik, 2005), family planning decision making (Ha, Jayasuriya, & Owen, 2005), an HIV prevention program in adolescents (Boutin-Foster et al., 2010; Diiorio et al., 2006), a nutrition education program (Powers, Struempler, Guarino, & Parmer, 2005; Shilts, Lamp, Horowitz, & Townsend, 2009), a poison prevention education program (Schwartz, Howland, Mercurio-Zappala, & Hoffman, 2003), prevention and reduction of aggressive behavior (Orpinas & Horne, 2004), prevention of childhood obesity (Canavera, Sharma, & Murnan, 2008–2009), problem-solving skills (Coates, Malouff, & Rooke, 2008; Sharma, Petosa, & Heaney, 1999; Shimazu, Kawakami, Irimajiri, Sakamoto, & Amano, 2005), a self-help physical activity intervention at the workplace (Griffin-Blake & DeJoy, 2006), a self-help weight management intervention (Tufano & Karras, 2005), self-regulation of driving among high-risk older drivers (Stalvey & Owsley, 2003), a sun protection intervention in preschoolers (Gritz et al., 2006), a smoking cessation program (Patten et al., 2009; Ramelson, Friedman, & Ockene, 1999), smoking prevention programs (Langlois, Petosa, & Hallam, 1999), a walking program (Rovniak, Hovell, Wojcik, Winett, & Martinez-Donate, 2005), and Web-assisted instruction for physical activity (Suminski & Petosa, 2006). **Table 7.3** summarizes these applications.

> *The field of health is changing from a disease model to a health model. It is just as meaningful to speak of levels of vitality and healthfulness as of degrees of impairment and debility. Health promotion should begin with goals not means. If health is the goal, biomedical interventions are not the only means to it.*
>
> —Bandura (2004, p. 143)

Some examples in which SCT has been used for secondary and tertiary prevention are for adherence to continuous positive airway pressure (CPAP) treatment for sleep apnea (Stepnowsky, Marler, Palau, & Annette Brooks, 2006), behavior change intervention after knee replacement (Harnirattisai & Johnson, 2005), a childhood asthma management program (McGhan, Wells, & Befus, 1998), a diabetes education program (Chapman-Novakofski & Karduck, 2005), dietary approaches to reducing hypertension (Rankins, Sampson, Brown, & Jenkins-Salley, 2005), intervention to improve the quality of life for women with breast cancer (Blacklock, Rhodes, Blanchard, & Gaul, 2010; Graves, Carter, Anderson, & Winett, 2003), a lifestyle program for leg ulcer patients (Heinen, Bartholomew, Wensing, Kerkhof, & Achterberg, 2006), mammography screening among American Indian women (Dignan et al., 2005), medication self-management among people with epilepsy (Diiorio et al., 2005; Diiorio et al., 2009), a physical activity program for prostate cancer patients (Taylor et al., 2006), promotion of female condom use in a sexually transmitted disease clinic (Artz et al., 2005), rehabilitation following myocardial infarction and coronary artery bypass grafting (Hiltunen et al., 2005), skin self-examination by

TABLE 7.3   Applications of Social Cognitive Theory in Primary Prevention
Active ergonomics training program in computer users
Family planning decision making
HIV prevention program in adolescents
Nutrition education program
Poison prevention education program
Prevention and reduction of aggressive behavior
Prevention of childhood obesity
Problem-solving skills
Self-help physical activity intervention at the workplace
Self-help weight management intervention
Self-regulation of driving among high-risk older drivers
Smoking cessation program
Smoking prevention programs
Sun protection intervention in preschoolers
Walking program
Web-assisted instruction for physical activity

patients at high risk for melanoma (Hay et al., 2006), and weight loss in overweight and obese women (Annesi, 2010; Klohe-Lehman et al., 2006). **Table 7.4** summarizes these applications.

LIMITATIONS OF SOCIAL COGNITIVE THEORY

Social cognitive theory is a robust behavioral theory, and its biggest advantage is that it can be applied easily. The other important dimension of this theory is that social structural factors are integrated with personal determinants, which is often not the case with other theories of behavior. However, like all theories, this theory has some limitations. Some critics have noted that the theory is about learning and is, therefore, more applicable for children. The theory is not specifically designed for changing

TABLE 7.4	Applications of Social Cognitive Theory in Secondary and Tertiary Prevention
Adherence to continuous positive airway pressure (CPAP) treatment for sleep apnea	
Behavior change intervention after knee replacement	
Childhood asthma management program	
Diabetes education program	
Dietary approaches to reducing hypertension	
Intervention to improve the quality of life for women with breast cancer	
Lifestyle program for leg ulcer patients	
Mammography screening among American Indian women	
Medication self-management among people with epilepsy	
Physical activity program for prostate cancer patients	
Promotion of female condom use in a sexually transmitted disease clinic	
Rehabilitation following myocardial infarction and coronary artery bypass grafting	
Skin self-examination by patients at high risk for melanoma	
Weight loss in overweight and obese women	

behavior. For example, the stages of change theory is specific about changing behaviors and provides indications of the different stages through which a person moves. SCT provides no such guidance.

The theory has many constructs, and often it is not possible to reify all these constructs, which tends to limit the theory's usage. Ideally, a theory should be parsimonious. Also, the single most important predictor of the theory is identified as self-efficacy. Often, the items that measure self-efficacy are very similar to the items that measure the behavior, thus adding to measurement bias. Further, questions meant to measure an individual's cognition in SCT often change and create the responder's thinking rather than tapping into how exactly that individual thinks to begin with. Prochaska (2006) has criticized SCT as lacking arrangement of constructs in mathematical relationships. As a result, different practitioners use different sets of constructs in different combinations. Finally, Prochaska (2006) notes that SCT-based interventions mainly target those who are prepared to change the behavior; in the process, such interventions miss a large majority of the population. A theory should provide guidance for change for people with varying levels of readiness.

APPLICATION EXERCISE

In this chapter we have presented several applications of social cognitive theory in behavioral research, in primary, secondary, and tertiary prevention. Choose an area of interest to you from these applications and read the full text article to see how the theory was used in that context. One such example is the study done by Sharma, Wagner, and Wilkerson (2005–2006) in the area of obesity prevention behaviors among children. They chose four obesity prevention behaviors: limiting television viewing, encouraging daily physical activity, increasing fruit and vegetable intake, and increasing water consumption. They chose selected constructs of social cognitive theory: expectations (multiplicative score of outcome expectations and outcome expectancies) for each of the four behaviors, self-efficacy for each of the four behaviors, and self-control for each of the four behaviors. They developed a 52-item valid and reliable scale that was administered to 159 fifth-grade students. Minutes of physical activity were predicted by self-efficacy to exercise and number of times taught at school ($R^2 = 0.072$). Hours of TV watching were predicted by number of times taught about healthy eating at school and self-control through goal setting ($R^2 = 0.055$). Glasses of water consumed were predicted by expectations for drinking water ($R^2 = 0.091$). Servings of fruits and vegetables consumed were predicted by self-efficacy of eating fruits and vegetables ($R^2 = 0.137$). This is a useful study that demonstrates how social cognitive theory has been used.

Locate the full text article for this study and prepare a 250 word critique on its methodology.

SKILL-BUILDING ACTIVITY

Let us see how we can apply SCT to the issue of developing problem-solving skills in upper elementary school children. **Figure 7.3** depicts each of the constructs from SCT and links these with educational processes and behavioral objectives to develop problem-solving skills.

We need to be parsimonious in our selection of constructs from the theory, so let's choose six constructs. The health education intervention would start by modifying the construct of situational perception by brainstorming about potential stressors that would require problem solving by the children. A lecture to build knowledge

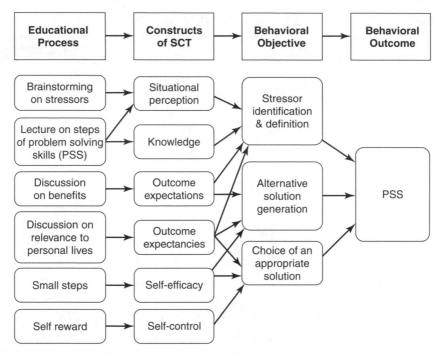

FIGURE 7.3 How social cognitive theory (SCT) has been used to modify problem solving skills.

about stressors and the steps of problem solving can be given. To modify outcome expectations, a discussion on the benefits of problem-solving skills can be organized. Some examples of these benefits could include increased popularity with friends, faster learning, better grades, more fun with family, and more fun at school. To modify outcome expectancies, the relevance of the anticipated outcomes to the students' personal lives can be discussed.

To modify self-efficacy, the steps of problem solving can be broken down into small steps. These steps could be as follows: (1) identify the stressor, (2) think of many ways to deal with each stressor, (3) think of all the good points about each way, (4) think of all the bad points about each way, and (5) choose one solution after looking at the good and bad points for several possible solutions. Messages that role models use these steps of problem solving can be used to reinforce self-efficacy. Stress management techniques can be practiced while applying the steps of problem solving, which also reinforces self-efficacy. Finally, to modify self-control, the children can be instructed to write goals for applying problem-solving skills and then reward themselves when they accomplish their goals.

Using this approach, plan a health education program for a behavior issue of your choice. Table 7.5 provides a set of questions to assist you in choosing educational methods that correspond to different constructs of social cognitive theory.

TABLE 7.5   Choosing the Educational Methods for Health Education Program Planning Using Social Cognitive Theory

1. What is the best educational method to facilitate knowledge?
   - Lecture
   - Informational talk
   - Fact sheets
   - Other

2. What is the best educational method to facilitate outcome expectations?
   - Discussion
   - Brainstorming
   - Role play
   - Simulation
   - Other

3. What is the best educational method to facilitate outcome expectancies?
   - Discussion
   - Brainstorming
   - Role play
   - Simulation
   - Other

4. What is the best educational method to facilitate situational perception?
   - Discussion
   - Brainstorming
   - Role play
   - Simulation
   - Other

5. What is the best educational method to facilitate changes in environment?
   - Making physical changes in the environment
   - Building social support
   - Providing access to health care
   - Other

(continued)

TABLE 7.5	**Choosing the Educational Methods for Health Education Program Planning Using Social Cognitive Theory (*Continued*)**

6. What is the best educational method to facilitate self-efficacy?
   - Demonstration
   - Role play
   - Video with a credible role model
   - Stress reduction techniques
     – Progressive muscle relaxation
     – Visual imagery
     – Autogenic training
     – Yoga/meditation
     – Other
   - Other

7. What is the best educational method to facilitate self-efficacy in overcoming impediments?
   - Demonstration
   - Role play
   - Video with a credible role model
   - Stress reduction techniques
     – Progressive muscle relaxation
     – Visual imagery
     – Autogenic training
     – Yoga/meditation
     – Other
   - Other

8. What is the best educational method to facilitate self-control?
   - Group formation
   - Coalition building
   - Registration of not-for-profit organization
   - Other

9. What is the best educational method to facilitate emotional coping?
   - Progressive muscle relaxation
   - Autogenic training
   - Yoga/meditation
   - Visual imagery
   - Other

SUMMARY

Albert Bandura, a professor of psychology at Stanford University, is the originator of social cognitive theory (previously called social learning theory). This theory explains human behavior as a triadic reciprocal causation among behavior, environment, and personal factors (such as cognitions, affect, and biological events). Five basic human capabilities describe human beings according to this theory: symbolizing capability (use of symbols in attributing meaning to experiences), vicarious capability (learning from observing other people's behavior and the consequences they face), forethought capability (most behavior is purposive and regulated by prior thoughts), self-regulatory capability (setting internal standards and self-evaluative reactions for one's behavior), and self-reflective capability (analysis of experiences and thinking about one's own thought processes).

The constructs of the theory include knowledge (learning facts and gaining insights related to an action, idea, object, person, or situation), outcome expectations (anticipation of the probable outcomes that would ensue as a result of engaging in the behavior), outcome expectancies (the value a person places on the probable outcomes that result from performing a behavior), situational perception (how a person perceives and interprets the environment around him- or herself), environment (physical or social circumstances or conditions that surround a person), self-efficacy (the confidence that a person has in his or her ability to pursue a behavior), self-efficacy in overcoming impediments (the confidence that a person has in overcoming barriers while performing a given behavior), goal setting or self-control (setting goals and developing plans to accomplish chosen behaviors), and emotional coping (techniques employed by the person to control the emotional and physiological states associated with acquisition of a new behavior). The constructs are amenable to modification by different educational methods. Social cognitive theory has been applied over the past 30 years in a variety of areas within health promotion and education.

IMPORTANT TERMS

emotional coping
environment
forethought capability
goal setting
outcome expectancies
outcome expectations
reciprocal determinism
self-control
self-efficacy

self-efficacy in overcoming
    impediments
self-reflective capability
self-regulatory capability
situational perception
social cognitive theory (SCT)
social learning theory
symbolizing capability
vicarious capability

REVIEW QUESTIONS

1. Describe the historical genesis of social cognitive theory.
2. Discuss reciprocal determinism.
3. Discuss the underpinnings of social cognitive theory.
4. What is self-efficacy and how can it be built?
5. Describe the constructs of social cognitive theory.
6. Discuss the limitations of social cognitive theory.
7. Apply social cognitive theory in changing a behavior of your choice for a target population of your choice.

WEBSITES TO EXPLORE

Albert Bandura: Biographical Sketch

http://www.des.emory.edu/mfp/bandurabio.html

This website, developed in 2004 and maintained by Frank Pajares at Emory University, provides a detailed biography of Albert Bandura along with links to various important events and accomplishments in the life of Albert Bandura. *Read the biography of Albert Bandura and prepare a reaction paper explaining what impressed you most about him.*

Albert Bandura

http://www.ship.edu/~cgboeree/bandura.html

This website, developed and maintained by George Boeree of Shippensburg University in Pennsylvania, provides a brief biography of Bandura and an interesting account of social learning theory. *Review this website and describe how social learning theory is used in therapy.*

Idea: Social Cognitive Theory Compared with Constructivism and Cooperative Learning

http://i-d-e-a.org/page109.html

This website presents an overview of social cognitive theory and compares it with the theory of constructivism and cooperative learning. As we have seen, in social cognitive theory self-efficacy, self-control, outcome expectations, and outcome expectancies are important factors related to behavior development. In constructivism, the learner actively constructs new ideas and interprets concepts based on current and past knowledge. In cooperative learning, the learner is actively engaged in the learning process. *Review this website and compare and contrast the three theoretical approaches.*

Overview of Social Cognitive Theory and Self-Efficacy

http://www.des.emory.edu/mfp/eff.html

Developed in 2002 and maintained by Frank Pajares at Emory University, this website briefly traces the origin of social cognitive theory, then talks about fundamental human capabilities and describes self-efficacy beliefs. *Review this website and comment on how self-efficacy beliefs influence human functioning.*

Social Cognitive Theory: Brief Video

http://video.google.com/videoplay?docid=-2953790276071699877

This website features a 4-minute video on social cognitive theory. Watch the Bobo doll experiment and the account of snake phobia therapy. *Share one important implication you discovered about SCT by watching this video.*

REFERENCES

Allport, G. W. (1937). *Personality: A psychological interpretation.* New York: Holt.

Annesi, J. J. (2009). Dose-response and self-efficacy effects of an exercise program on vigor change in obese women. *American Journal of the Medical Sciences, 339*(2), 127–132.

Artz, L., Macaluso, M., Kelaghan, J., Austin, H., Fleenor, M., Robey, L., et al. (2005). An intervention to promote the female condom to sexually transmitted disease clinic patients. *Behavior Modification, 29*(2), 318–369.

Bandura, A. (1969). *Principles of behavior modification.* New York: Prentice-Hall

Bandura, A. (1977). *Social learning theory*. Englewood Cliffs, NJ: Prentice-Hall.

Bandura, A. (1986). *Social foundations of thought and action.* Englewood Cliffs, NJ: Prentice-Hall.

Bandura, A. (Ed.). (1995). *Self-efficacy in changing societies.* New York: Cambridge University Press.

Bandura, A. (1997). *Self-efficacy: The exercise of control.* New York: W. H. Freeman.

Bandura, A. (2001a). Social cognitive theory: An agentic perspective. *Annual Review of Psychology, 52,* 1–26.

Bandura, A. (2001b). Social cognitive theory of mass communication. *Mediapsychology, 3,* 265–299.

Bandura, A. (2002). Social cognitive theory in cultural context. *Applied Psychology: An International Review, 51*(2), 269–290.

Bandura, A. (2004). Health promotion by social cognitive means. *Health Education and Behavior, 31,* 143–164.

Bandura, A. (2005). The primacy of self-regulation in health promotion. *Applied Psychology: An International Review, 54*(2), 245–254.

Bandura, A., & Walters, R. H. (1963). *Social learning and personality development*. New York: Holt, Rinehart and Winston.

Baranowski, T., Perry, C. L., & Parcel, G. S. (2002). How individuals, environments, and health behavior interact. Social cognitive theory. In K. Glanz, B. K. Rimer, & F. M. Lewis (Eds.), *Health behavior and health education: Theory, research, and practice* (3rd ed., pp. 165–184). San Francisco: Jossey-Bass.

Bere, E., & Klepp, K. I. (2005). Changes in accessibility and preferences predict children's future fruit and vegetable intake. *International Journal of Behavioral Nutrition and Physical Activity, 2,* 15.

Blacklock, R., Rhodes, R., Blanchard, C., & Gaul, C. (2010). Effects of exercise intensity and self-efficacy on state anxiety with breast cancer survivors. *Oncology Nursing Forum, 37*(2), 206–212.

Boutin-Foster, C., McLaughlin, N., Gray, A., Ogedegbe, A., Hageman, I., Knowlton, C., et al. (2010). Reducing HIV and AIDS through Prevention (RHAP): A theoretically based approach for teaching HIV prevention to adolescents through an exploration of popular music. *Journal of Urban Health*, Epub ahead of print. PMID: 20195778.

Burgess-Champoux, T., Marquart, L., Vickers, Z., & Reicks, M. (2006). Perceptions of children, parents, and teachers regarding whole-grain foods, and implications for a school-based intervention. *Journal of Nutrition Education and Behavior, 38*(4), 230–237.

Canavera, M., Sharma, M., & Murnan, J. (2008–2009). Development and pilot testing a social cognitive theory-based intervention to prevent childhood obesity among elementary students in rural Kentucky. *International Quarterly of Community Health Education, 29*(1), 57–70.

Carleton, R. A., Lasater, T. M., Assaf, A. R., Feldman, H. A., & McKinlay, S. (1995). The Pawtucket Heart Health Program: Community changes in cardiovascular risk factors and projected disease risk. *American Journal of Public Health, 85,* 777–785.

Chapman-Novakofski, K., & Karduck, J. (2005). Improvement in knowledge, social cognitive theory variables, and movement through stages of change after a community-based diabetes education program. *Journal of the American Dietetic Association, 105*(10), 1613–1616.

Coates, C., Malouff, J. M., & Rooke, S. E. (2008). Efficacy of written modeling and vicarious reinforcement in increasing use of problem-solving methods by distressed individuals. *The Journal of Psychology, 142*(4), 413–425.

Dignan, M. B., Burhansstipanov, L., Hariton, J., Harjo, L., Rattler, T., Lee, R., et al. (2005). A comparison of two Native American Navigator formats: Face-to-face and telephone. *Cancer Control, 12*(Suppl. 2), 28–33.

Diiorio, C., Escoffery, C., Yeager, K. A., McCarty, F., Henry, T. R., Koganti, A., et al. (2009). WebEase: Development of a Web-based epilepsy self-management intervention. *Preventing Chronic Disease, 6*(1), A28.

Diiorio, C., McCarty, F., & Denzmore, P. (2006). An exploration of social cognitive theory mediators of father-son communication about sex. *Journal of Pediatric Psychology, 31*(9), 917–927.

Diiorio, C., McCarty, F., Depadilla, L., Resnicow, K., Holstad, M. M., Yeager, K., et al. (2009). Adherence to antiretroviral medication regimens: A test of a psychosocial model. *AIDS and Behavior, 13*(1), 10–22.

Diiorio, C., Resnicow, K., McCarty, F., De, A. K., Dudley, W. N., Wang, D. T., et al. (2006). Keepin' it R.E.A.L.! Results of a mother-adolescent HIV prevention program. *Nursing Research, 55*(1), 43–51.

Diiorio, C., Shafer, P. O., Letz, R., Henry, T. R., Schomer, D. L., Yeager, K., et al. (2005). Project EASE: A study to test a psychosocial model of epilepsy medication management. *Epilepsy and Behavior, 5*(6), 926–936.

Dollard, J., & Miller, N. E. (1950). *Personality and psychotherapy.* New York: McGraw-Hill.

Farquhar, J. W. (1978). The community-based model of lifestyle intervention trials. *American Journal of Epidemiology, 108,* 103–111.

Farquhar, J. W., Fortmann, S. P., Maccoby, N., Haskell, W. I., Williams, P., Flora, J., et al. (1985). The Stanford five-city project: Design and methods. *American Journal of Epidemiology, 122*(2), 323–334.

Farquhar, J. W., Maccoby, N., Wood, P. D., Alexander, J. K., Breitrose, H., Brown, B. W., Jr., et al. (1977). Community education for cardiovascular health. *Lancet, 1,* 1192–1195.

Freud, S. (1960). *The ego and the id.* New York: Norton. (Original work published 1923)

Gilles, D. M., Turk, C. L., & Fresco, D. M. (2006). Social anxiety, alcohol expectancies, and self-efficacy as predictors of heavy drinking in college students. *Addictive Behaviors, 31*(3), 388–398.

Graves, K. D., Carter, C. L., Anderson, E. S., & Winett, R. A. (2003). Quality of life pilot intervention for breast cancer patients: Use of social cognitive theory. *Palliative and Support Care, 1*(2), 121–134.

Greene, B. L., DeJoy, D. M., & Olejnik, S. (2005). Effects of an active ergonomics training program on risk exposure, worker beliefs, and symptoms in computer users. *Work, 24*(1), 41–52.

Griffin-Blake, C. S., & DeJoy, D. M. (2006). Evaluation of social-cognitive versus stage-matched, self-help physical activity interventions at the workplace. *American Journal of Health Promotion, 20*(3), 200–209.

Gritz, E. R., Tripp, M. K., James, A. S., Harris, R. B., Mueller, N. H., Chamberlain, R. M., et al. (2006). Effects of a preschool staff intervention on children's sun protection: Outcomes of Sun Protection Is Fun! *Health Education and Behavior,* Epub. PMID: 16740505.

Ha, B. T., Jayasuriya, R., & Owen, N. (2005). Increasing male involvement in family planning decision making: Trial of a social-cognitive intervention in rural Vietnam. *Health Education Research, 20*(5), 548–556.

Harnirattisai, T., & Johnson, R. A. (2005). Effectiveness of a behavioral change intervention in Thai elders after knee replacement. *Nursing Research, 54*(2), 97–107

Hay, J. L., Oliverio, S. A., Dusza, S. W., Phelan, D. L., Ostroff, J. S., & Halpern, A. C. (2006). Psychosocial mediators of a nurse intervention to increase skin self-examination in patients at high risk for melanoma. *Cancer Epidemiology Biomarkers and Prevention, 15*(6), 1212–1216.

Heinen, M. M., Bartholomew, L. K., Wensing, M., Kerkhof, P., & Achterberg, T. (2006). Supporting adherence and healthy lifestyles in leg ulcer patients: Systematic development of the Lively Legs program for dermatology outpatient clinics. *Patient Education and Counseling, 61*(2), 279–291.

Hiltunen, E. F., Winder, P. A., Rait, M. A., Buselli, E. F., Carroll, D. L., & Rankin, S. H. (2005). Implementation of efficacy enhancement nursing interventions with cardiac elders. *Rehabilitation Nursing, 30*(6), 221–229.

Honda, K., & Gorin, S. S. (2006). A model of stage of change to recommend colonoscopy among urban primary care physicians. *Health Psychology, 25*(1), 65–73.

Kaewthummanukul, T., Brown, K. C., Weaver, M. T., & Thomas, R. R. (2006). Predictors of exercise participation in female hospital nurses. *Journal of Advanced Nursing, 54*(6), 663–675.

Kalichman, S. C., Cain, D., Fuhrel, A., Eaton, L., Di Fonzo, K., & Ertl, T. (2005). Assessing medication adherence self-efficacy among low-literacy patients: Development of a pictographic visual analogue scale. *Health Education Research, 20*(1), 24–35.

Klohe-Lehman, D. M., Freeland-Graves, J., Anderson, E. R., McDowell, T., Clarke, K. K., Hanss-Nuss, H., et al. (2006). Nutrition knowledge is associated with greater weight loss in obese and overweight low-income mothers. *Journal of American Dietetic Association, 106*(1), 65–75.

Koniak-Griffin, D., & Stein, J. A. (2006). Predictors of sexual risk behaviors among adolescent mothers in a human immunodeficiency virus prevention program. *Journal of Adolescent Health, 38*(3), 297.e1–11.

Langlois, M. A., Petosa, R., & Hallam, J. S. (1999). Why do effective smoking prevention programs work? Student changes in social cognitive theory constructs. *Journal of School Health, 69*(8), 326–331.

Luepker, R. V., Murray, D. M., Jacobs, D. R., Mittelmark, M. B., Bracht, N., Carlaw, R., et al. (1994). Community education for cardiovascular disease prevention: Risk factor changes in the Minnesota Heart Health Program. *American Journal of Public Health, 84*, 1383–1393.

Martino, S. C., Collins, R. L., Kanouse, D. E., Elliott, M., & Berry, S. H. (2005). Social cognitive processes mediating the relationship between exposure to television's sexual content and adolescents' sexual behavior. *Journal of Personality and Social Psychology, 89*(6), 914–924.

Mashegoane, S., Moalusi, K. P., Peltzer, K., & Ngoepe, M. A. (2004). The prediction of condom use intention among South African university students. *Psychological Reports, 95*(2), 407–417.

McGhan, S. L., Wells, H. M., & Befus, A. D. (1998). The "Roaring Adventures of Puff": A childhood asthma education program. *Journal of Pediatric Health Care, 12*(4), 191–195.

Mouttapa, M., Valente, T., Gallaher, P., Rohrbach, L. A., & Unger, J. B. (2004). Social network predictors of bullying and victimization. *Adolescence, 39*(154), 315–335.

Oliver, K., & Cronan, T. A. (2005). Correlates of physical activity among women with fibromyalgia syndrome. *Annals of Behavioral Medicine, 29*(1), 44–53.

Orpinas, P., & Horne, A. M. (2004). A teacher-focused approach to prevent and reduce students' aggressive behavior: The GREAT Teacher Program. *American Journal of Preventive Medicine, 26*(Suppl. 1), 29–38.

Patten, C. A., Petersen, L. R., Hughes, C. A., Ebbert, J. O., Morgenthaler Bonnema, S., Brockman, T. A., et al. (2009). Feasibility of a telephone-based intervention for support persons to help smokers quit: A pilot study. *Nicotine & Tobacco Research, 11*(4), 427–432.

Powers, A. R., Struempler, B. J., Guarino, A., & Parmer, S. M. (2005). Effects of a nutrition education program on the dietary behavior and nutrition knowledge of second-grade and third-grade students. *Journal of School Health, 75*(4), 129–133.

Prochaska, J. O. (2006). Is social cognitive theory becoming a transtheoretical model? A comment on Dijkstra et al. (2006). *Addiction, 101*, 916–917.

Ramelson, H. Z., Friedman, R. H., & Ockene, J. K. (1999). An automated telephone-based smoking cessation education and counseling system. *Patient Education and Counseling, 36*(2), 131–144.

Rankins, J., Sampson, W., Brown, B., & Jenkins-Salley, T. (2005). Dietary Approaches to Stop Hypertension (DASH) intervention reduces blood pressure among hypertensive African American patients in a neighborhood health care center. *Journal of Nutrition Education and Behavior, 37*(5), 259–264.

Rhodes, R. E., & Plotnikoff, R. C. (2005). Can current physical activity act as a reasonable proxy measure of future physical activity? Evaluating cross-sectional and passive prospective designs with the use of social cognition models. *Preventive Medicine, 40*(5), 547–555,

Rotter, J. B. (1954), *Social learning and clinical psychology*. Englewood Cliffs, NJ: Prentice-Hall.

Rovniak, L. S., Hovell, M. F., Wojcik, J. R., Winett, R. A., & Martinez-Donate, A. P. (2005). Enhancing theoretical fidelity: An e-mail-based walking program demonstration. *American Journal of Health Promotion, 20*(2), 85–95.

Schwartz, L., Howland, M. A., Mercurio-Zappala, M., & Hoffman, R. S. (2003). The use of focus groups to plan poison prevention education programs for low-income populations. *Health Promotion Practice, 4*(3), 340–346.

Sharma, M., & Deepak, S. (2003). An intercountry study of expectations, roles, attitudes and behaviors of community-based rehabilitation volunteers. *Asia Pacific Disability Rehabilitation Journal, 14*, 179–190.

Sharma, M., Mehan, M. B., & Surabhi, S. (2008–2009). Using social cognitive theory to predict obesity prevention behaviors among preadolescents in India. *International Quarterly of Community Health Education, 29*(4), 351–361.

Sharma, M., Petosa, R., & Heaney, C. A. (1999). Evaluation of a brief intervention based on social cognitive theory to develop problem solving skills among sixth grade children. *Health Education and Behavior, 26*, 465–477.

Sharma, M., Wagner, D. I., & Wilkerson, J. (2005–2006). Predicting childhood obesity prevention behaviors using social cognitive theory. *International Quarterly of Community Health Education, 24*(3), 191–203.

Shilts, M. K., Lamp, C., Horowitz, M., & Townsend, M. S. (2009). Pilot study: EatFit impacts sixth graders' academic performance on achievement of mathematics and English education standards. *Journal of Nutrition Education & Behavior, 41*(2), 127–131.

Shimazu, A., Kawakami, N., Irimajiri, H., Sakamoto, M., & Amano, S. (2005). Effects of Web-based psychoeducation on self-efficacy, problem solving behavior, stress responses and job satisfaction among workers: A controlled clinical trial. *Journal of Occupational Health, 47*(5), 405–413.

Skinner, B. F. (1953). *Science and human behavior*. New York: Macmillan.

Stalvey, B. T., & Owsley, C. (2003). The development and efficacy of a theory-based educational curriculum to promote self-regulation among high-risk older drivers. *Health Promotion Practice, 4*(2), 109–119.

Stepnowsky, C. J., Marler, M. R., Palau, J., & Annette Brooks, J. (2006). Social-cognitive correlates of CPAP adherence in experienced users. *Sleep Medicine, 7*(4), 350–356.

Suminski, R. R., & Petosa, R. (2006). Web-assisted instruction for changing social cognitive variables related to physical activity. *Journal of American College Health, 54*(4), 219–225.

Tavares, L. S., Plotnikoff, R. C., & Loucaides, C. (2009). Social-cognitive theories for predicting physical activity behaviours of employed women with and without young children. *Psychology, Health, & Medicine, 14*(2), 129–142.

Taylor, C. L., Demoor, C., Smith, M. A., Dunn, A. L., Basen-Engquist, K., Nielsen, I., et al. (2006). Active for Life After Cancer: A randomized trial examining a lifestyle physical activity program for prostate cancer patients. *Psychooncology, 15*(10), 847–862.

Tufano, J. T., & Karras, B. T. (2005). Mobile eHealth interventions for obesity: A timely opportunity to leverage convergence trends. *Journal of Medical Internet Research, 7*(5), e58.

Wang, S. L., Charron-Prochownik, D., Sereika, S. M., Siminerio, L., & Kim, Y. (2006). Comparing three theories in predicting reproductive health behavioral intention in adolescent women with diabetes. *Pediatric Diabetes, 7*(2), 108–115.

Young, D. R., Haskell, W. L., Jatulis, D. E., & Fortmann, S. P. (1993). Associations between changes in physical activity and risk factors for coronary heart disease in a community-based sample of men and women: The Stanford five-city project. *American Journal of Epidemiology, 138*, 205–216.

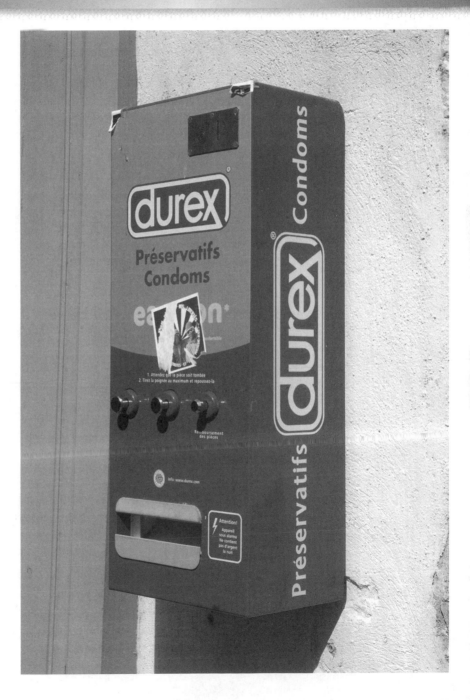

Social Marketing

- audience segmentation
- exchange theory
- marketing mix
- partnership
- place
- policy

- price
- product
- promotion
- publics
- purse strings
- social marketing

AFTER READING THIS CHAPTER YOU SHOULD BE ABLE TO

- Describe the historical genesis of social marketing
- List the constructs of social marketing
- Differentiate between commercial marketing and social marketing
- Summarize the applications of social marketing in health education and health promotion
- Identify key constructs from the social marketing model
- Apply the social marketing model to influence a health behavior of your choice

This chapter discusses the social marketing model. **Social marketing** is the use of commercial marketing techniques to help a target population acquire a beneficial health behavior (Weinreich, 1999). Social marketing is becoming a popular choice for influencing behavior in both the government and not-for-profit sectors in the United States and in many other countries around the world. In the field of health, some important applications of social marketing include family planning, recruiting blood donors, reducing infant mortality through oral rehydration, and preventing smoking in adolescents (Andreasen & Kotler, 2003). The primary difference between social marketing and commercial marketing is in their objectives. In social marketing, the primary purpose is to benefit the target audience and change behaviors that have social implications.

This chapter begins by describing the historical aspects of the genesis of social marketing. Next, we delineate the differences between commercial marketing and social marketing and describe the social marketing approach and the various constructs that make up this model. We then discuss applications of social marketing in health education and health promotion. Finally, we outline the limitations of social marketing and present a skill-building application.

HISTORICAL PERSPECTIVE

Social marketing had its origins in India, where it was used in the 1960s to promote a family planning program, particularly the use of condoms (Harvey, 1999). The process entailed subsidizing condoms and supplying them through existing commercial distribution networks, using the mass media, and using other retail marketing techniques (Thapa, Prasad, Rao, Severy, & Rao, 1994). Partnerships were formed with corporations such as Unilever and Brooke Bond Tea Company to market the Nirodh brand of condoms. Under the program, condoms sales exceeded one billion by the mid-1990s, a multifold increase from the initial years of the program. This continues to be one of the largest applications of social marketing in the world, and the program has been expanded to include other products such as oral contraceptives, oral rehydration solution, iron foliate, and female condoms.

> *Social marketing is the application of commercial marketing techniques to the analysis, planning, execution, and evaluation of programs designed to influence the voluntary behavior of target audiences in order to improve their personal welfare and that of their society.*
>
> —Andreasen (1995, p. 7)

In the 1950s, U.S. sociologist G. D. Wiebe (1951–1952) first suggested that marketing might be applied to "selling brotherhood" and other social ideas. This suggestion was incorporated in the work of Philip Kotler in the late 1960s. Kotler and Levy (1969) suggested that marketing was a pervasive societal activity that included all transactions. Kotler and Zaltman (1971) first defined social marketing as "the design, implementation, and control of programs calculated to influence the acceptability of social ideas and involving considerations of product planning, pricing, communication, distribution, and marketing research" (p. 5). However, interest in social marketing was lukewarm throughout the 1970s and most of the 1980s (Andreasen, 2003). The main type of social marketing that occurred was marketing of contraceptives, in which the product was just like a product in commercial marketing and a nominal price was involved. Not much marketing of ideas was done.

Social marketing made major advancements in the late 1980s and throughout the 1990s. In 1989, the first textbook on social marketing was published by Kotler and Roberto. They defined social marketing as a "social change technology involving the design, implementation, and control of programs aimed at increasing the acceptability of a social idea or practice in one or more groups of target adopters" (p. 24), thus placing social marketing in synchrony with health education and health promotion. In 1995, Andreasen defined social marketing as "the application of commercial marketing techniques to the analysis, planning, execution, and evaluation of programs designed to influence the voluntary behavior of target audiences in order to improve their personal welfare and that of their society" (p. 7). This definition brought the idea closer to health education and health promotion, where the purpose is also behavior change.

In 1994, the journal *Social Marketing Quarterly* was founded, and the Social Marketing Institute was founded in Washington, D.C. in 1999. The mission of the institute was to advance the science and art of social marketing. Some of the major social marketing initiatives in the 1990s were the U.S. Department of Agriculture's 5-a-Day campaign; the Centers for Disease Control and Prevention's campaign to inform health care professionals and the public that stomach ulcers were caused by the bacterium Helicobacter pylori and could be cured with antibiotics; North Carolina's statewide seat belt enforcement campaign, the "Click It or Ticket" program, which is still in use in other states; and a national breast-feeding promotional campaign through the Women, Infants, and Children (WIC) program (Social Marketing Institute, 2006).

> *Social marketing consists of a voluntary exchange between two or more parties, in which each is trying to further its own perceived self-interest while recognizing the need to accommodate the perceived self-interest of the other to achieve its own ends.*
>
> —Rothschild (1999)

In *Social Marketing in the 21st Century* Alan Andreasen (2006) laments that at present social marketing is in danger of being "pigeonholed as a downstream approach." He believes that most social marketing applications are geared toward rectifying bad behaviors, such as smoking, neglecting prenatal care, and so on. As a result, opportunities to use social marketing to foster positive behaviors are being lost. In any case, the social marketing approach is quite strong, as is evidenced by the growing number of publications and diverse applications using this model.

DIFFERENCES BETWEEN COMMERCIAL MARKETING AND SOCIAL MARKETING

The primary difference between social marketing and commercial marketing is in their objectives. In social marketing, the primary purpose is to benefit the target audience and change behaviors that have social implications. Andreasen and Kotler (2003) have identified additional differences between commercial marketing and social marketing (**Table 8.1**). The expectations in social marketing are more demanding, the scrutiny is done from a variety of sources, the idea that is sold is often totally new, and the educational level of the target audience is usually low. Social marketing often has to address what people do not want to change, has a high level of involvement between the marketer and the public, and often has invisible benefits or benefits that go to third parties. The rewards offered for making the recommended change are usually self-rewards, and budgets and the choice of products are limited.

TABLE 8.1	**Differences Between Commercial Marketing and Social Marketing**	
Attribute	**Commercial Marketing**	**Social Marketing**
Purpose	Making profits	Making behavior change for social causes
Expectations	Modest	Demanding, such as complete eradication of a problem or universal adoption of a behavior
Scrutiny	Usually done in the private sector	Done from a variety of sources: government, public, and funders
Novelty	Usually selling a known product	Sometimes selling an idea that is totally new (e.g., bacteria cause ulcers)
Education level	Variable and includes different sections	Usually vulnerable sections of audiences with low literacy
Distasteful behaviors	Usually caters to what public likes	Often has to address what people do not want to change (e.g., wearing a seat belt)
Involvement between marketer and public	Little	Often very high
Benefits	Clear in profits	Often invisible
Third parties	Direct benefits to people using the product	Often the benefits are to third parties, such as poor people
Self-rewards	Usually the rewards are external (e.g., discount better product)	Usually the rewards offered are internal or self-rewards (e.g., weight loss)
Budgets	Generous	Limited
Funding	Usually private	Usually government or not-for-profit foundations
Choices of products	Numerous	Limited

APPROACH AND CONSTRUCTS OF SOCIAL MARKETING

A core concept in marketing is developed in **exchange theory** (Thackeray & Brown, 2005). Exchange theory implies the transfer or transaction of something valuable between two individuals or groups (Flora, Schooler, & Pierseon, 1997). In social marketing, this transaction is voluntary and must be of benefit to the consumer (Lefebvre & Flora, 1988). The target audience must view the benefits as outweighing the costs for making the behavior change. For example, in a health promotion program that encourages participants to engage in physical activity, the costs to individuals would be loss of free time, loss of time to watch television, and so on. The benefits the social marketer offers must be more appealing than these losses, such as more energy to do things, the ability to lose weight, and so on.

There is no universal consensus regarding the social marketing model among social marketing professionals. Various authors have described different steps in social marketing. For example, Andreasen (1995) has defined six stages:

1. *Listening stage*. Background analysis and listening to the target audience.
2. *Planning stage*. The marketing mission, objectives, goals, and strategy are defined.
3. *Structuring stage*. A marketing organization, procedures, benchmarks, and feedback mechanisms are established.
4. *Pretesting stage*. Key program elements are tested.
5. *Implementing stage*. The strategy is put into effect.
6. *Monitoring stage*. Program progress is tracked.

Andreasen notes that the movement across these six stages is not linear but is an upward spiral process. The target audience is central in this planning process.

The National Cancer Institute (2005) has suggested four steps in a wheel of planning for social marketing: (1) planning and strategy development; (2) developing and pretesting concepts, messages, and materials; (3) implementing the program; and (4) assessing effectiveness and making refinements.

Weinreich (1999) has described a somewhat similar sequence of five steps: (1) planning, (2) message and material development, (3) pretesting, (4) implementation, and (5) evaluation. The first step, planning, entails four components: formative research, analysis, segmenting the target audience, and strategy development. **Formative research** involves collecting quantitative and qualitative data about the problem, its context, the attitudes and behaviors of the target audience, ways to reach the target audience, and existing messages and materials. In the analysis component, the problem, environment, and resources available for the program are analyzed. In **audience segmentation**, distinct groups of people who are similar to each other in particular characteristics and are thus likely to respond to messages in a similar way are identified. Segments may be based on such factors as geography, demography, medical history, personality characteristics, attitudes, behaviors, and so on. After identifying the segments, data about the target audience's knowledge, attitudes, and behavior is collected. Qualitative methods such as focus groups, in-depth interviews, and case studies or quantitative methods such as surveys are used in this component. The fourth component in the first step is *strategy development*, in which the goals and objectives are set and the social marketing mix is chosen. In marketing, the four Ps that define the **marketing mix** are product, price, place, and promotion. Weinreich (1999) has defined four additional Ps for social marketing: publics, partnership, policy, and purse strings.

The first P is **product**. In social marketing, the product is the behavior or offering that is intended to be adopted by the target audience. The product can be a physical product, such as condoms; a service, such as mammography; a practice, such as eating five or more servings of fruits and vegetables a day; or an intangible idea, such as environmental protection. The product must be able to fill a need felt by people and must be appealing and attractive. It is important to link potential benefits and subsequent benefits to the product, thereby making it attractive to the target audience. It is also important to find out about competing ideas (products) and to explain why the target audience would prefer the product being socially marketed. For example, if one were marketing physical activity, the competition would be from sedentary activities such as watching television or surfing the Internet. Knowing the competition allows one to plan counterarguments.

Price refers to the tangible and intangible things that the target audience has to give up in order to adopt the new idea (product). The price could be money, which is tangible, but often it is an intangible cost such as time, effort, or giving up an old way of life. Formative research should discover what the target audience considers to be the price for adopting the new behavior. This research should include an assessment of all barriers that confront the target population. Ways to minimize the costs and remove barriers must be considered in designing the strategy.

In commercial marketing, **place** refers to the distribution channels, or where and how customers will get the product. In social marketing, place refers to where the target audience will be exposed to messages about the behavior. For example, if we were advocating physical activity, we would need to determine whether the message would be delivered at the home of the person by a television spot, a newspaper article, or through the Internet. The message could also be given at the workplace, either on a bulletin board or by e-mail. The message could be given in community forums, such as the grocery store, local church, community center, or doctor's office. Messages need to be targeted to a particular place to be effective. Along with the messages, the product (idea or behavior) should be made available at that particular place. For example, if physical activity is to be done at home, then a stationary bike or treadmill should be available so the person can exercise while watching television. Distribution channels, or who will deliver the message, need to be decided. For example, if we want to promote physical activity, we could use a peer-to-peer network or counseling sessions through phone calls from the doctor's office.

Promotion is the mechanism by which one gets the message across to the target audience. Various techniques are used. Examples are advertisements, such as public service announcements (PSAs); public relations, such as writing letters to the editor or creating press releases; promotions, such as having a contest; media advocacy, such as holding a press event for policy change; personal selling, such as having a counseling session; special events, such as organizing a health fair; and entertainment, such as organizing a psychodrama.

The fifth P, **publics**, refers to both the primary and secondary audiences involved in the program. The primary audience is the target audience to whom the behavior change is targeted. In making their decisions, the members of the primary target audience may depend on other people. For example, in a smoking prevention program for adolescents, their parents, peers, and teachers would all be secondary audiences who need to provide the same messages. Policy makers are another secondary group that influence any decision and need to be involved.

Partnership refers to collaborating with multiple individuals or organizations who work on the same issue. No single organization has sufficient resources to significantly influence the huge outcome usually expected in social marketing. As a result, it makes sense for different organizations to form a coalition around the issue and then target it from different angles. Such collaborations can occur if two organizations either share the same goal or share the same target population.

Policy refers to creating the environmental supports needed to sustain the behavior change. For example, for promoting five or more servings of fruits and vegetables policies must be in place that allow vending machines to dispense such items and that make fruits and vegetables available at affordable rates. Some effective approaches for modifying policies are techniques such as advocacy, media advocacy, lobbying, and working with policy makers or legislators.

The final P is the **purse strings**, which refers to the amount of money available for the campaign. In social marketing, there is no profit to sustain the efforts. All efforts in social marketing depend on resources in the form of donations or grants; therefore, grant writing is an important aspect of running a social marketing campaign. Other sources of funding, including selling a tangible product, also must be considered. **Table 8.2** summarizes the eight Ps of social marketing, and **Figure 8.1** illustrates the social marketing model.

TABLE 8.2	Key Constructs of Social Marketing	
Construct	**Definition**	**How to Modify?**
Product	Behavior or offering that is intended for the target audience to adopt	Match with a need felt by the target audience Make it appealing and attractive Link potential benefits and subsequent benefits to the product Find out about the competing ideas (products) and why the target audience would prefer the product being socially marketed
Price	Tangible and intangible things that the target audience has to give up in order to adopt the new idea (product)	Find ways to minimize the costs Find ways to eliminate barriers
Place	Where the target audience will perform the behavior	Target messages at the particular place where the behavior will be performed Make the product (idea or behavior) available at that particular place Choose appropriate distribution channels, or who will deliver the message
Promotion	Mechanism by which one gets the message across to the target audience	Advertising Public relations Promotions Media advocacy Personal selling Special events Entertainment
Publics	Primary and secondary audiences involved in the program	Involve primary audiences Involve secondary audiences
Partnership	Establish collaboration with multiple individuals or organizations who work on the same issue	Build coalitions
Policy	Create the environmental supports needed to sustain the behavior change	Advocate, lobby, and create policies regarding the issue
Purse strings	Amount of money available for the campaign	Write grants Sell a tangible product

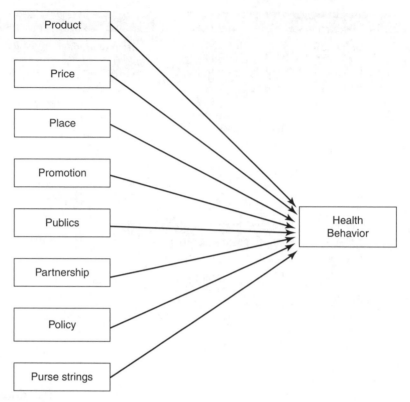

FIGURE 8.1   The social marketing model.

The second step in social marketing is *message and materials development.* This step has three components: identifying appropriate channels, developing effective messages, and developing creative strategy. Identifying appropriate channels entails identifying where the target population will be performing the behavior (place) and then matching the channels. For example, if physical activity is to be performed at community centers, then the channels of health fairs at the community center, community center newsletter announcements, billboard announcements, and so on need to be organized. The step of developing effective messages needs to use some of the behavioral theories elaborated in this book, such as the health belief model, transtheoretical model, theory of reasoned action, theory of planned behavior, social cognitive theory, and the diffusion of innovations model. Developing creative strategy entails being creative in packaging the set of messages and materials.

The third step in social marketing is *pretesting*. Some of the aspects that need to be checked while pretesting the materials are their acceptability by the target audience, attractiveness to the target population, comprehension by the target population, completeness, and appropriateness for the target population. Techniques such as focus groups, nominal groups, central location interviews, questionnaires, and expert review can be used.

The fourth step in social marketing is *implementation*, in which the strategy is put into action. The final stage is evaluation. A variety of designs and methods can be used in the evaluation step, such as a posttest only design, a single group pretest/posttest design, or an experimental design with a control group. In terms of methods, self-reports as well as observational methods can be effective.

> *Social Marketing is a larger idea than social promotion and advertising. We need to highlight the importance of the other three Ps, product, price, and place, in determining whether a social marketing campaign will be successful. We must add the idea that client behavior analysis, segmentation, and positioning are critical concepts in developing our social marketing approach.*
>
> —Kotler (2005, p. 147)

APPLICATIONS OF SOCIAL MARKETING

Social marketing has been used in a variety of applications in health education and health promotion. These applications include an antitobacco campaign (Lin & Hullman, 2005; Perusco et al., 2010), a campaign to improve antibiotic use (Goossens et al., 2006), a campaign to reduce the stigma of mental illness (Corrigan & Gelb, 2006), a community-wide physical activity campaign (Regcr-Nash et al., 2006; Rissel et al., 2010), designing a cancer prevention program (Miner, White, Lubenow, & Palmer, 2005; Sinclair, & Foley, 2009), a diabetes prevention program (Bachar et al., 2006; HEALTHY study group et al., 2009), an educational program aimed at improving prescribing for hypertension (Horn et al., 2006), family health advocacy for pregnant and parenting women (Baffour, Jones, & Contreras, 2006), increasing cervical cancer screening (Bethune, & Lewis, 2009; Millett, Zelenyanszki, Furlong, & Binysh, 2005), increasing condom use (Meekers, Agha, & Klein, 2005; Piot et al., 2010), increasing female condom use (Bull et al., 2008; Meekers & Richter, 2005), increasing syphilis awareness (Stephens, Bernstein, McCright, & Klausner, 2010; Vega & Roland, 2005), increasing use of bicycle helmets (Ludwig, Buchholz, & Clarke, 2005), iron-folic acid supplementation in Cambodian women (Crape et al., 2005), leprosy elimination in Sri Lanka (Williams, Dewapura, Gunawardene, & Settinayake, 1998), nutrition education in preschoolers (Young, Anderson, Beckstrom, Bellows, & Johnson, 2004), physical activity promotion in adolescent girls (Staten, Birnbaum, Jobe, & Elder, 2006), promoting insecticide-treated nets in Africa (De Allegri et al., 2010; Maxwell, Rwegoshora, Magesa, & Curtis, 2006), promoting iron nutrition for at-risk infants (Verrall, Napash, Leclerc, Mercure, & Gray-Donald, 2006), promoting preconceptional use of folic acid (Quinn, Hauser, Bell-Ellison, Rodriguez, & Frias, 2006), recruiting men who have sex with men for HIV research (Silvestre et al., 2006), reducing marijuana and alcohol use among adolescents (Slater et al., 2006), a self-help weight management intervention (Tufano & Karras, 2005), and a tractor rollover protection structure (ROPS) campaign (Sorensen, Jenkins, Bayes, & Clark, May, 2010). **Table 8.3** summarizes these applications.

> *For decades the health sector has watched as big companies have used marketing to wreak havoc on public health. Social marketing enables us to fight fire with fire.*
>
> —Hastings and McDermott (2006, p. 1212)

LIMITATIONS OF SOCIAL MARKETING

Social marketing is a useful model that is still being refined. There are definite advantages to this approach, such as extensive formative research, pretesting of the components before implementation, and the use of the marketing mix. However, like all other models and theories, social marketing has some limitations. First, in public health, the goal is to reach as many people as possible; however, in social marketing, audience segmentation and the use of tailored messages filter out many people who may be in need of the services or behavior change. Second, social marketing requires a lot of lead time for extensive formative research and pretesting (Marshall, Bryant, Keller, & Fridinger, 2006). Often the program planners do not have that much time and need to implement the intervention faster; they also often do not have the resources to expend on preplanning.

Social marketing has been labeled "motivational manipulation," especially by thinkers from third world countries (Banerji, 1986). Delivery of health education programs as social marketing campaigns that rely on technomanagerial approaches often drains resources that could be used to build the basic infrastructure in developing countries. Sometimes the solutions advocated by social marketing in these situations are Band-Aid solutions that do not address the root causes and do not involve community participation. Almost always, the social marketer decides what behaviors will constitute improvement; community members do not have much say. This unequal playing field between marketers and public poses ethical dilemmas as well (Grier & Bryant, 2005).

TABLE 8.3   Applications of the Social Marketing Model in Health Education and Health Promotion

Antitobacco campaign

Campaign to improve antibiotic use

Campaign to reduce the stigma of mental illness

Community-wide physical activity campaign

Designing cancer prevention programs

Diabetes prevention program

Educational program aimed at improving prescribing for hypertension

Family health advocacy for pregnant and parenting women

Increasing cervical cancer screening

Increasing condom use

Increasing female condom use

Increasing syphilis awareness

Increasing use of bicycle helmets

Iron-folic acid supplementation in Cambodian women

Leprosy elimination in Sri Lanka

Nutrition education in preschoolers

Physical activity promotion in adolescent girls

Promoting insecticide-treated nets in Africa

Promoting iron nutrition for at-risk infants

Promoting preconception use of folic acid

Recruiting men who have sex with men for HIV research

Reducing marijuana and alcohol use among adolescents

Self-help weight management intervention

Tractor rollover protection structure (ROPS) campaign

Andreasen (2006) noted that social marketing as an approach to social change lacks clarity. There are multiple definitions, the field is not well differentiated and lacks academic stature, and there is a lack of appreciation of social marketing at top levels. These observations are based on empirical research from more than 300 personal

> *Social marketing needs to be marketed to major social action groups, both governmental and nongovernmental, so that these groups will seek more social marketing consultants and offer more funding for social marketing campaigns. This will convince marketing students and marketing professionals that they can find a challenging and remunerative career in social marketing.*
>
> —Kotler (2005, p. 147)

interviews, 100 field questionnaires, and two focus groups conducted by Social Marketing Institute researchers.

Social marketing is more effective for behaviors that need to be changed once or only a few times, but is less effective for behaviors that must be repeated and maintained over a period of time (Evans, 2006). Finally, Peattie and Peattie (2003) noted that social marketing depends too much on commercial marketing for its theoretical underpinnings and must formulate its own theoretical basis. They suggested that the four Ps be renamed as follows: social proposition (product), costs (price), accessibility (place), and communication (promotion).

APPLICATION EXERCISE

In this chapter we have provided several examples of applications of the social marketing model. Choose an area that interests you and locate the full text article of that application. You will be able to see how social marketing has been applied in that application. One such example is the study by Rissel and colleagues (2010) who developed, implemented, and evaluated the Cycling Connecting Communities (CCC) project in Sydney, Australia. The project was based on the social marketing model. It utilized various techniques such as organizing bike rides and related events, teaching courses for cycling skills, distributing cycling maps of the area to residents, and covering cycling events in the local press. For evaluation they employed a quasi-experimental design. Pre- and postintervention telephone surveys with an interval of 24 months were administered to experimental group residents in Fairfield and Liverpool and to a demographically similar comparison group in Bankstown. The results demonstrated statistically significant ($p \leq 0.05$) awareness levels of the Cycling Connecting Communities project in the experimental group (13.5%) as compared to the comparison group (8.0%). The rates of cycling in the experimental group (32.9%) were also significantly higher than those in the comparison group (9.7%). The bicycle paths were used more by the experimental group (28.3%) than by the comparison group (16.2%), which was also statistically significant ($p \leq 0.05$). This study shows how a project based on the social marketing model can successfully influence health behaviors.

Locate the full text article of this study and prepare a critique of 250 words.

SKILL-BUILDING ACTIVITY

Let us see how we can apply the social marketing model to the issue of promoting physical activity among middle-aged women. Let us assume that formative research and audience segmentation have identified the target audience as African American women. **Figure 8.2** provides a diagrammatic depiction of the application of social marketing to this example.

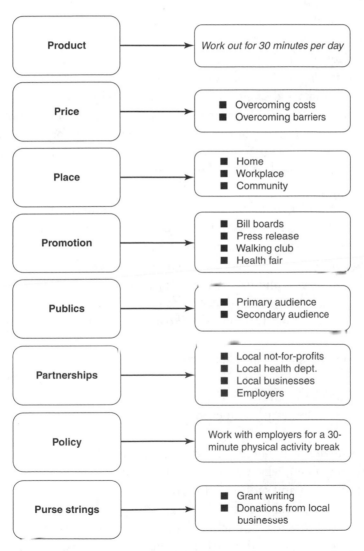

FIGURE 8.2 How the social marketing mix can be used to promote physical activity.

The first construct that needs to be determined is product. We need to articulate a specific behavior, which could be defined as 30 minutes of moderate-intensity physical activity on at least five days a week (preferably all days). Some activities that might appeal to this audience are brisk walking, doing yard work, swimming, riding a bicycle, and dancing. A brief message that could appeal is "Work out for 30 minutes a day." The message would need to be pretested and refined with the members of the target audience.

The second construct that needs to be reified is price. Modification of costs and barriers needs to be done. Some potential costs are time, child care, health club dues, discomfort, and missing a favorite TV show. These could be countered by emphasizing that the activity takes only 30 minutes, initially reimbursing child care costs, offering a subsidized fee for health clubs or finding activities that can be done at home, clarifying that discomfort disappears with regular activity, and designing activities around the TV. Some potential barriers include lack of motivation, lack of skills, having no one to exercise with, and unsafe neighborhoods. These could be countered by having self-rewards, providing free lessons, having participants exercise in pairs or with a peer or a spouse, and stressing that participants should exercise at times and places when it is safe.

The place for giving out the message could be at home through television, newspaper, or the Internet. Or it could be at the workplace through a bulletin board, e-mail, or a supervisor's memo. It could also be community outlets such as a grocery store, shopping mall, church, community center, or doctor's office. Community outlets, especially churches or community centers, are generally good choices for this target audience.

Promotion can be done through a billboard campaign in the community that shows the message "Work out for 30 minutes a day" and the image of an African American woman engaged in physical activity. Additional promotion can be done through a press release for all community outlets, such as newspapers, television channels, and radio shows. In addition, a walking club can be formed and promoted in the community. A community-based event such as a health fair can be used to launch the walking club.

The fifth construct is publics. The primary audience for this campaign would be African American women, who would be targeted with the message. The secondary audience would be peers and spouses, who would need to be mobilized to help participants adhere to the physical activity routine.

To modify the construct of partnership, the organization initiating this program would need to work with local nonprofit agencies, such as the American Heart Association, American Cancer Society, local health department, local businesses, employers, and local gyms. Ideally, a coalition could be formed to which everyone can contribute systematically.

To modify policy, if feasible, the organization can work with employers to allow time for being physically active while at work. For example, a break of 30 minutes can be given to women for walking while they are at the office. The final construct is purse strings, which would involve the organization writing a grant to obtain funding. In-kind donations from local businesses can also be obtained.

Using this approach, you can plan to work on designing a social marketing–based campaign for a health behavior issue in a target audience of your choice. **Table 8.4** provides a set of questions to assist you in shaping the constructs of the social marketing mix.

SUMMARY

Social marketing is the use of commercial marketing techniques to help a target population acquire a beneficial health behavior. Social marketing had its origins in India in the 1960s for promoting the family planning program by marketing condoms. In the United States the approach began to be used in the 1970s; it is at present a useful technique for behavior change.

Social marketing differs from commercial marketing in that social marketing is more demanding, the scrutiny is done from a variety of sources, the idea that is sold is often totally new, and the educational level of the target audience is usually low. Also, social marketing often has to address what people do not want to change, has high involvement between the marketer and the public, and often has invisible benefits or benefits that go to third parties. The rewards offered for making the recommended change are self-rewards, and budgets and the choice of products are limited. A salient concept in social marketing is that of exchange theory, which implies the voluntary transfer or transaction of something valuable between two parties. The benefits to the consumer must be underscored.

Social marketing goes through five steps: (1) planning, (2) message and material development, (3) pretesting, (4) implementation, and (5) evaluation. In planning, audience segmentation and marketing mix are important. In audience segmentation, distinct groups of people who are similar to each other in particular characteristics and are thus likely to respond to messages in a similar way are identified. In marketing mix, the product (behavior), price (costs and barriers), place, and promotion are considered. Social marketing adds a further four Ps: publics, partnership, policy, and purse strings. The social marketing model has been widely applied in health education and health promotion programs.

TABLE 8.4   Shaping the Constructs of the Social Marketing Mix for Health Education Program Planning

1. What should be considered while developing the product?
   - One-time behavior or continuing behavior
   - Low-involvement behavior or high-involvement behavior
   - Individual decision involved in behavior or group decision involved in behavior
   - Creativity of the message
   - Appeal of the message
   - Attractiveness of the message

2. What should be considered while developing the price?
   - Costs
   - Ways to counteract costs
   - Barriers
   - Ways to counteract barriers

3. What should be considered while developing the place?
   - Home avenues
     - Television
     - Newspaper
     - Mail
     - Internet
   - Community avenues
     - Supermarkets
     - Shopping malls
     - Community centers
     - Churches
   - Workplace avenues
     - Bulletin boards
     - E-mail
     - Memos
   - Other avenues

4. What should be considered while developing the promotion?
   - Advertising options
   - Public relations opportunities
   - Promotional avenues
   - Media advocacy opportunities
   - Personal selling options
   - Special events
   - Entertainment events

TABLE 8.4 Shaping the Constructs of the Social Marketing Mix for Health Education Program Planning (*Continued*)

5. What should be considered while developing the publics?
   - Primary audience delineation
   - Secondary audience delineation

6. What should be considered while developing the partnerships?
   - Local health department
   - Local not-for-profit organizations working on same or similar topics
   - Local not-for-profit organizations working with same target audience
   - Local businesses
   - Other

7. What should be considered while developing the policy?
   - Agenda framing
   - Identifying policy makers
   - Opportunities to meet policy makers and legislators
   - Other

8. What should be considered while developing the purse strings?
   - Grant writing
   - Donations from local businesses
   - Selling tangible products
   - Other

IMPORTANT TERMS

audience segmentation	price
exchange theory	product
formative research	promotion
marketing mix	publics
partnership	purse strings
place	social marketing
policy	

REVIEW QUESTIONS

1. Describe the historical genesis of social marketing.
2. Differentiate between social marketing and commercial marketing.
3. Define audience segmentation.

4. Describe the constructs of the social marketing model.
5. Apply the social marketing model to influence a health behavior of your choice.
6. Discuss the limitations of the social marketing model.

WEBSITES TO EXPLORE

Academy for Educational Development

http://www.aed.org/Approaches/SocialMarketing/index.cfm

This is the website of Academy for Education Development, founded in 1961. The academy is a not-for-profit organization dedicated to solving important social problems and building the capacity of individuals, communities, and institutions to become more self-sufficient. The academy works in education, health, and providing economic opportunities for the underserved in the United States and developing countries throughout the world. Various projects by this organization have used social marketing. *Visit this website and read about at least two social marketing projects supported by this organization. What factors contributed to the success of these projects?*

Centers for Disease Control & Prevention (CDC): Health Information Campaigns

http://www.cdc.gov/healthmarketing/

This is the website of the Centers for Disease Control and Prevention (CDC), which documents several health communication campaigns including an appropriate antibiotic use campaign (Get Smart); One Test Two Lives campaign for testing for HIV in pregnancy; Prevention Is Care campaign for preventing transmission by HIV-infected persons;Choose Your Cover campaign, which is a skin cancer prevention and education campaign; and many others. *Read at least two accounts and comment on the extent of the application of the social marketing model.*

Social Marketing.com

http://www.social-marketing.com/

This website is developed and maintained by Nedra Kline Weinreich, the author of *Hands on Social Marketing. A Step-by-Step Guide.* The website links to workshops she conducts, her book, several articles about social marketing, other social marketing and health websites, and her contact information. *Review this website and explore the links mentioned here. Document at least two new ideas you learned about social marketing.*

Social Marketing for Leprosy

http://www.novartisfoundation.org

The website maintained by the Novartis Foundation for Sustainable Development discusses various issues and applications related to social marketing. In the website's search engine type "social marketing" and read several articles including those about leprosy stigma reduction in Sri Lanka and the fight against tuberculosis in Tanzania. *Summarize how social marketing was able to eliminate the stigma associated with leprosy in Sri Lanka.*

Social Marketing Institute

http://www.social-marketing.org/index.html

With a grant from the Robert Wood Johnson Foundation in 1999, the Social Marketing Institute was formed with the mission of advancing the science and practice of social marketing. The institute provides on-site team-based strategic guidance to programs, organizations, businesses, and foundations that apply social marketing approaches; carries out and disseminates research on social marketing best practices; provides training and education in social marketing; sponsors academic research; and provides connections and leadership to social change professionals, commercial marketers, academics, and funders. *Navigate this website and read more about the social marketing success stories of peptic ulcer, the Click It or Ticket campaign, Florida's antismoking campaign, the oral rehydration campaign in Honduras, and many others. Which story did you like most and why?*

Social Marketing Listserver

listproc@listproc.georgetown.edu

This listserv is maintained at Georgetown University by Dr. Alan Andreasen for people with an interest in social marketing. *If you are interested in sharing information, asking questions, or offering comments on social marketing, please feel free to send them to this group.*

REFERENCES

Andreasen, A. A. (1995). *Marketing social change: Changing behavior to promote health, social development, and the environment.* San Francisco: Jossey-Bass.

Andreasen, A. A. (2003). The life trajectory of social marketing. Some implications. *Marketing Theory, 3*(3), 293–303.

Andreasen, A. A. (2006). *Social marketing in the 21st century*. Thousand Oaks, CA: Sage.

Andreasen, A. R., & Kotler, P. (2003). *Strategic marketing for non-profit organizations* (6th ed.). Upper Saddle River, NJ: Prentice-Hall.

Bachar, J. J., Lefler, L. J., Reed, L., McCoy, T., Bailey, R., & Bell, R. (2006). Cherokee Choices: A diabetes prevention program for American Indians. *Preventing Chronic Disease, 3*(3), A103.

Baffour, T. D., Jones, M. A., & Contreras, L. K. (2006). Family health advocacy: An empowerment model for pregnant and parenting African American women in rural communities. *Family and Community Health, 29*(3), 221–228.

Banerji, D. (1986). *Social sciences and health service development in India: Sociology of formation of an alternative paradigm.* New Delhi, India: Lok Paksh.

Bethune, G. R., & Lewis, H. J. (2009). Let's talk about smear tests: Social marketing for the National Cervical Screening Programme. Public Health, 123(Suppl. 1), e17–22.

Bull, S. S., Posner, S. F., Ortiz, C., Beaty, B., Benton, K., Lin, L., et al. (2008). POWER for reproductive health: Results from a social marketing campaign promoting female and male condoms. *The Journal of Adolescent Health*, 43(1), 71–78.

Corrigan, P., & Gelb, B. (2006). Three programs that use mass approaches to challenge the stigma of mental illness. *Psychiatric Services, 57*(3), 393–398.

Crape, B. L., Kenefick, E., Cavalli-Sforza, T., Busch-Hallen, J., Milani, S., & Kanal, K. (2005). Positive impact of a weekly iron-folic acid supplement delivered with social marketing to Cambodian women: Compliance, participation, and hemoglobin levels increase with higher socio-economic status. *Nutrition Reviews, 63*(12, Pt. 2), S134–S138.

De Allegri, M., Marschall, P., Flessa, S., Tiendrebéogo, J., Kouyaté, B., Jahn, A., et al. (2010). Comparative cost analysis of insecticide-treated net delivery strategies: Sales supported by social marketing and free distribution through antenatal care. *Health Policy & Planning, 25*(1), 28–38.

Evans, W. D. (2006). How social marketing works in health care. *British Medical Journal, 332*, 1207–1210.

Flora, J. A., Schooler, C., & Pierseon, R. M. (1997). Effective health promotion among communities of color: The potential of social marketing. In M. E. Goldberg, M. Fishbein, & S. E. Middlestadt (Eds.), *Social marketing: Theoretical and practical perspectives* (pp. 353–373). Mahwah, NJ: Lawrence Erlbaum.

Goossens, H., Guillemot, D., Ferech, M., Schlemmer, B., Costers, M., van Breda, M., et al. (2006). National campaigns to improve antibiotic use. *European Journal of Clinical Pharmacology, 62*(5), 373–379.

Grier, S., & Bryant, C. A. (2005). Social marketing in public health. *Annual Review of Public Health, 26*, 319–339.

Harvey, P. D. (1999). *Let every child be wanted: How social marketing is revolutionizing contraceptive use around the world.* Westport, CT: Auburn House.

Hastings, G., & McDermott, L. M. (2006). Putting social marketing into practice. *British Medical Journal, 332*, 1210–1212.

HEALTHY study group, Hirst, K., Baranowski, T., DeBar, L., Foster, G. D., Kaufman, F., et al. (2009). HEALTHY study rationale, design and methods: Moderating risk of type 2 diabetes in multi-ethnic middle school students. *International Journal of Obesity, 33*(Suppl. 4), S4–S20.

Horn, F. E., Maudryk, J. A., Mackson, J. M., Wutzke, S. E., Weekes, L. M., & Hyndman, R. J. (2006). Measurement of changes in antihypertensive drug utilization following primary care educational interventions. *Pharmacoepidemiology and Drug Safety*. Epub PMID: 16634120

Kotler, P. (2005). *According to Kotler: The world's foremost authority on marketing answers your questions*. New York: American Management Association.

Kotler, P., & Levy, S. J. (1969). Broadening the concept of marketing. *Journal of Marketing, 33*, 10–15.

Kotler, P., & Roberto, E. (1989). *Social marketing: Strategies for changing public behavior*. New York: Free Press.

Kotler, P., & Zaltman, G. (1971). Social marketing: An approach to planned social change. *Journal of Marketing, 35*, 3–12.

Lefebvre, R. C., & Flora, J. A. (1988). Social marketing and public health intervention. *Health Education Quarterly, 15*, 299–315.

Lin, C. A., & Hullman, G. A. (2005). Tobacco-prevention messages online: Social marketing via the Web. *Health Communication, 18*(2), 177–193.

Ludwig, T. D., Buchholz, C., & Clarke, S. W. (2005). Using social marketing to increase the use of helmets among bicyclists. *Journal of American College Health, 54*(1), 51–58.

Marshall, R. J., Bryant, C., Keller, H., & Fridinger, F. (2006). Marketing social marketing: Getting inside those "big dogs' heads" and other challenges. *Health Promotion Practice, 7*, 206–212.

Maxwell, C., Rwegoshora, R., Magesa, S., & Curtis, C. (2006). Comparison of coverage with insecticide-treated nets in a Tanzanian town and villages where nets and insecticide are either marketed or provided free of charge. *Malaria Journal, 5*(1), 44.

Meekers, D., Agha, S., & Klein, M. (2005). The impact on condom use of the "100% Jeune" social marketing program in Cameroon. *Journal of Adolescent Health, 36*(6), 530.

Meekers, D., & Richter, K. (2005). Factors associated with use of the female condom in Zimbabwe. *International Family Planning Perspectives, 31*(1), 30–37.

Millett, C., Zelenyanszki, C., Furlong, C., & Binysh, K. (2005). An evaluation of a social marketing campaign to reduce the number of London women who have never been screened for cervical cancer. *Journal of Medical Screening, 12*(4), 204–205.

Miner, J. W., White, A., Lubenow, A. E., & Palmer, S. (2005). Geocoding and social marketing in Alabama's cancer prevention programs. *Preventing Chronic Disease, 2*, A17.

National Cancer Institute. (2005). *Theory at a glance: A guide for health promotion practice* (2nd ed.). Washington, DC: U.S. Department of Health and Human Services. Retrieved May 20, 2006, from http://www.nci.nih.gov/theory/pdf

Peattie, S., & Peattie, K. (2003). Ready to fly solo? Reducing social marketing's dependency on commercial marketing theory. *Marketing Theory, 3*, 365–385.

Perusco, A., Poder, N., Mohsin, M., Rikard-Bell, G., Rissel, C., Williams, M., et al. (2010). Evaluation of a comprehensive tobacco control project targeting Arabic-speakers residing in south west Sydney, Australia. *Health Promotion International*. Epub ahead of print, PMID: 20189945

Piot, B., Mukherjee, A., Navin, D., Krishnan, N., Bhardwaj, A., Sharma, V., et al. (2010). Lot quality assurance sampling for monitoring coverage and quality of a targeted condom social marketing programme in traditional and non-traditional outlets in India. *Sexually Transmitted Infections, 86*(Suppl. 1), i56–i61.

Quinn, G. P., Hauser, K., Bell-Ellison, B. A., Rodriguez, N. Y., & Frias, J. L. (2006). Promoting pre-conceptional use of folic acid to Hispanic women: A social marketing approach. *Maternal and Child Health Journal, 10*(5), 403–412.

Reger-Nash, B., Fell, P., Spicer, D., Fisher, B. D., Cooper, L., Chey, T., et al. (2006). BC Walks: Replication of a communitywide physical activity campaign. *Preventing Chronic Disease, 3*(3), A90.

Rissel, C. E., New, C., Wen, L. M., Merom, D., Bauman, A. E., & Garrard, J. (2010). The effectiveness of community-based cycling promotion: Findings from the Cycling Connecting Communities project in Sydney, Australia. *The International Journal of Behavioral Nutrition and Physical Activity, 7*(1), 8.

Rothschild, M. L. (1999). Carrots, sticks, and promises: A conceptual framework for the management of public health and social issue behaviors. *Journal of Marketing, 63*, 24–37.

Silvestre, A. J., Hylton, J. B., Johnson, L. M., Houston, C., Witt, M., Jacobson, L., et al. (2006). Recruiting minority men who have sex with men for HIV research: Results from a 4-city campaign. *American Journal of Public Health, 96*(6), 1020–1027.

Sinclair, C., & Foley, P. (2009). Skin cancer prevention in Australia. *British Journal of Dermatology, 161*(Suppl. 3), 116–123.

Slater, M. D., Kelly, K. J., Edwards, R. W., Thurman, P. J., Plested, B. A., Keefe, T. J., et al. (2006). Combining in-school and community-based media efforts: Reducing marijuana and alcohol uptake among younger adolescents. *Health Education Research, 21*(1), 157–167.

Social Marketing Institute. (2006). *Success stories.* Retrieved July 10, 2006, from http://www.social-marketing.org/success.html

Sorensen, J. A., Jenkins, P., Bayes, B., Clark, S., & May, J. J. (2010). Cost-effectiveness of a ROPS social marketing campaign. *Journal of Agricultural Safety and Health, 16*(1), 31–40.

Staten, L. K., Birnbaum, A. S., Jobe, J. B., & Elder, J. P. (2006). A typology of middle school girls: Audience segmentation related to physical activity. *Health Education and Behavior, 33*(1), 66–80.

Stephens, S. C., Bernstein, K. T., McCright, J. E., & Klausner, J. D. (2010). Dogs Are Talking: San Francisco's social marketing campaign to increase syphilis screening. *Sexually Transmitted Diseases, 37*(3), 173–176.

Thackeray, R., & Brown, K. M. (2005). Social marketing's unique contributions to health promotion practice. *Health Promotion Practice, 6*, 365–368.

Thapa, S., Prasad, C. V., Rao, P. H., Severy, L. J., & Rao, S. R. (1994). Social marketing of condoms in India. *Advances in Population: Psychosocial Perspective, 2*, 171–204.

Tufano, J. T., & Karras, B. T. (2005). Mobile eHealth interventions for obesity: A timely opportunity to leverage convergence trends. *Journal of Medical Internet Research, 7*(5), e58.

Vega, M. Y., & Roland, E. L. (2005). Social marketing techniques for public health communication: A review of syphilis awareness campaigns in 8 U.S. cities. *Sexually Transmitted Diseases, 32*(Suppl. 10), S30–S36.

Verrall, T., Napash, L., Leclerc, L., Mercure, S., & Gray-Donald, K. (2006). Community-based communication strategies to promote infant iron nutrition in northern Canada. *International Journal of Circumpolar Health, 65*(1), 65–78.

Weinreich, N. K. (1999). *Hands on social marketing: A step-by-step guide*. Thousand Oaks, CA: Sage.

Wiebe, G. D. (1951-1952). Merchandising commodities and citizenship on television. *Public Opinion Quarterly, 15*, 679–691.

Williams, P. G., Dewapura, D., Gunawardene, P., & Settinayake, S. (1998). Social marketing to eliminate leprosy in Sri Lanka. *Social Marketing Quarterly, 4*(4), 27–31.

Young, L., Anderson, J., Beckstrom, L., Bellows, L., & Johnson, S. L. (2004). Using social marketing principles to guide the development of a nutrition education initiative for preschool-aged children. *Journal of Nutrition Education and Behavior, 36*(5), 250–257.

CHAPTER 9

Diffusion of Innovations

AFTER READING THIS CHAPTER YOU SHOULD BE ABLE TO

- Describe the historical genesis of the diffusion of innovations theory
- List the constructs of the diffusion of innovations theory
- Summarize the applications of the diffusion of innovations theory in public health
- Identify methods to modify constructs from the diffusion of innovations theory
- Apply the diffusion of innovations theory for changing a health behavior of your choice

The diffusion of innovations theory is a model that has been thoroughly tested. The term **diffusion** refers to the process by which a new idea, object, or practice filters through various channels in a community over time (Rogers, 2003). It is a special form of communication in which the idea that is being conveyed is new. The term **innovations** refers to the new ideas, objects, or practices that are to be adopted. The hallmark of the diffusion of innovations theory is that it deals with the dissemination of new ideas and their adoption by people in a systematic manner. In addition, diffusion of innovations theory is a tool for social change. Once a new idea is infused into a community, change becomes inevitable.

This chapter begins by describing the historical aspects of the genesis of the diffusion of innovations theory. We then describe the approach taken by the diffusion of innovations theory and the various constructs that make up this theory. We discuss the applications of the diffusion of innovations theory in public health and the limitations of the theory, and then present a skill-building application.

> *Communication is essential for social change. . . . Social change is the process by which alteration occurs in the structure and function of a social system. National revolution, invention of a new manufacturing technique, founding of a village improvement council, adoption of birth control methods by a family—all are examples of social change.*
>
> —Rogers and Shoemaker (1971, p. 7)

HISTORICAL PERSPECTIVE

The diffusion of innovations theory can be traced back to the early 1900s, when Gabriel Tarde, a French sociologist and legal scholar, wrote *The Laws of Imitation* (Tarde, 1903/1969), which looked at factors that helped innovations spread. He used the term *imitation*, which is similar to the present-day term *adoption* (Rogers, 2003), to describe how innovations were accepted. Georg Simmel, a German philosopher and sociologist who was a contemporary of Tarde, introduced the notion of a *stranger*, who is a member of a system but not strongly attached to it. This concept was used later on in diffusion of innovations theory. Tarde's and Simmel's propositions were followed by the work of anthropologist Clark Wissler (1923), who studied the diffusion of horses from Spanish explorers to American Indian tribes in the Plains. Wissler found that the introduction of horses caused the peaceful Indian tribes to go to war with neighboring tribes.

Empirical work with the diffusion of innovations theory began with a hybrid seed corn study conducted by rural sociologists Bryce Ryan and Neal Gross at Iowa State University (Ryan & Gross, 1943; Valente & Rogers, 1995). Hybrid seeds were developed in 1928. Their use increases a harvest by more than 20%, yet only a small number of farmers initially adopted the hybrid corn. Full diffusion of this innovation took almost 12 years, with the average farmer taking 7 years to progress from initial awareness to full-scale adoption of planting the whole field with hybrid seed. The main dependent variable was innovativeness (the degree to which an individual adopts early as compared with others). The cumulative number of farmers adopting the hybrid corn plotted against time formed an S-shaped curve; when plotted on a frequency basis, it formed a normal bell-shaped curve. Mass media were found to be important in the awareness stage, whereas interpersonal communication was more important at the persuasion stage (Rogers & Singhal, 1996).

Throughout the 1940s and 1950s, the diffusion of innovations theory was popular in rural sociology. In the 1950s, Everett Rogers, while pursuing his doctoral studies in rural sociology at Iowa State, became interested in the diffusion theory and worked on his dissertation in that area. In 1962, he wrote the *Diffusion of Innovations*; at that time there were 405 publications on this theory (Rogers, 2004). In 2003, when the fifth edition of this book was published, more than 5200 applications of this theory had been published in various fields (Rogers, 2003). Interested readers may consult this book for detailed information on this theory. Everett Rogers is the foremost authority on this theory and teaches at the University of New Mexico.

The applications of the diffusion of innovations theory in public health, health promotion, and health education began with immunization campaigns and family planning programs. From the 1960s onward, the diffusion of innovations theory was used to speed up the adoption of family planning methods in Latin America, Africa, and Asia. Recent impetus for applying the diffusion of innovations theory in public health has come from the HIV/AIDS epidemic. In the mid-1980s, the STOP AIDS intervention based on the diffusion of innovations theory was implemented and tested in San Francisco (Rogers & Shefner-Rogers, 1999). One of the components of this intervention was to identify opinion leaders who were bartenders at gay bars and train them in HIV prevention among gay men. This approach is now being evaluated in developing countries. In 2000, Malcolm Gladwell wrote *The Tipping Point: How Little Things Can Make a Big Difference*, in which he defined the "tipping point" as the moment when something unique becomes common. This is the purpose of the diffusion of innovations.

> *The diffusion model has now been around for a long time, almost 60 years. Is diffusion dead or dying? It is not declining. The number of diffusion publications completed per year continues to hold steady. Unlike most models of human behavior that begin to fade after some years of use, the diffusion model continues to attract strong interest from scholars.*
>
> —Rogers (2004, p. 19)

CONSTRUCTS OF THE DIFFUSION OF INNOVATIONS THEORY

An **innovation** refers to an idea, practice, or product (including services) that is perceived as new by an individual or other unit of adoption (Rogers, 2003). It does not matter how long this idea, practice, or product has been around. What matters is that the person who is adopting it *perceives* it as new. The newness of an innovation can be with regard to knowledge, persuasion, or the decision to adopt. Newness regarding knowledge refers to the situation in which the potential adopter was not previously aware of the product, practice, or idea. Newness regarding persuasion refers to the situation in which the potential adopter has not been previously contacted by anyone about the product, practice, or idea. Finally, newness regarding the decision to adopt pertains to the situation in which the potential adopter has not formed a positive or negative attitude about using the product, practice, or idea. Innovations are of three types: (1) *incremental innovations*, which reflect a relatively small improvement over previous products; (2) *distinctive innovations*, which represent significant improvement but do not entail any new technology or approach; and (3) *breakthrough innovations*, which are based on a new technology or approach (Schumann, Prestwood, Tong, & Vanston, 1994).

Innovations have several attributes (Frerichs, 1994; Greenhalgh, Robert, Bate, Macfarlane, & Kyriakidou, 2005; Rogers, 2003; Tornatzky & Klein, 1982). See **Table 9.1** for additional information on the attributes described here:

- **Perceived relative advantage**: Perception regarding how much better the new product, idea, or practice is than the one it will replace
- **Compatibility**: Perception of the innovation's consistency with the values, past experiences, and needs of potential adopters
- **Complexity**: Perception of the degree of difficulty in understanding and using the new idea, practice, or product
- **Demonstrability**: The degree to which an innovation may be experimented with on a limited basis
- **Clarity of results**: The degree to which outcomes of an innovation are clearly visible
- **Costs**: The tangible and intangible expenses incurred in the adoption of a new idea, practice, or product
- **Reversibility**: The ability and degree to which the status quo can be reinstated by ceasing to use the innovation
- **Pervasiveness**: The degree to which an innovation requires changes or adjustments by other elements in the social system
- **Reinvention**: The degree to which a potential adopter can adapt, refine, or modify the innovation to suit his or her needs

These characteristics of innovations usually serve as independent variables in studies using this theory (Wolfe, 1994).

The second construct of the diffusion of innovations theory is **communication channels** (Rogers, 2003). These are the links between those who possess know-how regarding the innovation and those who have not yet adopted that innovation. They are the means by which messages are transferred between individuals. Communication

TABLE 9.1 Key Attributes of Innovations		
Attribute	**Definition**	**How to Modify?**
Perceived relative advantage	The perception regarding how much better the new product, idea, or practice is than the one it will replace	Increase the perception that the innovation is advantageous in monetary terms, social terms, or other respect.
Compatibility	The perception of the innovation's consistency with the values, past experiences, and needs of potential adopters	Make the idea consistent with the prevalent norms and values.
Complexity	The perception of the degree of difficulty in understanding and using the new idea, practice, or product	Simplify the idea, practice, or product.
Demonstrability	The degree to which an innovation may be experimented with on a limited basis	Provide an opportunity to try the idea, practice, or product either in small units or in total.
Clarity of results	The degree to which outcomes of an innovation are clearly visible	Disseminate information on the results of the innovation and make it more visible.
Costs	The tangible and intangible expenses incurred in the adoption of a new idea, practice, or product	Minimize costs as far as possible.
Reversibility	The ability and degree to which the status quo can be reinstated by ceasing to use the innovation	Make innovations reversible.
Pervasiveness	The degree to which an innovation requires changes or adjustments by other elements in the social system	Minimize changes in other parts.
Reinvention	The degree to which a potential adopter can adapt, refine, or modify the innovation to suit his or her needs	Allow for modification(s) by the user.

channels are of three kinds: (1) *mass media channels*, such as television, radio, and newspapers; (2) *interpersonal channels*, which require face-to-face interaction between two or more individuals; and (3) *interactive communication channels*, such as the Internet. Mass media channels are the swiftest, reach a large number of people, and are especially advantageous in building awareness or knowledge about the innovation. Interpersonal channels are especially helpful in persuading a potential adopter. Therefore, in the initial stages of adoption one should use mass media channels, followed by interpersonal and interactive channels to reinforce the message and persuade the potential adopter.

The third construct of the diffusion of innovations theory is **time** (Rogers, 2003), which refers to the interval between becoming aware of an idea and adopting the idea. This can take from days to years, depending on the innovation. The time construct is involved with diffusion of innovations in three ways: (1) the innovation-decision process, (2) adopter categories, and (3) rate of adoption (Rogers, 2003). The *innovation-decision process* is a five-step process:

1. Gaining knowledge about the innovation
2. Being persuaded about the innovation
3. Deciding whether to adopt or reject the innovation
4. Implementing the innovation (putting it to use)
5. Confirming step: either reversing the decision or adopting the innovation

Adopter categories indicate people's willingness to adopt an innovation and have a bell-shaped distribution. The initial adopters are the innovators (2.5%), people who adopt quickly. Innovators by nature are adventurous, cosmopolitan, have geographically dispersed contacts, are high risk takers, and have a high tolerance for uncertainty and failure. The second category consists of the early adopters (13.5%). Early adopters are well-respected opinion leaders and well-integrated and judicious individuals. The early-majority category (34%) consists of people who are deliberate, highly connected within a peer system, and are ahead of the average. These adopters are followed by the late majority (34%). Late-majority adopters are skeptical, responsive to economic necessity, responsive to social norms, have limited economic resources, and have a low tolerance for uncertainty. The final group are the laggards (16%). Laggards are more traditional in their disposition, are relatively isolated, have precarious economic situations, and are suspicious of change.

The *rate of adoption* refers to the speed with which an innovation is adopted. If we plot the cumulative frequency against time, an S-shaped curve is obtained, which is the rate of adoption (**Figure 9.1**). The diffusion rate usually serves as the dependent variable in studies using the diffusion of innovations theory (Wolfe, 1994).

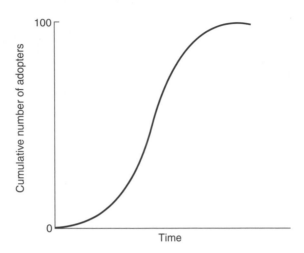

FIGURE 9.1   The S-shaped curve of diffusion.

The fourth construct of the diffusion of innovations theory is the **social system** (Berwick, 2003; Rogers, 2003). A social system implies people in a society connected by a common goal and is composed of individuals, groups, organizations, or communities. An important aspect of the social system is how similar the group members are. Similarity among group members is called **homophily**. Innovations spread faster among homophilous groups (Cain & Mitman, 2002; Rogers, 2003). Hence, to enhance the rate of diffusion of an innovation, identify the degree of homophily in the target audience and use homophilous agents to spread the message.

Another aspect of the social system is the use of **social networks**, which are person-centered webs of social relationships (Heaney & Israel, 2002) that provide friendship, advice, communication, and support (Valente, 1996). Social networks can be physical or virtual (i.e., in the cyberworld). The configuration of social networks through which innovations diffuse governs the pace and extent of diffusion. For example, in the 1960s, studies showed that diffusion of the practice of tetracycline prescription occurred faster among physicians with denser social networks than for isolated physicians (Cain & Mitman, 2002). To hasten diffusion, identify and utilize physical and virtual networks and create new networks.

The third aspect of the social system is the **change agent**, an individual who influences a potential adopter's decision about innovation in a favorable way (Haider &

Kreps, 2004). An example of a change agent might be a health educator at a health department. The change agent must be used to favorably influence the decision. The fourth aspect of social systems is **opinion leaders**, individuals who are influential in a community and sway the beliefs and actions of their colleagues in either a positive or negative direction (Locock, Dopson, Chambers, & Gabbay, 2001). These are individuals who have greater exposure to new ideas through the media, have greater social participation, have higher social status, and are more innovative (Rogers & Shoemaker, 1971). To hasten diffusion, identify true opinion leaders and involve them in the campaign. Opinion leaders have been used in heart health trials, such as the Stanford five-city project (Farquahar et al., 1990) and the North Karelia project (Puska et al., 1986).

These characteristics of the social system usually serve as independent variables in studies using this theory (Wolfe, 1994). **Table 9.2** summarizes the key constructs of the diffusion of innovations theory, along with ways to modify them.

To apply these constructs of the diffusion of innovations theory for health programming, Dearing (2004) has suggested a nine-step process. The first step is selecting the topic, in which the area of concern with high societal need and fewer previous programs is selected. Next is identifying the program population, in which the target population is selected. The third step is deriving a sample of best practices, in which the best existing products pertaining to the topic are identified. The fourth step is identifying intermediary networks. In this step, potential adopters are identified; there must be existing communication within this network. The fifth step is identifying opinion leaders in the intermediary network. Opinion leaders, as we have seen, are individuals who are influential in a community. They can be identified by sociometric questionnaires (in which respondents characterize their relations with others in the network), participant observation, expert interviews, or self-reports. Opinion leaders typically consist of 5 to 6% of the network membership. The sixth step is collecting pretest data, such as characteristics of members of the community and pretest opinions about the product. The next step is creation of a decision support tool, in which potential adopters can assess alternative best-practice products. The eighth step is to set up research design conditions, in which network members can be assigned to different conditions in which different variables are manipulated. The final step is posttest measurement, in which a posttest similar to the pretest can be administered and the rate of adoption in different conditions calculated. **Table 9.3** summarizes these steps.

A similar model for the diffusion of innovations theory in public health organizations, FOMENT, has been suggested by Muhiuddin Haider of George Washington

TABLE 9.2   Key Constructs of the Diffusion of Innovations Theory

Construct	Definition	How to Modify?
Innovation	An idea, practice, or product (including services) that is perceived as new by an individual or other unit of adoption	Increase the perception that innovation is advantageous in monetary terms, social terms, or in other respects. Make the idea consistent with the prevalent norms and values. Simplify the idea, practice, or product. Provide opportunity to try the idea, practice, or product either in small units or in total. Disseminate information on results of the innovation and make it more visible. Minimize costs as far as possible. Make innovations reversible. Minimize changes in other parts of the social system. Allow for modification(s) by the user.
Communication channels	The link between those who have know-how regarding the innovation and those who have not yet adopted the innovation	Use mass media for building awareness. Use interpersonal channels for persuasion.
Time	The interval between becoming aware of an idea and adopting the idea	Facilitate adoption over time.
Social system	People in a society connected by a common goal	Facilitate adoption from person to person. Use homophilous agents to spread the message. Use social networks. Use change agents. Use opinion leaders.

TABLE 9.3	Steps for Applying the Diffusion of Innovations Theory for Health Programming

1. Select the topic.

2. Identify the program population.

3. Derive a sample of best practices.

4. Identify intermediary networks.

5. Identify opinion leaders in the intermediary network.

6. Collect pretest data.

7. Create a decision support tool.

8. Set up research design conditions.

9. Measure the rate of adoption and participants' opinions posttest.

University (Haider & Kreps, 2004). FOMENT is an acronym in which *F* stands for *focus* on a specific behavior change; *O* for *organization* of the behavior change program; *M* for *management*, which supports and approves the behavior change program; *E* for an *environment* that is conducive to behavior change; *N* for a *network* to diffuse innovations at the individual and organizational levels; and *T* for the *technology* available to diffuse innovations.

> *Improving the application of the Diffusion of Innovations model in the field of public health can lead to advances in health promotion and disease prevention on a global level.*
>
> —Haider and Kreps (2004, p. 3)

APPLICATIONS OF THE DIFFUSION OF INNOVATIONS THEORY

The diffusion of innovations theory has been used in a variety of applications in public health, health promotion, and health education. Most of the published studies on the diffusion of innovations theory use cross-sectional surveys of adopters done after they have adopted the innovation and pertain to a single innovation (Meyer, 2004). Some examples of the application of this theory for public health are adopting and implementing a picture archiving communication system (PACS) in hospitals (Pare & Trudel, 2007); adopting novel medication regimes for diabetes management (De Civita & Dasgupta, 2007; Pugh, Anderson, Pogach, & Berlowitz, 2003); adopting telemedicine in rural areas (Helitzer, Heath, Maltrud, Sullivan, & Alverson, 2003); designing Students Together Against Negative Decisions (STAND), a peer educator training curriculum for sexual risk reduction (Smith, Dane, Archer, Devereaux, & Katner, 2000; Smith & DiClemente, 2000); enriching a gerontology curriculum (Dorfman & Murty, 2005); implementing change strategy for primary care treatment of depression (Dietrich et al., 2004); implementing computerized provider order entry (CPOE) in the outpatient setting (Ash et al., 2006); implementing family planning in developing countries (Murphy, 2004; Sharma & Sharma, 1996; Vaughan & Rogers, 2000); implementing health counseling intervention in the cardiology outpatient clinic (Harting et al., 2005); implementing the National Quality Measurement and Reporting System (NQMRS) (McGlynn, 2003); implementing patient education in community pharmacies (Pronk, Blom, Jonkers, & Van Burg, 2001); implementing a sun protection program (Buller et al., 2005); implementing technology implementation systems to promote patient safety (Karsh, 2004); implementing telehomecare technology in community care (Hebert & Korabek, 2004); incorporating genomic medicine into primary care (Suther & Goodson, 2004); increasing Internet use by family physicians (Chew, Grant, & Tote, 2004); interpreting primary care physicians attitude regarding rotavirus immunization (Agyeman et al., 2009); predicting radon testing (Peterson & Howland, 1996); predicting smoking cessation (Deprey et al., 2009; Kuntsche & Gmel, 2005); reducing the spread of sexually transmitted diseases and HIV infection (Backer & Rogers, 1998; Bertrand, 2004; Valente & Fosados, 2006; Swendeman & Rotheram-Borus, 2010); translating research on diabetes self-management interventions into practice (Leeman, Jackson, & Sandelowski, 2006); using acetylcholinesterase inhibitors in Alzheimer's disease (Ruof, Mittendorf, Pirk, & von der Schulenburg, 2002); using decision support systems (DSS) by child welfare workers (Foster & Stiffman, 2009); using patient-driven computers in primary care services (Shakeshaft & Frankish, 2003); and using voodoo practitioners in Haiti to educate people about HIV/AIDS (Barker, 2004). **Table 9.4** summarizes these applications.

> *Examples of potentially constructive innovations in health care can be as simple as ensuring that an improved drug regimen published in a refereed journal article immediately becomes the norm in a practice group, or as complex as redesigning an entire scheduling system to better conform to sound principles from queuing theory.*
>
> —Berwick (2003, p. 1969)

LIMITATIONS OF THE DIFFUSION OF INNOVATIONS THEORY

The diffusion of innovations theory has been in existence for quite some time and has been tested empirically and refined. It offers several advantages in guiding the adoption of something that is novel or new. However, like all other models and theories, this approach has some limitations. In health promotion and education, there are few real innovations (Tornatzky & Fleischer, 1990). People often know about the issues

TABLE 9.4   Applications of the Diffusion of Innovations Theory in Public Health

Adopting and implementing a picture archiving communication system (PACS) in hospitals

Adopting novel medication regimens for diabetes management

Adopting telemedicine in rural areas

Designing Students Together Against Negative Decisions (STAND), a peer educator training curriculum for sexual risk reduction

Enriching a gerontology curriculum

Implementing change strategy for primary care treatment of depression

Implementing computerized provider order entry (CPOE) in the outpatient setting

Implementing family planning in developing countries

Implementing health counseling intervention in the cardiology outpatient clinic

Implementing a National Quality Measurement and Reporting System (NQMRS)

Implementing patient education in community pharmacies

Implementing a sun protection program

Implementing technology implementation systems to promote patient safety

Implementing telehomecare technology in community care

Incorporating genomic medicine into primary care

Increasing Internet use by family physicians

Interpreting primary care physicians attitude regarding rotavirus immunization
Predicting radon testing

Predicting smoking cessation

Reducing the spread of sexually transmitted diseases and HIV infection

Translating research on diabetes self-management interventions into practice

Using acetylcholinesterase inhibitors in Alzheimer's disease

Using decision support systems (DSS) by child welfare workers

Using patient-driven computers in primary care services

Using voodoo practitioners in Haiti to educate people about HIV/AIDS and may have tried the behavior. For example, almost all smokers know that smoking is injurious to their health, and many have tried to quit. So quitting is not an innovation for them. Use of the diffusion of innovations theory is challenging in these circumstances.

Public health interventions are preventive in nature, whereby the individual has to adopt the new idea today to avoid the likelihood of a negative consequence occurring at a later date. For example, a smoker would need to quit smoking today to prevent development of lung cancer 20 or so years later. Such a long interval poses special challenges, and diffusion occurs more slowly (Rogers, 2002). It needs to be kept in mind that diffusion of innovations in health is a complex process that occurs at multiple levels, across many different settings, and utilizes different strategies (Oldenburg & Parcel, 2002; Parcel, Perry, & Taylor, 1990).

Oftentimes in health promotion and health education, the interventions are designed for lower socioeconomic groups, people with low literacy levels, and other vulnerable community members. The adoption and diffusion process is easier and smoother in the wealthier and more highly educated populations than in the vulnerable populations, which present a number of challenges and barriers. As a consequence, the gap between the haves and the have-nots widens even further.

Another issue with the diffusion of innovations theory is pro-innovation bias (Rogers, 2003). This refers to the preconception that an innovation should be diffused and adopted by all members of society in a rapid manner without rejection or reinvention. This is often not possible with many health promotion and education objectives. For example, it is virtually impossible at present to think that no one will smoke or that everyone will engage in 30 minutes of physical activity every day. Rogers (2003) suggested conducting research while the innovation is still being adopted rather than waiting for it to be completely adopted, studying unsuccessful innovations and examining the broader context in which an innovation diffuses.

> *Diffusion is a multifaceted perspective about social change. Scholars dating at least to Georg Simmel and Gabriel Tarde 100 years ago theorized about imitative behavior at the level of small groups and within communities, and the relation between these micro-level processes to macro-level social change in which sectors, networks, and cities change.*
>
> —Dearing (2004, p. 24)

Finally, Nutley, Davies, and Walter (2002) have talked about the limitations of focusing on linear-stage models of decision making with the diffusion of innovations theory. Seldom does the adoption of innovation follow a linear path as suggested in the theory. Often the path is uneven, and results that fit the S-shaped curve are not achieved (Chattoe & Gilbert, 1997; Mohr, 1987; Rosegger, 1996). Hence Nutley, Davies, and Walter (2002) advocate a nonlinear, dynamic process that pays more attention to systemic context and norms. In this regard, Westarp (2003) has suggested relational and structural models. Relational models analyze how direct contacts between participants in networks influence the decision to adopt or not adopt an innovation, whereas structural models focus on the pattern of all relationships and show how the structural characteristics of a social system determine the diffusion process.

APPLICATION EXERCISE

In this chapter, we have introduced several applications of the diffusion of innovations model in public health. Choose any area that interests you and locate the full text article of that application to see how the model has been used. One such application is by Deprey and colleagues (2009), who have described the activities of the Oregon Tobacco Quit Line (OTQL). The *innovation* that the project had was the Nicotine patch. They distributed a two-week starter kit of this patch free of charge to their callers for $2\frac{1}{2}$ months (*time*). The *communication channels* they used were radio programs, word of mouth, e-mails, and letters to public and private sector partners. The *social systems* they tapped were health plans, local policy makers, media sources, and referral sources such as health care providers. Some of the outcomes of the intervention were increased media attention, a 12 times increase in calls to the program, and a reach to 1.3% of the smokers.

Read the full text article and prepare a critique of 250 words on this application.

SKILL-BUILDING ACTIVITY

Let us see how we can apply the diffusion of innovations theory in health education and health promotion. Currently in the profession of health education and health promotion, the National Commission for Health Education Credentialing (NCHEC) provides a certification system. Other professions, such as physicians, nurses, and dietitians, are registered practitioners. Let us assume we want to start the innovation of "registered health educators."

In applying the diffusion of innovations theory, we would first look at the construct of innovation and its attributes. The first attribute is perceived relative advantage. For all existing and prospective health educators, this innovation should seem advantageous. Employers could be convinced to give a nominal raise to those who become registered health educators, thus providing a monetary advantage. The social status that comes with being a registered member of the profession would need to be underscored. The ability to write the credential RHEd with one's name would need to be marketed. The second attribute is compatibility. This innovation is in direct synchrony with the previous innovation of Certified Health Education Specialist (CHES) and should build on that to be successful. The third attribute is that of complexity. The process should be similar to that of becoming a CHES, and thus not very complex. The simpler the process, the better its chances of adoption. The fourth attribute, demonstrability, would not be possible with this innovation. The fifth attribute is that of clarity of results. The results of several years of success with CHES and with registration in other disciplines could be shared. The sixth attribute is costs, which would have to be kept at a nominal rate similar to that involved with CHES. The seventh attribute of reversibility would be easy: a person who does not want to be registered would simply abstain from paying the annual dues. The eighth attribute is that of pervasiveness. To influence this attribute, employers would need to make adjustments by endorsing the idea of registered health educators and mandating that only such individuals be hired in health education jobs. The ninth attribute, reinvention, does not apply to this innovation.

The second construct is that of communication channels. Mass mailing of information about the innovation (registration for health educators) would need to be sent to existing CHES practitioners, the 258 institutions of higher education that award degrees in health education, and all major employers who hire health educators (e.g., county health departments, state health departments, major hospitals, major school systems, and large companies with health and wellness units). Interpersonal communication using people who have adopted the innovation would also need to be done. A website detailing the innovation would need to be set up.

The third construct is that of time. The flow of time would involve the five-step process of providing knowledge about the innovation, persuading health educators about the innovation, helping health educators decide about the innovation, starting the first batch of registered health educators, and then confirming their continuation as registered health educators. A count of people adopting the innovation can be kept so that a rate of adoption curve can be plotted.

The fourth construct is that of the social system. The first aspect of the social system is homophily. Health educators comprise diverse groups. Thus the first task would be to decrease the diversity and make the innovation appeal to the common attributes of all health educators. The second aspect is social networks. Health educators who have adopted the innovation can be used to spread the message to other health educators. The electronic network of health educators (HEDIR) can also be used in this process. The third aspect of the social system is the change agent. The leadership at the National Commission for Health Education Credentialing should take up the task of coordinating and sending the necessary information and becoming change agents. The fourth aspect of the social system is opinion leaders, who would be composed of supervisors at workplaces and department chairs at the various institutions of higher education.

Using this approach, you can plan to work on spreading any innovation using the diffusion of innovations theory. **Table 9.5** provides a set of questions to consider when setting up your plan.

TABLE 9.5   Shaping Constructs of the Diffusion of Innovations Theory for Health Education Program Planning

1. What should be considered while developing the innovation?
   - Increase perceived relative advantage
   - Increase compatibility
   - Decrease complexity
   - Give opportunity for demonstrability
   - Show clarity of results
   - Minimize costs
   - Allow for reversibility
   - Work on factors affecting pervasiveness
   - Allow for reinvention

2. What should be considered while developing the communication channels?
   - Mass media
   - Interpersonal
   - Interactive

3. What should be considered while developing the time?
   - Innovation-decision process
   - Rate of adoption
   - Adopter categories

4. What should be considered while developing the social system?
   - Homophily
   - Social networks
   - Change agents
   - Opinion leaders

SUMMARY

The diffusion of innovations theory deals with adoption of a new idea, practice, or object over a period of time. The origins of this theory are almost 100 years old, but the first empirical study was done by Bryce Ryan and Neal Gross at Iowa State University with hybrid corn seed in the 1940s. They studied the adoption process and the characteristics of the farmers who adopted the hybrid corn seed. Their work had implications not only in agriculture but also for a variety of disciplines, including health promotion and health education.

The four main constructs of the diffusion of innovations theory are innovation, communication channels, time, and social system. Several attributes of innovation are perceived relative advantage (perception about how much better the new product, idea, or practice is than the one it will replace), compatibility (the perception regarding the innovation's consistency with the values, past experiences, and needs of potential adopters), complexity (the perception of the degree of difficulty in understanding and using the new idea, practice, or product), demonstrability (the degree to which an innovation may be experimented with on a limited basis), clarity of results (the degree to which the outcomes of an innovation are clearly visible), costs (the tangible and intangible expenses incurred in the adoption of a new idea, practice, or product), reversibility (the ability and degree to which the status quo can be reinstated by ceasing to use the innovation), pervasiveness (the degree to which an innovation requires changes or adjustments by other elements in the social system), and reinvention (the degree to which a potential adopter can adapt, refine, or modify the innovation to suit his or her needs).

The communication channels are of three kinds: (1) mass media channels, such as television, radio, and newspapers; (2) interpersonal channels, which require face-to-face interaction between two or more individuals; and (3) interactive communication channels, such as the Internet.

The time construct is involved with the diffusion of innovations in three ways: (1) the innovation-decision process, (2) adopter categories, and (3) rate of adoption. The social system construct comprises homophily (similarity among group members), social networks (person-centered webs of social relationships), change agents (people who influence a potential adopter's decision about innovation in a favorable way), and opinion leaders (influential individuals in a community who sway the beliefs and actions of their colleagues in either a positive or negative direction). The diffusion of innovations theory has been widely applied in public health.

IMPORTANT TERMS

change agent
clarity of results
communication channels
compatibility
complexity
costs
demonstrability
diffusion
homophily

innovation
opinion leaders
perceived relative advantage
pervasiveness
reinvention
reversibility
social networks
social system
time

REVIEW QUESTIONS

1. Describe the historical genesis of the diffusion of innovations theory.
2. Discuss any five attributes of innovations.
3. What does the acronym FOMENT mean in the context of diffusion of innovations?
4. Describe the four constructs of the diffusion of innovations theory.
5. Discuss the limitations of the diffusion of innovations theory.
6. Apply the diffusion of innovations theory for spreading any innovation of your choice.

WEBSITES TO EXPLORE

CORE Diffusion of Innovations Initiative

http://www.coregroup.org/our-technical-work/initiatives/diffusion-of-innovations

This is the website of CORE Group, a membership association of international nongovernmental organizations (NGOs) that promotes and improves the health of children and women in developing countries through collaborative NGO action and learning. This website presents some applications of diffusion of innovations theory, including a practical guide for Africa on Vitamin A supplementation, a guide for community-based volunteer health educators, the partnership defined quality (PDQ) approach, a barrier analysis manual, a Census-Based, Impact-Oriented (CBIO) approach, and a safe motherhood program. *Review this website and read more about each of these six interventions. Which one interested you most and why?*

Diffusion of Innovations and Outreach

http://nnlm.gov/archive/pnr/eval/rogers.html

This website presents an article by Everett M. Rogers and Karyn L. Scott titled, "The Diffusion of Innovations Model and Outreach from the National Network of Libraries of Medicine to Native American Communities," which was written in 1997. The article summarizes lessons from 300 outreach projects. *Review this website and comment on outreach models and outreach strategies.*

Emergent Themes in the Sustainability of Primary Health Care Innovation

http://www.mja.com.au/public/issues/183_10_211105/sib10729_fm.html

This website synthesizes the findings of five studies of sustainability of primary health care innovation across six domains (political, institutional, financial, economic, client, and workforce). Three major themes emerge from their analysis. *Review these three themes. What can you say about generalization for diffusion of innovations from this review?*

Internet Use Among Doctors

http://www.stfm.org/fmhub/fm2004/October/Fiona645.pdf

This website presents a study by Chew and colleagues (2004) regarding the adoption of Internet use by family physicians using the diffusion of innovations theory. It summarizes the results about a survey of family physicians with regard to their Internet use and various strategies to increase the use. *Read this study and comment on how family physicians incorporate the Internet in their practice.*

Milbank Quarterly Article

http://www.milbank.org/quarterly/8204feat.html

This website summarizes an article that addressing the question, "How can we spread and sustain innovations in health service delivery and organization?" The article describes both the content and the process used in arriving at the conclusions. *Read the article and identify key factors for sustaining innovations in health service organizations.*

National Aeronautics and Space Administration (NASA) Library

http://www.hq.nasa.gov/office/hqlibrary/ppm/ppm39.htm

The NASA headquarters library website summarizes articles and technical reports, books, and Internet sources on diffusion of innovations theory. The website was organized in 2000. *Review this website and locate a source or Internet site. Read and summarize what you learned.*

National Center for the Study of Adult Learning & Literacy (NCSALL)

http://www.ncsall.net/?id=246

The National Center for the Study of Adult Learning & Literacy website summarizes the diffusion of innovations theory. NCSALL is a federally funded research and development center focusing on adult learning. Read the account on the website and identify key components of the diffusion of innovations theory.

REFERENCES

Agyeman, P., Desgrandchamps, D., Vaudaux, B., Berger, C., Diana, A., Heininger, U., et al. (2009). Interpretation of primary care physicians' attitude regarding rotavirus immunisation using diffusion of innovation theories. *Vaccine, 27*(35), 4771–4775.

Ash, J. S., Sittig, D. F., Dykstra, R. H., Guappone, K., Carpenter, J. D., & Seshadri, V. (2006). Categorizing the unintended sociotechnical consequences of computerized provider order entry. *International Journal of Medical Informatics.* Epub PMID: 16793330.

Backer, T. E., & Rogers, E. M. (1998). Diffusion of innovations theory and work-site AIDS programs. *Journal of Health Communication, 3*(1), 17–28.

Barker, K. (2004). Diffusion of innovations: A world tour. *Journal of Health Communication, 9*(Suppl. 1), 131–137.

Bertrand, J. T. (2004). Diffusion of innovations and HIV/AIDS. *Journal of Health Communication, 9*(Suppl. 1), 113–121.

Berwick, D. M. (2003). Disseminating innovations in health care. *Journal of the American Medical Association, 289,* 1969–1975.

Buller, D. B., Andersen, P. A., Walkosz, B. J., Scott, M. D., Cutter, G. R., Dignan, M. B., et al. (2005). Randomized trial testing a worksite sun protection program in an outdoor recreation industry. *Health Education and Behavior, 32*(4), 514–535.

Cain, M., & Mitman, R. (2002). *Diffusion of innovation in health care. Oakland, CA: California Health Care Foundation.* Retrieved July 20, 2006, from http://www.iftf.org/docs/SR-778_Diffusion_of_Innovation_in_HC.pdf.

Chattoe, E., & Gilbert, N. (1997). *Modelling the adoption of AEMs as an innovation diffusion process.* Retrieved July 20, 2006, from http://wwwlisc.clermont.cemagref.fr/ImagesProject/Results/models/Diffusion%20Model/dolomieu.html.

Chew, F., Grant, W., & Tote, R. (2004). Doctors on-line: Using diffusion of innovations theory to understand Internet use. *Family Medicine, 36*(9), 645–650.

Dearing, J. W. (2004). Improving the state of health programming by using diffusion theory. *Journal of Health Communication, 9,* 21–36.

De Civita, M., & Dasgupta, K. (2007). Using diffusion of innovations theory to guide diabetes management program development: An illustrative example. *Journal of Public Health, 29*(3), 263–268.

Deprey, M., McAfee, T., Bush, T., McClure, J. B., Zbikowski, S., & Mahoney, L. (2009). Using free patches to improve reach of the Oregon Quit Line. *Journal of Public Health Management and Practice, 15*(5), 401–408.

Dietrich, A. J., Oxman, T. E., Williams, J. W., Jr., Kroenke, K., Schulberg, H. C., Bruce, M., et al. (2004). Going to scale: Re-engineering systems for primary care treatment of depression. *Annals of Family Medicine, 2*(4), 301–304.

Dorfman, L. T., & Murty, S. A. (2005). A diffusion of innovations approach to gerontological curriculum enrichment: Institutionalizing and sustaining curricula change. *Gerontology and Geriatrics Education, 26*(2), 35–50.

Farquahar, J. W., Fortmann, S. P., Flora, J. A., Taylor, C. B., Haskell, W. L., Williams, P. T., et al. (1990). Effects of a communitywide education on cardiovascular disease risk factors: The Stanford five-city project. *Journal of the American Medical Association, 264*, 359–365.

Foster, K. A., & Stiffman, A. R. (2009). Child welfare workers' adoption of decision support technology. *Journal of Technology in Human Services, 27*(2), 106–126.

Frerichs, G. R. (1994). The diffusion of innovations. In S. J. Levy, G. R. Frerichs, & H. L. Gordon (Eds.), *The Dartnell's marketing manager's handbook* (3rd ed., pp. 774–785). Chicago: Dartnell.

Gladwell, M. (2000). *The tipping point: How little things can make a big difference.* Boston: Little Brown.

Greenhalgh, T., Robert, G., Bate, P., Macfralane, F., & Kyriakidou, O. (2005). *Diffusion of innovations in health service organizations: A systematic literature review.* Malden, MA: Blackwell.

Haider, M., & Kreps, G. L. (2004). Forty years of diffusion of innovations: Utility and value in public health. *Journal of Health Communication, 9*, 3–11.

Harting, J., van Assema, P., Ruland, E., van Limpt, P., Gorgels, T., van Ree, J., et al. (2005). Implementation of an innovative health service: A "real-world" diffusion study. *American Journal of Preventive Medicine, 29*(2), 113–119.

Heaney, C. A., & Israel, B. A. (2002). Social networks and social support. In K. Glanz, B. K. Rimer, & F. M. Lewis (Eds.), *Health behavior and health education: Theory, research, and practice* (3rd ed., pp. 185–209). San Francisco: Jossey-Bass.

Hebert, M. A., & Korabek, B. (2004). Stakeholder readiness for telehomecare: Implications for implementation. *Telemedicine Journal and e-Health, 10*(1), 85–92.

Helitzer, D., Heath, D., Maltrud, K., Sullivan, E., & Alverson, D. (2003). Assessing or predicting adoption of telehealth using the diffusion of innovations theory: A practical example from a rural program in New Mexico. *Telemedicine Journal and e-Health, 9*(2), 179–187.

Karsh, B. T. (2004). Beyond usability: Designing effective technology implementation systems to promote patient safety. *Quality and Safety in Health Care, 13*(5), 388–394.

Kuntsche, S., & Gmel, G. (2005). The smoking epidemic in Switzerland: An empirical examination of the theory of diffusion of innovations. *Sozial und Praventivmedizin, 50*(6), 344–354.

Leeman, J., Jackson, B., & Sandelowski, M. (2006). An evaluation of how well research reports facilitate the use of findings in practice. *Journal of Nursing Scholarship, 38*(2), 171–177.

Locock, L., Dopson, S., Chambers, D., & Gabbay, J. (2001). Understanding the role of opinion leaders in improving clinical effectiveness. *Social Science and Medicine, 53*, 745–757.

McGlynn, E. A. (2003). An evidence-based national quality measurement and reporting system. *Medical Care, 41*(Suppl. 1), I8–I15.

Meyer, G. (2004). Diffusion methodology: Time to innovate. *Journal of Health Communication, 9*, 59–69.

Mohr, L. B. (1987). Innovation theory. In J. M. Pennings & A. Buitendam (Eds.), *New technology as organizational innovation* (pp. 13–31). Cambridge, MA: Ballinger.

Murphy, E. (2004). Diffusion of innovations: Family planning in developing countries. *Journal of Health Communication, 9*(Suppl 1), 123–129.

Nutley, S., Davies, H., & Walter, I. (2002). *Learning from the diffusion of innovations.* Retrieved July 21, 2006, from http://www.st-andrews.ac.uk/~ruru/Learning%20from%20the%20Diffusion%20of%20Innovations.pdf

Oldenburg, B., & Parcel, G. S. (2002). Diffusion of innovations. In K. Glanz, B. K. Rimer, & F. M. Lewis (Eds.), *Health behavior and health education: Theory, research, and practice* (3rd ed., pp. 312–334). San Francisco: Jossey-Bass.

Parcel, G. S., Perry, C. L., & Taylor, W. C. (1990). Beyond demonstration: Diffusion of health promotion interventions. In N. Bracht (Ed.), *Health promotion at the community level.* Thousand Oaks, CA: Sage.

Pare, G., & Trudel, M. C. (2007). Knowledge barriers to PACS adoption and implementation in hospitals. *International Journal of Medical Informatics, 76*(1), 22–33.

Peterson, E. W., & Howland, J. (1996). Predicting radon testing among university employees. *Journal of Air and Waste Management Association, 46*(1), 2–11.

Pronk, M. C., Blom, A. T., Jonkers, R., & Van Burg, A. (2001). The diffusion process of patient education in Dutch community pharmacy: An exploration. *Patient Education and Counseling, 42*(2), 115–121.

Pugh, M. J., Anderson, J., Pogach, L. M., & Berlowitz, D. R. (2003). Differential adoption of pharmacotherapy recommendations for type 2 diabetes by generalists and specialists. *Medical Care Research and Review, 60*(2), 178–200.

Puska, P., Koskela, K., McAlister, A., Mayranen, H., Smolander, A., Moisio, S., et al. (1986). Use of lay opinion leaders to promote the diffusion of health innovations in a community programme: Lessons learned from the North Karelia project. *Bulletin of the World Health Organization, 64*(3), 437–446.

Rogers, E. M. (2002). Diffusion of preventive interventions. *Addictive Behaviors, 27,* 989–993.

Rogers, E. M. (2003). *Diffusion of innovations* (5th ed.). New York: Free Press.

Rogers, E. M. (2004). A prospective and retrospective look at the diffusion model. *Journal of Health Communication, 9,* 13–19.

Rogers, E. M., & Shefner-Rogers, C. L. (1999). Diffusion of innovations and HIV/AIDS prevention research. In W. N. Elwood (Ed.), *Power in the blood: A handbook on AIDS, politics, and communication* [electronic resource, pp. 405–414]. Mahwah, NJ: Lawrence Erlbaum.

Rogers, E. M., & Shoemaker, F. F. (1971). *Communication of innovations: A cross cultural approach* (2nd ed.). New York: Free Press.

Rogers, E. M., & Singhal, A. (1996). Diffusion of innovations. In M. B. Salwen & D. W. Stacks (Eds.), *An integrated approach to communication theory and research* (pp. 409–420). Mahwah, NJ: Lawrence Erlbaum.

Rosegger, G. (1996). *The economics of production and innovation: An industrial perspective* (3rd ed.). Oxford, UK: Butterworth Heinemann.

Ruof, J., Mittendorf, T., Pirk, O., & von der Schulenburg, J. M. (2002). Diffusion of innovations: Treatment of Alzheimer's disease in Germany. *Health Policy, 60*(1), 59–66.

Ryan, B., & Gross, N. C. (1943). The diffusion of hybrid seed corn in two Iowa communities. *Rural Sociology, 8,* 15–24.

Schumann, P. A., Prestwood, D.C.L., Tong, A. H., & Vanston, J. H. (1994). *Innovate! Straight path to quality, customer delight, and competitive advantage.* New York: McGraw-Hill.

Shakeshaft, A. P., & Frankish, C. J. (2003). Using patient-driven computers to provide cost-effective prevention in primary care: A conceptual framework. *Health Promotion International, 18*(1), 67–77.

Sharma, V., & Sharma, A. (1996). Training of opinion leaders in family planning in India: Does it serve any purpose? *Revue d'épidémiologie et de santé publique, 44*(2), 173–180.

Smith, M. U., Dane, F. C., Archer, M. E., Devereaux, R. S., & Katner, H. P. (2000). Students Together Against Negative Decisions (STAND): Evaluation of a school-based sexual risk reduction intervention in the rural South. *AIDS Education and Prevention, 12*(1), 49–70.

Smith, M. U., & DiClemente, R. J. (2000). STAND: A peer educator training curriculum for sexual risk reduction in the rural South. Students Together Against Negative Decisions. *Preventive Medicine, 30*(6), 441–449.

Suther, S. G., & Goodson, P. (2004). Texas physicians' perceptions of genomic medicine as an innovation. *Clinical Genetics, 65*(5), 368–377.

Swendeman, D., & Rotheram-Borus, M. J. (2010). Innovation in sexually transmitted disease and HIV prevention: Internet and mobile phone delivery vehicles for global diffusion. *Current Opinion in Psychiatry, 23*(2), 139–144.

Tarde, G. (1969). *The laws of imitation* (E. C. Parsons, Trans.). New York: Dover. (Original work published 1903)

Tornatzky, L. G., & Fleischer, M. (1990). *The process of technological innovation.* Lexington, MA: Lexington Books.

Tornatzky, L. G., & Klein, K. J. (1982). Innovation characteristics and innovation adoption-implementation: A meta analysis of findings. *IEEE Transactions on Engineering Management, 29,* 28–45.

Valente, T. W. (1996). Social network thresholds in the diffusion of innovations. *Social Networks, 18,* 69–89.

Valente, T. W., & Fosados, R. (2006). Diffusion of innovations and network segmentation: The part played by people in promoting health. *Sexually Transmitted Diseases, 33*(Suppl. 7), S23–S31.

Valente, T. W., & Rogers, E. M. (1995). The origins and development of the diffusion of innovations paradigm as an example of scientific growth. *Science Communication, 16,* 242–273.

Vaughan, P. W., & Rogers, E. M. (2000). A staged model of communication effects: Evidence from an entertainment-education radio soap opera in Tanzania. *Journal of Health Communication, 5*(3), 203–227.

Westarp, F. V. (2003). *Modeling software markets: Empirical analysis, network simulations, and marketing implications.* New York: Physica-Verlag.

Wissler, C. (1923). *Man and culture.* New York: Thomas Y. Crowell.

Wolfe, R. A. (1994). Organizational innovation: Review, critique, and suggested research directions. *Journal of Management Studies, 31,* 407–431.

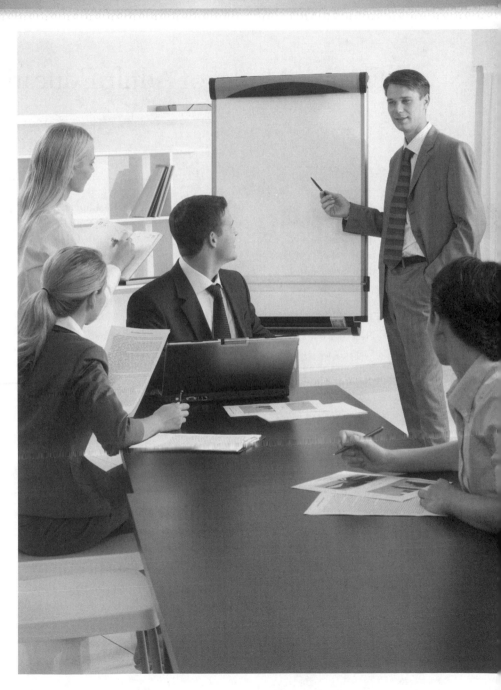

CHAPTER 10

Freire's Model of Adult Education

KEY CONCEPTS

- codification
- conscientization
- critical consciousness
- dialogue
- informal education
- popular education

- praxis
- problematization or problem posing
- SHOWED model
- social reality
- transformation

AFTER READING THIS CHAPTER YOU SHOULD BE ABLE TO

- Describe Paulo Freire's contribution to adult education
- List five constructs from Freire's adult education model
- Explain the application of Freire's model in health education
- Identify educational methods and match these to modify each construct from Freire's model to influence a health behavior
- Apply Freire's model to design an intervention to change a health behavior of your choice

Paulo Freire (1921–1997) was a Brazilian educator, philosopher, and political activist who worked in the area of adult literacy. His book *Pedagogy of the Oppressed* (Freire, 1970b) is currently one of the most cited books in education in Asia, Africa, and South America (Smith, 2005). His model is also popular in the United States, where it has been used for community organization, health education, and social work in addition to adult education. His model is often employed by those who work with oppressed people and use informal education or popular education. **Informal education** is based on experiential learning (learning from one's experiences), uses simple conversation, and can take place in any setting. **Popular education** is similar to informal education; it is need based, does not have a hierarchical relationship between learners and facilitators, builds on community knowledge, and aims at political action (Hamilton & Cunningham, 1989). Freire's model is sometimes referred to as the *theory of liberation education* (Freire, 1985).

Freire believed that education was a means of freeing people from the "culture of silence" that is widely prevalent among the masses, especially in nonindustrialized countries (Freire, 1970b). The essence of Freire's teaching is **dialogue**, or becoming adept at two-way communication. He believed that the individual deprived of dialogue was oppressed. He looked at dialogue as the process and practice of liberation. Since dialogue is the essence of the Freirean approach, the latter is also called *participatory research* (Cornwall & Jewkes, 1995). The second hallmark of Freirean methodology is the fundamental technique of **problematizing**, or **problem posing**. This approach is essentially the opposite of traditional education, which Freire labeled "banking education" (Freire, 1970b). Banking education provides ready-made answers or solutions to problems and does not allow people to think for themselves. The emphasis of the problem-posing approach lies in raising questions without providing any predetermined answers. The students reflect and arrive at the answers themselves.

> *Paulo Freire was a Brazilian educator whose book* Pedagogy of the Oppressed *is one of the most cited books in education in Asia, Africa, and South America.*
>
> —Smith, 2005

HISTORICAL PERSPECTIVE

Paulo Freire was born in 1921 in northeast Brazil in a well-to-do middle-class family that was severely affected by the Great Depression (1929–1939). His father died when Paulo was only 13 years old, and the family suffered from many difficulties during that period. With great efforts he attended the Recifé University and studied law, philosophy, and linguistics. Thereafter, he worked as a legal assessor in trade unions for a number of years but gradually drifted toward the field of education. In 1963, he became the director of the National Literacy Program in Brazil. This program led to political upheaval in its time because it overturned the traditional electoral base (in Brazil at the time, only the literate could vote).

Freire's work is considered to be an important example of education being used to bring about social change. In the 1970s, his book *Pedagogy of the Oppressed* (Freire, 1970b) and its reviews in Harvard publications established Freire as a radical, revolutionary pedagogue. Through his work as a consultant in the Office of Education of the World Council of Churches he became active in the struggles of several nonindustrialized countries, mostly in Africa. In the 1980s, he returned to Brazil, and with the help of the mayor of São Paulo, in 1989 he started a literacy program based on his theory of education that combined the church and the university. He was scheduled to teach at Harvard in September of 1997, but he died of a heart attack in May of that year at the age of 76.

Paulo Freire's work in literacy enabled illiterate people in Brazil to gain the right to vote, which is a great example of using education for political action.

Some of Freire's other well-known books are *Cultural Action for Freedom* (1970a), *Education for Critical Consciousness* (1973), *Education: The Practice of Freedom* (1976), *The Politics of Education: Culture, Power and Liberation* (1985), *Pedagogy of Hope: Reviving Pedagogy of the Oppressed* (1995), and *Pedagogy of the Heart* (1997).

APPROACH OF FREIRE'S MODEL

The Freirean model uses a three-phase process, which is summarized in **Table 10.1**. Although this approach appears to be simple, it is often difficult in practice because helping people reflect on their experiences requires a high degree of facilitation. The first phase in this approach is the *naming phase*, in which the facilitators and learners reflect on the question "What is the problem?" or "What is the question under discussion?" This has also been called the *listening stage*. It is conducted in equal partnership with the community members to identify problems and determine priorities (Gugushe, 1996). For example, when applying this theory with a group of overweight high school students, the group may identify their problem as being overweight or may identify the problem as spending too much time using computers and other media.

The second phase is the *reflection phase*, in which the facilitator poses the question "How do we explain this situation?" or "Why is this the case?" This phase is also called the *dialogue stage*. The discussion objects in this stage are often called **codes**, and the process itself **codification**. The codes are created to structure a discussion or problem-posing dialogue around the main issue or issues. A code is a physical representation of an identified community issue in any form. It could be a case study, role play, story, slide show, photograph, song, or so on. An effective code exemplifies a problematic situation with many facets so that participants can express their emotional and social responses to it. The emphasis is on bringing out the inner emotions of participants as much as possible.

TABLE 10.1   Three Phases of the Freirean Model

Phase	Main Question for Reflection
1: Naming (listening stage)	What is the problem?
2: Reflection (dialogue stage)	How do we explain this situation?
3: Action	What can be done to change this situation?

In some training programs, facilitators help in this reflection by using a five-step questioning strategy (debriefing) in which participants, after undergoing the codification process, are asked to (1) describe what they see and feel, (2) as a group define the many levels of the problem, (3) share similar experiences from their lives, (4) question why this problem exists, and (5) develop action plans to address the problem (Gugushe, 1996). For example, in a group of overweight high school students, the facilitators might implement a role play in which the various problems, such as being teased by fellow classmates, inability to participate in some activities in which they would like to participate, and not being comfortable with their body appearance, could be brought out and stir emotions in the participants. These emotions would then be used by the facilitator to initiate learning and to encourage participants to move to the next step, action.

The third phase is the *action phase*, characterized by the question "What can be done to change this situation?" or "What options do we have?" The unique feature of this pedagogical approach is that it is *process centered* as opposed to being outcome centered or product centered. It does not prescribe the attainment of any acceptable end product in the beginning; rather, it focuses on the approach that needs to be followed. In the example of working with a group of overweight high school students, the health educator needs to arrive at an action plan, but the specific content of that action plan is up to the group. The group might choose teasing about the problem of overweight as the most significant issue and develop a strategy of peer education, or the group might see physical inactivity as the major issue and develop an approach for becoming more physically active.

Another practical method for applying this model and remembering all the facilitation steps has been described by Wallerstein and Bernstein (1988). They applied Freire's ideas to alcohol and substance abuse prevention programs in youth and coined the acronym SHOWED. Their **SHOWED model** is depicted in **Table 10.2**.

TABLE 10.2   SHOWED Model: A Practical Way to Apply the Freirean Model
What do we see here?
What is really happening?
How does the story relate to our lives?
Why did the person acquire the problem?
How is it possible for this person to become empowered?
What can we do about it?

CONSTRUCTS OF FREIRE'S MODEL

As discussed in earlier chapters, when using theories to design health education and health promotion programs, it is very important to organize the ideas from the theory into discrete constructs or building blocks that can be distinctly identified. This is particularly challenging with Freire's model because no source clearly identifies the constructs from his model. This chapter identifies five main concepts of Freire's theory that can be used by health education programs and presents these as key constructs (**Table 10.3**). These concepts are illustrated in **Figure 10.1**.

The first construct of Freire's model is *dialogue*, described as an authentic exchange between the learners and educators (or, for health education, between health educators and those in need of behavior change or their families). Dialogue entails real, concrete awareness of the context of facts (**social reality**). This reality or context

TABLE 10.3 Key Constructs of Freire's Model		
Construct	**Definition**	**How to modify?**
Dialogue	Two-way exchange between learners and educators	• Opportunity for two-way communication (e.g., open group discussion)
Conscientization	Identification of underlying systemic forces of oppression	• Identification of oppressive sources (e.g., brainstorming on root causes) • Working together as change agents (e.g., team-building activities) • Personalizing the issue (e.g., using role plays to generate emotions)
Praxis	Reflective action or active reflection	• Working on a specific project (e.g., a pilot project assignment)
Transformation	Relationship that identifies one as a political and social being	• Discussing political and social implications of chosen issues (e.g., use of case studies)
Critical consciousness	Political organization of those adversely affected	• Organizing those affected to take action (e.g., creation of a not-for-profit group)

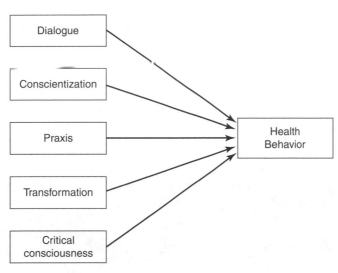

FIGURE 10.1   Constructs of Freire's model.

must come from the perspective of the clients. This construct can be applied in health education settings by providing opportunities to have a two-way discussion between health educators and the people needing behavior change or their families. The discussion must explore the root causes of their behaviors. The techniques of brainstorming, small group discussion, large group discussion, and online discussion forums can be employed in this regard.

Evaluation of health education programs using the Freirean model is mostly done qualitatively (Sharma, 2001). However, quantitative measurement is also possible. To quantitatively evaluate the construct of dialogue, some of the dimensions that can be measured are the extent of two-way communication through self-reports, the extent of problem posing through an objective evaluation of the transcript or video of the discussions, and the extent of joint discovery of the social reality as measured by either self-reports or analysis of the end products of dialogue. **Table 10.4** summarizes the quantitative indicators for different constructs of the Freirean model and their methods of measurement.

Dialogue cannot exist without humility.

—Paulo Freire (1970b)

The second construct is **conscientization**, or efforts to identify and address the underlying systemic forces of oppression and inequality. Freire (1970b) calls conscientization a process of "humanization" or an effort to enlighten people about the obstacles preventing them from a clear perception of reality. For health education, it refers to

TABLE 10.4   Quantitative Indicators for Different Constructs of the Freirean Model and Their Methods of Measurement

Construct	Quantitative Indicators	Method of Measurement
Dialogue	• Extent of two-way communication • Extent of problem posing • Extent of joint discovery of social reality	• Self-reports • Evaluation of the transcript or video • Self-reports or analysis of the end products of dialogue
Conscientization	• Extent of identification of oppressive sources • Extent of working together as change agents • Extent to which the key issue influences each person at a personal level	• Self-reports or evaluation of transcript or video • Self-reports or evaluation of products generated and tasks completed • Self-reports
Praxis	• Extent of participation and reflection in project planning, implementation and evaluation • Extent of perceived utility of the project	• Self-reports or assessment of actual products • Self-reports
Transformation	• Extent of focus on issue from the perspective of the people with the unhealthy behavior • Extent of unison on a collective viewpoint	• Self-reports • Self-reports
Critical consciousness	• Extent of cooperation among members; joint identification with the articulated issues, mission, and vision of the group • Extent of communication within the group • Extent of political organization of the group	• Self-reports • Self-reports or evaluation of video • Self-reports or analysis of the tasks completed

identification of the root causes of unhealthy behaviors, which can be done by techniques such as brainstorming or reflecting on case studies. The second component of this construct is working together as change agents. This can be achieved by using team-building activities such as the broken squares game, team juggling game, and so on (Business Fundamentals, 2005). Finally, to influence this construct, the health educator needs to personalize the issue for the participants as much as possible. This can be done by using techniques such as role plays or simulations to generate emotions.

After implementation of this construct in community-based rehabilitation programs, the extent of identification of oppressive sources can be measured by self-report or by checking the transcripts or video recordings. The extent of working together as change agents can be evaluated by self-report or gauged by the products generated and tasks completed. Finally, the extent to which the key issue influences each participant at a personal level can be ascertained by a self-report questionnaire.

The third construct of Freire's model is **praxis**, which refers to what Freire (1985) calls "reflective action" or "active reflection." It is the method of tying together theory and practice. Often we find that a gap exists between preaching (theory) and practice. The purpose of this construct is to narrow that gap and possibly eliminate it. In technical terms, praxis is the linkage between epistemology (source of knowledge) and ontology (reality). In health education interventions, it can be used when the participants work on a specific project and accomplish some tasks. An example could be joint creation of an action plan for behavior change and collective evaluation of it. Some of the researchable aspects that process and impact evaluation can assess for this construct include extent of participation in project planning, extent of reflection in project planning, extent of participation in project implementation, extent of reflection in project implementation, extent of participation in project evaluation, extent of reflection in project evaluation, and extent of perceived utility of the project. All of these can be gauged by self-reports or assessment of actual products.

The fourth construct of the Freirean model is **transformation**. Freire (1976) describes this as the process of changing *objects* (who have a naive consciousness of reality) into *subjects* (who see the theory behind the reality). It connotes independence, status, and integrity. It implies possession of "social consciousness," or being in a relationship that identifies one as a political and social being. In transformation, the solution is not to "integrate" people into the structure of oppression but to transform the structure so that they can become "beings for themselves" (Freire, 1970b). In simple terms, it means making people more aware of the political aspects of any issue.

This construct can be applied in health education by providing participants with opportunities for self-reflection followed by discussion. Educational techniques such as case studies are quite useful in influencing this construct. For example, a group of

high school smokers could start to understand the profit-making motive of the tobacco industry through a case study in which they learn how the industry buys adver-

*Education is never neutral. . . .
Either it conforms or it
transforms.*

—Paulo Freire (1985)

tising on various media and lobbies legislators to get its
products sanction, visibility, and coverage. Finally, they
can become cognizant of how these issues influence smoking behaviors. Evaluators of health education programs
can measure the extent of focus on the issue from the perspective of the people negatively affected by the unhealthy

behavior, and the extent of unison on a collective viewpoint. These dimensions can be
measured by self-reports.

The final construct of the Freirean model is **critical consciousness**. In essence,
this refers to the political organization of those adversely affected. This can be applied
in health education by building cooperation between health educators and persons
with disabilities, fostering unity on issues, developing effective communication, and
augmenting the process of political organization to change policies and legislation. In
health education programs, it often leads to formation of a not-for-profit group. Evaluators of health education programs can measure the extent of cooperation among
members; the extent of joint identification with the articulated issues, mission, and vision of the group; the extent of communication within the group; and the extent of political organization of the group. These dimensions can be measured by self-reports.

APPLICATIONS OF FREIRE'S MODEL IN HEALTH EDUCATION

The first application of Paulo Freire's work in health education and health promotion
in the United States began in the 1980s in a study by Wallerstein and Bernstein
(1988). They developed a youth-centered, intergenerational, experiential prevention
program called the Adolescent Social Action Program (ASAP) in New Mexico. The program aimed at preventing substance abuse, particularly alcohol, in youth. The
program was found to be useful in influencing several process variables, such as empathy, critical thinking, and belief in group action, and some impact variables, such as
extent of participation in social action among the participants (Wallerstein & Sanchez-
Merki, 1994). Over the years, the program, which started in one school, was successfully
extended to several other schools utilizing the peer-to-peer model (Wallerstein,
Sanchez-Merki, & Dow, 1997).

Since the initial application in the 1980s, the model has been used in a variety of
applications in health education and promotion, both for individual-level behavior
change and for community-level changes. **Table 10.5** summarizes these applications
in health education and promotion. Freire's model has been used in breast cancer

TABLE 10.5   Applications of Freire's Model in Health Education and Health Promotion

Breast cancer control

Breast-feeding promotion

Building health literacy

Community organization

Evaluation of coalitions

Evaluation of worker safety programs

HIV/AIDS prevention

Improving decision making

Informing policy makers of the status of community health through community-taken photographs

Intercultural health promotion

Malaria prevention and control

Oral health promotion

Nutrition education

Participatory development of health education materials

Participatory program planning

Participatory evaluation

Patient education

Peer-to-peer approach for reproductive health

People with mental illness

Preparation of health educators

Preparation of nurse educators

Reducing nutritional inequities

Self-care education

Sexually transmitted diseases (STD) education

Training health functionaries

Work with abused women

control (Mishra et al., 1998), breast-feeding promotion (Daghio, Vezzani, & Ciardullo, 2003), building health literacy (Kickbusch, 2001; Nutbeam, 2000; Schillinger, 2001; Wang, 2000), community organization (Flick, Reese, Rogers, Fletcher, & Sonn, 1994; Minkler & Wallerstein, 1997), evaluation of coalitions (Sharma, 2002), evaluation of worker safety programs (Cole, 2002; McQuiston, 2000; Weinger & Lyons, 1992), HIV/AIDS prevention (Campbell, 2004; Gil, 1998; Laver, van der Borne, & Kok, 2005-2006; Miranda & Barroso, 2007), improving decision making (Wittmann-Price, 2004), informing policy makers of the health situation in the community through community-taken photographs (Wang & Burris, 1994), intercultural health promotion (Ditton, 2005), malaria prevention and control (Geounuppakul, Butraporn, Kunstadter, Leemingsawat, & Pacheun, 2007), oral health promotion (Gugushe, 1996; Watt, 2002), nutrition education (Krawinkel, Mahr, Wuestefeld, & ten Haaf, 2005), participatory development of health education materials (Rudd & Comings, 1994), participatory program planning (Campbell & Jovchelovitch, 2000; Laverack & Labonte, 2000), participatory evaluation (Sharma & Deepak, 2001), patient education (Fahrenfort, 1987; Roter, 2000; Waters, 2000), a peer-to-peer approach for reproductive health (United Nations Educational, Scientific, and Cultural Organization, 2003), people with mental illness (Bellamy & Mowbray, 1998; Caragata, 2000; Rindner, 2004; Wells, Miranda, Bruce, Alegria, & Wallerstein, 2004), preparation of health educators (Helitzer & Wallerstein, 1999), preparation of nurse educators (Chalmers & Bramadat, 1996; Chiesa & Fracolli, 2007; Delia Rojo, Villela Bueno, & Silva, 2008; Hartrick, Lindsey, & Hills, 1994; Liimatainen, Poskiparta, Karhila, & Sjögren, 2001; Rush, 1997), reducing nutritional inequities (Travers, 1997), self-care education (Levin, 1999), education about sexually transmitted diseases (Dal Sasso, Pedrini, & Branco, 2004), training of health functionaries (Fonn & Xaba, 2001; Labonte, Feather, & Hills, 1999), and work with abused women (Mann, 1987).

The model has been applied with different racial and ethnic subgroups. For example, it has been used with African Americans (Waters, 2000), Native Americans (Davis & Reid, 1999), rural Chinese women (Wang & Burris, 1994), Hispanic girls (Gil, 1998), and South African health workers (Fonn & Xaba, 2001).

> *Education must begin with the solution of the teacher-student contradiction, by reconciling the poles of the contradiction so that both are simultaneously teachers and students.*
>
> Freire (1970b, p. 53)

LIMITATIONS OF FREIRE'S MODEL

Like all the models and theories discussed in this book, the Freirean model has some limitations. Freire has often been criticized for his contorted manner of writing and his obscurantism, which makes interpretation of concepts difficult and measurement complex. The terminology that has been used in this chapter is evidence that Freire's writing style is not very easy and lends itself to multiple interpretations.

Freire's viewpoints are often considered too utopian or ideal. There is excessive idealism in the descriptions of knowing and of learners and educators participating as equals. Such participation is seldom achieved in real-world settings. It is often very difficult for a more educated person (educator) to shed his or her ego and begin to learn from the participants.

Freire presents a circular logic and demonstrates confusing repetitiveness in his writing style. As a consequence, it is difficult to differentiate the constructs of this model so that they are mutually exclusive. To use a theory, educators need all the ideas to be separate from each other so that they can be measured and evaluated distinctly.

The model has also been criticized for requiring social manipulation, which has been used to domesticate people rather than liberate them. Finally, the choice of codes (such as words and songs) in the dialogue step is purposively done so that there are no neutral words; instead, the codes challenge the social reality. This adds a bias to the scientific inquiry. In a way, the model is making people think and react in a predetermined fashion. Therefore, the political and social purpose inherent in the model can be challenged as being manipulative.

APPLICATION EXERCISE

In this chapter, we have introduced several applications of Freire's model in health education and health promotion. Choose an application in an area that interests you and locate the full text article of that application. Analyze how the model was used in that context. One such application is by Geounuppakul and colleagues (2007) in the area of malaria prevention and control in Chiang Mai Province, Thailand. They used Freire's model to empower a women's group for prevention and control of malaria in an experimental community. Their sample included 45 women. The activities in the empowerment program included building self-esteem and self-confidence and utilization of insecticide-treated nets (ITN) to prevent and control malaria. A total of 10 participatory meetings were organized. The study collected qualitative data through focus-group discussions, observations, and in-depth interviews with women, their husbands, and youths at risk for malaria. Data were collected before the intervention and after 3, 6, 9, and 12 months following the intervention from the experimental and a control community. It was found that in the experimental community malaria prevention behaviors, use of ITN, and self-esteem and self-confidence levels improved and were higher than in the control community. Definitive plans were made by the women in the experimental community that included protecting the family, giving malaria-related education, controlling mosquitoes, and using ITNs. They also linked this activity to an income generation program.

Locate the full text article of this application and prepare a critique of 250 words.

SKILL-BUILDING ACTIVITY

Let us see how we can apply Freire's model to the issue of unhealthy eating behaviors in high school students. **Figure 10.2** depicts each of the constructs from the Freirean model and links these with the educational processes and behavioral objectives in this example to modify the eating behavior of the students.

The health education intervention would start by modifying the construct of dialogue, which can be done through a discussion among students, their parents, school teachers, and administrators. The discussion could be organized outside of school hours, and the facilitator would need to ensure that it is conducted in an egalitarian

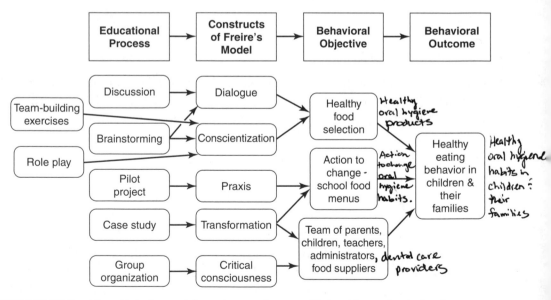

FIGURE 10.2   How Freire's model can be used to modify healthy eating behavior.

manner. One or more sessions might be used to build initial rapport and then to identify problems regarding eating behaviors.

Brainstorming can be used to build conscientization and explore the root causes of eating problems and their consequences. Role plays on these aspects and team-building exercises can be used to further modify this construct. The construct of praxis can be modified by having participants implement a pilot project related to healthy eating. The specific nature of the pilot project needs to be decided by the participants, but an example could be reading food labels and researching the caloric information of all food products used in the school and finding low-fat alternatives for each high-fat product. To modify the transformation construct, political and social awareness needs to be increased, which can be done through a case study. For example, the reasons certain food products are included in school menus and others are excluded can be explored. Finally, to raise critical consciousness, the action group of students, teachers, administrators, parents, food providers, and service personnel can form themselves into a regular unit to monitor healthy food products in the school.

Using Freire's model, work on a health behavior issue for a target group of your choice. **Table 10.6** provides a set of questions to assist you in choosing an educational method that corresponds to each of the different constructs.

SUMMARY

Paulo Freire (1921–1997), a Brazilian educator, is well known for his work using popular education to build adult literacy. In addition to adult education, his model has been used in community organization, development fields, social work, and health education. The three phases in his method are naming, reflection, and action.

The constructs of his theory are dialogue (two-way communication), conscientization (exploration of root causes of the problem), praxis (action and reflection), transformation (comprehension of political and social causes), and critical consciousness (formation of an organization). Dialogue can be facilitated through small group discussion, large group discussion, or online discussion. Conscientization can be facilitated by brainstorming, discussion, role play, simulation, and team-building exercises. Praxis can be facilitated by providing opportunities to develop action plans or implement pilot projects. Transformation can be facilitated by case studies, field visits, and so on. Critical consciousness can be developed by forming groups, building coalitions, and forming organizations.

TABLE 10.6   Choosing the Educational Methods for Health Education Program Planning Using Freire's Model

1. What is the best educational method to facilitate dialogue?
   - Small group discussion
   - Large group discussion
   - Online discussion
   - Other

2. What is the best educational method to facilitate conscientization?
   - Discussion
   - Brainstorming
   - Role play
   - Simulation
   - Team-building exercises
   - Other

3. What is the best educational method to facilitate praxis?
   - Pilot project
   - Other

4. What is the best educational method to facilitate transformation?
   - Case study
   - Field visit
   - Other

5. What is the best educational method to facilitate critical consciousness?
   - Group formation
   - Coalition building
   - Registration of not-for-profit organization
   - Other

IMPORTANT TERMS

codes	popular education
codification	praxis
conscientization	problematization (problem posing)
critical consciousness	SHOWED model
dialogue	social reality
informal education	transformation

REVIEW QUESTIONS

1. Discuss the three-phase approach of the Freirean model.
2. What does the acronym SHOWED mean in the context of the Freirean model?
3. Briefly describe the five constructs of Freire's model.
4. Differentiate between praxis and transformation.
5. How can critical consciousness be modified?
6. Using Freire's model, work to modify a health behavior issue for a target group of your choice.

WEBSITES TO EXPLORE

An Interview with Paulo Freire

http://aurora.icaap.org/talks/freire.html

This website presents an interview conducted with Paulo Freire in 1990. *Read this interview and discuss his views on conscientization.*

Informal Education

http://www.infed.org/

This is the encyclopedia of informal education website. Type "Paul Freire" into the search engine and read the webpage that discusses Freire and informal education. *Read this account and reflect on the critique of Freire's work. To what extent do you agree or disagree with that critique?*

Paulo Freire Institute

http://www.paulofreire.org/

This is the bilingual website of the Paulo Freire Institute (PFI), which is an international not-for-profit organization consisting of a network of people and institutions from 24 countries. The institute conducts research; offers courses; consults with groups; produces, edits, and publishes works based on Freirian thought; and promotes events related to Freirian thought. *Explore this website and summarize the present activities of this institute.*

Paulo Freire Institute at UCLA

http://www.paulofreireinstitute.org/index.html

Paulo Freire himself first suggested such an institute in 1994, and it was finally formed in 2001. The purpose of the institute is to advance Freire's pedagogy by bringing together scholars, activists, and teachers from around the world. *Explore this website and compare it to the eight other institutes on Paulo Freire from around the world. Write a summary of what you found out.*

Review of Paulo Freire's Books

http://fcis.oise.utoronto.ca/~daniel_schugurensky/freire/freirebooks.html

This website presents reviews of at least 20 books written by Paulo Freire. *Choose any one book by Freire from your library and read it. Then read the review of that book. To what extent do you agree with the reviewer?*

REFERENCES

Bellamy, C. D., & Mowbray, C. T. (1998). Supported education as an empowerment intervention for people with mental illness. *Journal of Community Psychology, 26,* 401–413.

Business Fundamentals. (2005). *Team building activities.* Retrieved January 1, 2006, from http://www.businessfundamentals.com/TeamBuilding.htm

Campbell, C. (2004). Creating environments that support peer education: Experiences from HIV/AIDS prevention in South Africa. *Health Education, 104,* 197–200.

Campbell, C., & Jovchelovitch, S. (2000). Health, community and development: Towards a social psychology of participation. *Journal of Community and Applied Social Psychology, 10,* 255–270.

Caragata, L. (2000). Using popular education groups: Can we develop a health promotions strategy for psychiatric consumers/survivors? *Canadian Journal of Community Mental Health, 19,* 5–20.

Chalmers, K. I., & Bramadat, I. J. (1996). Community development: Theoretical and practical issues for community health nursing in Canada. *Journal of Advanced Nursing, 24,* 719–726.

Chiesa, A. M., & Fracolli, L. A. (2007). An educational process to strengthen primary care nursing practices in São Paulo, Brazil. *International Nursing Review, 54*(4), 398–404.

Cole, H. P. (2002). Cognitive-behavioral approaches to farm community safety education: A conceptual analysis. *Journal of Agricultural Safety and Health, 8,* 145–159.

Cornwall, A., & Jewkes, R. (1995). What is participatory research? *Social Science and Medicine, 41,* 1667–1676.

Daghio, M. M., Vezzani, M. D., & Ciardullo, A. V. (2003). Impact of an educational intervention on breastfeeding. *Birth, 30,* 214–215.

Dal Sasso, G.T.M., Pedrini, D., & Branco, I. (2004). *Interactive media of health education in sexually transmitted diseases (STDs).* Retrieved December 31, 2005, from http://cmbi.bjmu.edu.cn/news/report/2004/medinfo2004/pdffiles/papers/348_d040005155.pdf

Davis, S. M., & Reid, R. (1999). Practicing participatory research in American Indian communities. *American Journal of Clinical Nutrition, 69,* 755S–759S.

Delia Rojo, M., Villela Bueno, S. M., & Silva, E. C. (2008). Conceptions of nursing students on health promotion related to psychoactive substances. *Revista Latino Americana de Enfermagem, 16,* 627–633.

Ditton, M. (2005). *Research plan for intercultural health promotion education*. Retrieved December 31, 2005, from http://conference.herdsa.org.au/2005/pdf/non_refereed/075.pdf

Fahrenfort, M. (1987). Patient emancipation by health education: An impossible goal? *Patient Education and Counseling, 10*, 25-37.

Flick, L. H., Reese, C. G., Rogers, G., Fletcher, P., & Sonn, J. (1994). Building community for health: Lessons from a seven-year-old neighborhood/university partnership. *Health Education Quarterly, 21*, 369–380.

Fonn, S., & Xaba, M. (2001). Health workers for change: Developing the initiative. *Health Policy and Planning, 16*(Suppl. 1), 13–18.

Freire, P. (1970a). *Cultural action for freedom*. Cambridge, MA: Harvard Educational Review and Center for the Study of Development and Social Change.

Freire, P. (1970b). *Pedagogy of the oppressed*. New York: Continuum.

Freire, P. (1973). *Education for critical consciousness*. New York: Continuum.

Freire, P. (1976). *Education: The practice of freedom*. London: Writers and Readers Cooperative.

Freire, P. (1985). *The politics of education: Culture, power and liberation*. South Hadley, MA: Bergin and Garvey.

Freire, P. (1995). *Pedagogy of hope: Reviving pedagogy of the oppressed*. New York: Continuum.

Freire, P. (1997). *Pedagogy of the heart*. New York: Continuum.

Geounuppakul, M., Butraporn, P., Kunstadter, P., Leemingsawat, S., & Pacheun, O. (2007). An empowerment program to enhance women's ability to prevent and control malaria in the community, Chiang Mai Province, Thailand. *The Southeast Asian Journal of Tropical Medicine and Public Health, 38*(3), 546–559.

Gil, V. E. (1998). Empowerment rhetoric, sexual negotiation, and Latinas' AIDS risk: Research implications for prevention health education. *International Quarterly of Community Health Education, 18*, 9–27.

Gugushe, T. S. (1996). An overview of Paulo Freire's perspective on health education. *Journal of the Dental Association of South Africa, 51*, 734–736.

Hamilton, E., & Cunningham, P. M. (1989). Community-based adult education. In S. B. Merriam & P. M. Cunningham (Eds.), *Handbook of adult and continuing education*. San Francisco: Jossey-Bass

Hartrick, G., Lindsey, E., & Hills, M. (1994). Family nursing assessment: Meeting the challenge of health promotion. *Journal of Advanced Nursing, 20*, 85–91.

Helitzer, D., & Wallerstein, N. (1999). A proposal for a graduate curriculum integrating theory and practice in public health. *Health Education Research, 14*, 697–706.

Kickbusch, I. S. (2001). Health literacy: Addressing the health and education divide. *Health Promotion International, 16*, 289–297.

Krawinkel, M. B., Mahr, J., Wuestefeld, M., & ten Haaf, J. (2005). Nutrition education for illiterate children in southern Madagascar: Addressing their needs, perceptions and capabilities. *Public Health Nutrition, 8*, 366–372.

Labonte, R. Feather, J., & Hills, M. (1999). A story/dialogue method for health promotion knowledge development and evaluation. *Health Education Research, 14*, 39–50.

Laver, S. M., van der Borne, B., & Kok, G. (2005-2006). Using theory to design an intervention for HIV/AIDS prevention in farm workers in rural Zimbabwe.1994–95. *International Quarterly of Community Health Education, 25*(1-2), 135–148.

Laverack, G., & Labonte, R. (2000). A planning framework for community empowerment within health promotion. *Health Policy and Planning, 15*, 255–262.

Levin, L. S. (1999). Patient education and self-care. *International Journal of Self Help and Self Care, 1*, 21–31.

Liimatainen, L., Poskiparta, M., Karhila, P., & Sjögren, A. (2001). The development of reflective learning in the context of health counselling and health promotion during nurse education. *Journal of Advanced Nursing, 34*, 648–658.

Mann, B. (1987).Working with battered women: Radical education or therapy? In E. Pence (Ed.), *In our best interest: A process for personal and social change* (pp. 104–116). Duluth: Minnesota Program Development.

McQuiston, T. H. (2000). Empowerment evaluation of worker safety and health education programs. *American Journal of Industrial Medicine, 38*, 584–597.

Minkler, M., & Wallerstein, N. (1997). Improving health through community organizing and community building: A health education perspective. In M. Minkler (Ed.), *Community organizing and community building for health* (pp. 30–52). New Brunswick, NJ: Rutgers University Press.

Miranda, K. C., & Barroso, M. G. (2007). HIV/AIDS counseling: Analysis based on Paulo Freire. *Revista Latino Americana de Enfermagem, 15*(1), 100–105.

Mishra, S. I., Chavez, L. R., Magana, J. R., Nava, P., Burciaga, V. R., & Hubbell, F. A. (1998). Improving breast cancer control among Latinas: Evaluation of a theory-based educational program. *Health Education and Behavior, 25*, 653–670.

Nutbeam, D. (2000). Health literacy as a public health goal: A challenge for contemporary health education and communication strategies into the 21st century. *Health Promotion International, 15*, 259–267.

Rindner, E. C. (2004). Using Freirean empowerment for health education with adolescents in primary, secondary, and tertiary psychiatric settings. *Journal of Child and Adolescent Psychiatric Nursing, 17*, 78–84.

Roter, D. (2000). The medical visit context of treatment decision-making and the therapeutic relationship. *Health Expectations, 3*, 17–25.

Rudd, R. E., & Comings, J. P. (1994). Learner developed materials: An empowering product. *Health Education Quarterly, 21*, 313–327.

Rush, K. L. (1997). Health promotion ideology and nursing education. *Journal of Advanced Nursing, 25*, 1292–1298.

Schillinger, D. (2001). Improving the quality of chronic disease management for populations with low functional health literacy: A call to action. *Disease Management, 4*, 103–109.

Sharma, M. (2001). Freire's adult education model: An underutilized model in alcohol and drug education? [Editorial]. *Journal of Alcohol and Drug Education, 47*(1), 1–3.

Sharma, M. (2002, July). *Using Freire's model for impact evaluation of coalitions in health and human services*. Paper presented at the summer residency of Walden University at Indiana University, Bloomington, IN.

Sharma, M., & Deepak, S. (2001). A participatory evaluation of community-based rehabilitation program in North Central Vietnam. *Disability and Rehabilitation, 23*, 352–358.

Smith, M. K. (2005). *Paulo Freire*. Retrieved December 29, 2005, from http://www.infed.org/thinkers/et-freir.htm

Travers, K. D. (1997). Reducing inequities through participatory research and community empowerment. *Health Education and Behavior, 24*, 344–356.

United Nations Educational, Scientific, and Cultural Organization. (2003), *Peer approach in adolescent reproductive health education: Some lessons learned*. Bangkok, Thailand: Author.

Wallerstein, N., & Bernstein, E. (1988). Empowerment education: Freire's ideas adapted to health education. *Health Education Quarterly, 15*, 379–394.

Wallerstein, N., & Sanchez-Merki, V. (1994). Freirian praxis in health education: Research results from an adolescent prevention program. *Health Education Research, 9*, 105–118.

Wallerstein, N., Sanchez-Merki, V., & Dow, L. (1997). Freirian praxis in health education and community organizing. A case study of an adolescent prevention program. In M. Minkler (Ed.), *Community organizing and community building for health* (pp. 195–211). New Brunswick, NJ: Rutgers University Press.

Wang, R. (2000). Critical health literacy: A case study from China in schistosomiasis control. *Health Promotion International, 15*, 269–274.

Wang, C., & Burris, M. A. (1994). Empowerment through photo novella: Portraits of participation. *Health Education Quarterly, 21*, 171–186.

Waters, C. M. (2000). End-of-life care directives among African Americans: Lessons learned—a need for community-centered discussion and education. *Journal of Community Health Nursing, 17*, 25–37.

Watt, R. G. (2002). Emerging theories into the social determinants of health: Implications for oral health promotion. *Community Dentistry and Oral Epidemiology, 30*, 241–247.

Weinger, M., & Lyons, M. (1992). Problem-solving in the fields: An action-oriented approach to farmworker education about pesticides. *American Journal of Industrial Medicine, 22*, 667–690.

Wells, K., Miranda, J., Bruce, M. L., Alegria, M., & Wallerstein, N. (2004). Bridging community intervention and mental health services research. *American Journal of Psychiatry, 161*, 955–963.

Wittmann-Price, R. A. (2004). Emancipation in decision-making in women's health care. *Journal of Advanced Nursing, 47*, 437–445.

GLOSSARY

action stage: Stage of change in which a person has made meaningful change in the past six months with regard to adopting a healthy behavior or quitting an unhealthy behavior.

advocacy: Health advocacy is about creating a shift in public opinion and mobilizing essential resources to support any issue or policy that affects the health of a community or constituency.

analytical epidemiology: Study of the determinants of health, such as behaviors and environments.

assessment protocol for excellence in public health (APEXPH) model: A public health planning model suitable for the local level that consists of three parts: organizational capacity assessment, community process, and completing the cycle.

attitude toward the behavior: A person's overall feeling of like or dislike toward any given behavior.

attitudes: Relatively constant feelings, predispositions, or set of beliefs directed toward an idea, object, person, or situation.

audience segmentation: Identifying distinct groups of people who are similar to each other in particular characteristics and thus likely to respond to messages in a similar way.

awareness: Becoming conscious of an action, idea, object, person, or situation.

behavior: Any overt action, conscious or unconscious, performed by an individual that has a measurable frequency, intensity, and duration; a category of actions with a specification of target, action, context, and time (TACT).

behavioral beliefs: Belief that performing a given behavior will lead to certain outcomes.

behavioral intention: The thought to perform the behavior, which is an immediate determinant of the given behavior.

beliefs: Statements of perceived facts or impressions about the world.

CDCynergy: A multimedia health communication planning model developed by the Centers for Disease Control and Prevention, based on a CD-ROM with tailored versions, that comprises six phases: problem definition and description, problem analysis, communication program planning, program and evaluation development, program implementation and management, and feedback.

certified health education specialist (CHES): An individual who meets the required health education training qualifications, has successfully passed the certification exam, and meets continuing education requirements.

certified in public health (CPH): A graduate from a Council on Education for Public Health (CEPH) accredited school or program of public health who has successfully completed a knowledge and skill test in public health conducted by the National Board of Public Health Examiners (NBPHE).

challenge: A component of hardiness that refers to a willingness to undertake change and confront new activities and obtain opportunities for growth.

change agent: An individual who influences a potential adopter's decision about an innovation in a favorable way.

chronic strains: Chronic stressors that result from the responses of one social group to another, such as overt or covert, intentional or unintentional discriminatory behavior due to race, ethnicity, or so forth.

chronic stressors: Type of stressors that are ongoing and last for a sustained period of time. These include persistent life difficulties, role strains, chronic strains, community-wide strains, and daily hassles.

clarity of results: The degree to which outcomes of an innovation are clearly visible.

coalition: Grouping of separate organizations in a community united to pursue a common goal related to health or other matters affecting a large number of people.

code: A physical representation of an identified community issue in a form such as a case study, role play, story, slide show, photograph, song, or so on.

code of ethics for health educators: Written document for professional conduct of health educators that delineates responsibilities to the public, profession, and employers and responsibilities regarding the delivery of health education, research and evaluation, and professional preparation.

codification: The process of creating codes to structure a discussion that highlights problems.

commitment: A component of hardiness that refers to the tendency to involve oneself in whatever one encounters, or a feeling of deep involvement in the activities of life.

communication channels: The links between those who have know-how regarding an innovation and those who have not yet adopted that innovation; the means by which messages are transferred between individuals.

community: A collection of people identified by a set of shared values.

community development: A stage in which local initiative and leadership in a community has been organized and stimulated to a level at which change in health or other matters is occurring.

community empowerment: Process whereby individuals gain mastery over their lives in the context of changing their social and political environments.

community mobilization: Persuading community members to attend or participate in any activity planned by the health educator. Its purpose is to enhance awareness of a given issue at the community level.

community organization: Process in which community members identify needs, set objectives, prioritize issues, develop plans, and implement projects for community improvement in health and related matters.

community participation: When community members actively participate in planning or implementing projects.

community-wide strains: Chronic stressors that operate at an ecological level, such as residing in a high-crime neighborhood.

compatibility: The perception of an innovation's consistency with the values, past experiences, and needs of potential adopters.

complexity: The perception of the degree of difficulty in understanding and using a new idea, practice, or product.

comprehensibility: A component of the theory of sense of coherence that refers to the extent to which perceived stressors make cognitive sense, implying that there is some set structure, consistency, order, clarity, and predictability.

comprehensive health education model (CHEM): An older model of health education that consists of six steps: involving people, setting goals, defining problems, designing plans, conducting activities, and evaluating results.

conscientization: A term coined by Paulo Freire and a distinct construct of his ideology that refers to the process of identification of the root causes of any problem.

consciousness raising: An experiential process of change in the transtheoretical model that entails raising awareness of the causes, consequences, and cures for a particular problem.

contemplation stage: Stage of change in which a person is considering change in the foreseeable future, but not immediately; usually defined as between one and six months.

contingency management: See *reinforcement management.*

control: A component of hardiness that refers to the belief that one causes the events of one's life and can influence the environment.

control beliefs: Beliefs about internal and external factors that may inhibit or facilitate the performance of a behavior.

coping: Purposive, psychological mechanisms for dealing with stressors.

costs: In diffusion of innovations theory, the tangible and intangible expenses incurred in the adoption of a new idea, practice, or product.

counterconditioning: A behavioral process of change in the transtheoretical model that requires learning a new, healthier behavior in place of the old, unhealthy behavior.

critical consciousness: A construct of the Freirean model that refers to the development of the political organization of those adversely affected by the problem.

cues to action: Precipitating forces that make a person feel the need to take action.

daily hassles: Chronic stressors that include everyday problems, such as getting stuck in traffic.

decisional balance: The construct of the transtheoretical model that addresses the relative importance placed by an individual on the advantages (pros) of behavior change as opposed to the disadvantages (cons).

defense mechanisms: The devices that the mind uses to alter an individual's perception of situations that disturb the internal milieu or mental balance.

demonstrability: The degree to which an innovation may be experimented with on a limited basis.

descriptive epidemiology: Study of the time, place, and population attributes of a health problem through the collection of data such as mortality (death), morbidity (illness), and disability rates.

development of social norms: Creating social acceptance for a practice, behavior, condition, policy, law, or environment that may affect health in a community.

dialogue: A construct of the Freirean model that refers to two-way communication between learners and educators.

diffusion: The process by which a new idea, object, or practice filters through various channels in a community over time.

dramatic relief: An experiential process of change in the transtheoretical model that enhances emotional arousal about one's behavior and emphasizes the relief that can come from changing it.

emotional coping: Techniques employed by a person to control the emotional and physiological states associated with acquisition of a new behavior.

emotion-focused coping: Method of dealing with a stressor in which the focus is inward and involves altering the way one thinks or feels about a situation or an event.

enabling factors: Antecedents to behavioral or environmental change that allow a motivation or environmental policy to be realized (e.g., availability of resources, accessibility, laws, or skills).

environment: Physical or social circumstances or conditions that surround a person.

environmental reevaluation: An experiential process of change in the transtheoretical model that involves both affective and cognitive components regarding how the behavior affects one's environment and how changing the behavior would influence the environment.

event-based models: Models of stress that underscore the role of life events in the causation of stress.

exchange theory: Marketing theory of voluntary transfer or transaction of something valuable between two individuals or groups.

forethought capability: The proposition that most behavior is purposive and regulated by prior thoughts.

formative research: In social marketing, collecting quantitative and qualitative data about a problem, its context, the attitudes and behaviors of the target audience, ways to reach the target audience, and existing messages and materials.

general adaptation syndrome: The three-stage physiological response (alarm reaction, resistance, and exhaustion) of any organism that encounters nonspecific stimuli.

goal setting: A determinant of behavior composed of setting goals and developing plans to accomplish chosen behaviors.

hardiness: A personality trait that is found to predict better coping with stressors; it consists of three components: commitment, control, and challenge.

health: A means to achieve desirable goals in life while maintaining a multidimensional (physical, mental, social, political, economic, and spiritual) equilibrium that is operationalized for individuals as well as for communities.

health behavior: Actions with a potentially measurable frequency, intensity, and duration performed at the individual, interpersonal, organizational, community, or public policy level for primary, secondary, or tertiary prevention. See also *preventive behaviors*.

health belief model (HBM): Theory designed to exclusively predict health behaviors based on the constructs of perceived susceptibility, perceived severity, perceived benefits, perceived costs, cues to action, and self-efficacy.

health education: Systematic application of a set of techniques to voluntarily and positively influence health through changing the antecedents of behavior (awareness, information, knowledge, skills, beliefs, attitudes, and values) in individuals, groups, or communities.

health literacy: The capacity of an individual to obtain, interpret, and understand basic health information and services and the competence to use such information and services in ways that are health enhancing.

health promotion: Process of empowering people to improve their health by providing educational, political, legislative, organizational, social, and community supports.

helping relationships: A behavioral process of change in the transtheoretical model that entails developing caring, open, trusting, and accepting relationships that help in adherence to the healthy behavior.

homophily: The degree of similarity among group members.

illness behaviors: Actions taken by a person who feels sick and indulges in the behavior for the purpose of defining the state of his or her health and for discovering suitable remedies.

informal education: Type of education that uses experiential learning (i.e., learning from one's experiences) and simple conversation and can take place in any setting.

information: The collection of facts related to an action, idea, object, person, or situation.

innovation: A new idea, object, or practice that is to be adopted.

intervention mapping: A health promotion and education planning model that comprises six steps: needs assessment or problem analysis; creating matrices of change objectives; selecting theory-based intervention methods and practical strategies; developing an organized program; planning for adoption, implementation, and sustainability of the program; and generating an evaluation plan.

knowledge: Learning facts and gaining insights related to an action, idea, object, person, or situation.

legislation: A law passed by elected officials at the local, state, or federal level.

levels of change: Five distinct but interrelated levels of psychological problems that can be addressed in psychotherapy: symptom/situational problems, maladaptive cognitions, current interpersonal conflicts, family/system conflicts, and intrapersonal conflicts.

life change events: See *life events.*

life events: A distinct category of stressors that are discrete, major happenings affecting or having the potential to influence one's body, mind, family, or community (e.g., death of a family member). Also known as life change events.

lobbying: Working with and influencing policy makers to develop an issue or policy that affects the health of a given community.

maintenance stage: Stage of change in which the person has maintained the changed behavior for a period of time, usually considered as six or more months.

manageability: A component of the sense of coherence that refers to the extent to which one feels that the resources under one's control are adequate to meet the demands posed by the stressors.

marketing mix: The combination of product, price, place, and promotion.

meaningfulness: A component of the sense of coherence that refers to the extent to which one feels that life makes sense emotionally and that at least some of the stressors in life are worth investing energy in and are worthy of commitment and engagement.

model: An eclectic, creative, simplified, and miniaturized application of concepts for addressing problems.

model for health education planning (MHEP): One of the older models of health education planning; it comprises six phases: program initiation, needs assessment, goal setting, planning/programming, implementation, and evaluation.

model for health education planning and resource development (MHEPRD): A five-phase model of health education planning developed in the 1980s that consists of the following phases: health education plans, demonstration programs, operational programs, research programs, and information and statistics.

motivation to comply: Degree to which a person wants to act in accordance with the perceived wishes of those significant in his or her life.

multilevel approach to community health (MATCH) model: A health education planning model that consists of five phases: goals selection, intervention planning, program development, implementation preparations, and evaluation.

networking: Creating interdependent relationships with individuals, groups, and organizations to accomplish mutually set objectives in health or other matters.

nonevents: Absence of events that have the potential for causing stress; these include desired or anticipated events that do not occur, desired events that do not occur even though their occurrence is normative for people of a certain group, and situations in which a person has nothing to do.

normative beliefs: A person's beliefs about how other people who are significant in his or her life would like him or her to behave.

opinion leaders: Influential individuals in a community who sway the beliefs and actions of their colleagues in either a positive or negative direction.

optimism: A personality disposition that refers to the tendency to expect the best possible outcome or think about the most hopeful aspects of any situation.

outcome evaluations: Value a person places on each outcome resulting from performance of a given behavior.

outcome expectancies: Value a person places on the probable outcomes that result from performing a behavior.

outcome expectations: Anticipation of the probable outcomes that would ensue as a result of engaging in the behavior under discussion.

partnership: Establishment of collaboration with multiple partners who will work on the same issue.

PEN-3 model: A culturally appropriate planning model that is composed of three interrelated and interdependent dimensions, each with an acronym of PEN: (1) health education (person, extended family, and neighborhood); (2) educational diagnosis of health behavior (perceptions, enablers, nurturers); and (3) cultural appropriateness of health behavior (positive, exotic, and negative).

perceived barriers: Beliefs concerning the actual and imagined costs of following a new behavior.

perceived behavioral control: How much a person feels he or she is in command of enacting the given behavior.

perceived benefits: Beliefs in the advantages of the methods suggested for reducing the risk or seriousness of the disease or harmful state resulting from a particular behavior.

perceived power: A person's perception about how easy or difficult it is to perform the behavior in each condition identified in his or her control beliefs.

perceived relative advantage: The perception regarding how much better a new product, idea, or practice is than the one it will replace.

perceived severity: Subjective belief in the extent of harm that can result from an acquired disease or harmful state as a result of a particular behavior.

perceived susceptibility: Subjective belief regarding a person's likelihood of acquiring a disease or reaching a harmful state as a result of indulging in a particular behavior.

perceived threat: The combination of perceived susceptibility and perceived severity.

persistent life difficulties: Chronic stressors that include life events lasting longer than six months, such as long-term disability.

pervasiveness: The degree to which an innovation requires changes or adjustments by other elements in the social system.

place: The distribution channels, or where and how customers are going to get the product.

planned approach to community health (PATCH) model: A health planning model developed by the Centers for Disease Control and Prevention that comprises five phases: mobilizing the community, collecting and organizing data, choosing health priorities, developing a comprehensive intervention plan, and evaluating results.

policy: Creating the environmental supports needed to sustain a behavior change.

policy development: The process of developing a policy with ramifications for affecting the health of communities.

popular education: Type of education that is based on community needs, fosters equal relationship between learners and teachers, builds on a community's experience, and aims at social change.

praxis: A construct of the Freirean model that refers to the method of tying together theory and practice; also known as active reflection or reflective action.

PRECEDE-PROCEED model: A health promotion and health education model with eight phases: social assessment and situational analysis, epidemiological assessment, educational and ecological assessment, administrative and policy assessment and intervention alignment, implementation, process evaluation, impact evaluation, and outcome evaluation. The acronym PRECEDE stands for predisposing, reinforcing, and enabling constructs in educational/environmental diagnosis and evaluation. The acronym PROCEED stands for policy, regulatory, and organizational constructs in educational and environmental development.

precontemplation stage: Stage of change in which a person is not considering change in the foreseeable future, usually defined as the next six months.

predisposing factors: Factors that are antecedents to behavioral change and that provide motivation for the behavior (e.g., knowledge, beliefs, attitudes, values, perceptions).

preparation stage: Stage of change in which a person is planning for change in the immediate future, usually defined as in the next month.

preventive behaviors: Actions taken by a healthy person for the purpose of preventing disease or detecting disease in an asymptomatic phase. See also *health behavior*.

price: The tangible and intangible things that the target audience has to give up in order to adopt the new idea (product).

primary appraisal: A process in which a person determines the severity of the stressor and makes an assessment regarding whether he or she is in trouble; one of the constructs of theories of stress and coping.

primary prevention: Preventive actions that are taken prior to the onset of disease or an injury with a view to removing the possibility of their ever occurring.

problem posing: See *problematization*.

problematization: The essence of Freirean methodology; it includes emphasis on raising questions without providing any predetermined answers. The participants have to reflect and arrive at answers themselves. Also known as problem posing.

problem-focused coping: Method of dealing with a given stressor by one's ability to think and to alter the environmental event or situation.

product: In social marketing, the behavior or offering that is intended for the target audience to adopt.

promotion: The mechanism by which one gets a message across to a target audience.

publics: The primary and secondary audiences involved in a social marketing program.

purse strings: The amount of money available at one's disposal for a social marketing campaign.

reappraisal: The feedback loop by which a person determines whether the effects of the stressor have been effectively negated; one of the constructs of theories of stress and coping.

recent life events: Discrete major life happenings that have occurred within the past year.

reciprocal determinism: The triadic reciprocity of causation among personal factors, environment, and behavior.

reinforcement management: A behavioral process of change in the transtheoretical model that utilizes reinforcements and punishments for taking steps in a particular direction.

reinforcing factors: Factors that follow a behavior and provide continuing rewards for sustenance of the behavior (e.g., family, peers, teachers, employers, health providers, community leaders, decision makers).

reinvention: The degree to which potential adopters of an innovation can adapt, refine, or modify the innovation to suit their needs.

remote life events: Discrete major life happenings that have occurred in the distant past, beyond one year.

response-based model: Model of stress that underscores the role of responses arising out of stress.

reversibility: In the diffusion of innovations theory, the ability and degree to which the status quo can be reinstated by ceasing to use the innovation.

role strains: Chronic stressors that include either strain from performing specific roles (such as parenting, working, being in a relationship) or performing a multiplicity of roles at the same time.

secondary appraisal: A process in theories of stress and coping in which a person determines how much control he or she has over the stressor. If control is high, then no stress develops; if control is low, then stress develops.

secondary prevention: Actions that block the progression of an injury or disease at its incipient stage.

self control: See *goal setting*.

self-efficacy: The confidence that a person has in his or her ability to pursue a behavior.

self-efficacy in overcoming impediments: Confidence that a person has in overcoming barriers while performing a given behavior.

self-liberation: A behavioral process of change in the transtheoretical model that entails belief that one can change and a commitment and recommitment to act on that change.

self-reevaluation: An experiential process of change in the transtheoretical theory that involves both affective and cognitive components and includes a person's assessment of his or her self-image with the new behavior.

self-reflective capability: Human attribute that entails analysis of experiences and thinking about one's own thought processes.

self-regulatory capability: Human attribute that entails setting internal standards and self-evaluative reactions for one's behavior.

sense of coherence: A theory that purports that comprehensibility, manageability, and meaningfulness in life improve coping with stress.

SHOWED model: A mnemonic acronym of the phases of Freirean methodology for facilitating a discussion. The steps are as follows: What do we see here? What is really happening? How does the story relate to our lives? Why does the person have the problem? How is it possible for the person to become empowered? What can we do about it?

sick role behaviors: Actions taken for the purpose of getting well by people who are sick.

situational perception: How one perceives and interprets the environment around oneself.

skill: Act involving physical movement, coordination, and use of the motor function.

social cognitive theory (SCT): Theory that posits a triadic reciprocity among behavior, environment, and cognitive personal factors.

social learning theory: Theory that posits that learning takes place from imitation, reinforcements, and self-control.

social liberation: An experiential process of change in the transtheoretical theory that refers to an increase in social opportunities or alternatives.

social marketing: The use of commercial marketing techniques to help in acquisition of a behavior that is beneficial for the health of a target population.

social networks: Person-centered webs of social relationships.

social reality: Awareness of the context of facts. This context must be from the perspective of the participants or clients.

social support: The help obtained through social relationships and interpersonal exchanges.

social system: People in a society connected by a common goal.

stages of change: Discrete phases in the transtheoretical model through which a person transits when undergoing change of a behavior. The stages consist of precontemplation, contemplation, action, and maintenance.

stimulus control: A behavioral process of change in the transtheoretical model that involves modifying the environment to increase cues for healthy behavior and decrease cues for unhealthy behavior.

stress: The response of the body and mind, including behaviors, as a result of encountering stressors, interpreting them, and making judgments about controlling or influencing the outcomes of these events.

stressors: Various external events that pose actual or perceived threats to the body or mind.

subjective norm: One's belief that most of the significant others in one's life think one should or should not perform a particular behavior.

symbolizing capability: Human attribute that entails the use of symbols in attributing meaning to experiences.

temptation: The urge to engage in unhealthy behavior when confronted with a difficult situation.

termination: The point in the transtheoretical model at which the person has completely quit the habit, has no temptation to relapse, and is fully self-efficacious to continue with the change.

tertiary prevention: Those actions taken after the onset of disease or an injury with a view to assisting diseased or disabled people.

theory of planned behavior (TPB): A theory of behavior that posits that intention precedes behavior and is determined by the attitude toward the behavior, subjective norms, and perceived behavioral control.

theory of reasoned action (TRA): A theory of behavior that posits that intention precedes behavior and is determined by the attitude toward the behavior and subjective norms.

time: In the diffusion of innovations theory, the interval between becoming aware of an idea and adopting it.

transactional model: Model of stress and coping that is characterized by the interaction of a person with the environment in four stages: primary appraisal, secondary appraisal, coping, and reappraisal.

transformation: A construct of the Freirean methodology that implies comprehension of the political and social causes of any given problem.

transtheoretical model (TTM): A model of behavior change that posits that people move through five stages of change, from precontemplation (not thinking about change) to maintenance (acquisition of the healthy behavior), in which they are aided through 10 processes of change and the constructs of decisional balance, self-efficacy, and overcoming temptation.

type A personality: Personality type that is characterized by a hurrying nature, exercising control over people and things, sense of urgency, and challenging nature.

type B personality: Personality type that is characterized by a more laid back lifestyle and a more relaxed disposition than a type A personality.

value expectancy theories: Theories that postulate that a behavior depends on the importance placed by an individual on an outcome (value) and the individual's estimate of the likelihood that a given action will result in that outcome (expectancy).

values: Enduring beliefs or systems of beliefs that a specific mode of conduct or end state of behavior is personally or socially preferable.

vicarious capability: Human attribute that entails the ability to learn from observing other people's behavior and the consequences that they face.

INDEX